# HOPE

## among the

**S**

The B ... cripture

Published by Brazos Press
a division of Baker Book House Company
P.O. Box 6287, Grand Rapids, MI 49516-6287
www.brazospress.com

Printed in the United States of America

Library of Congress Cataloging-in-Publication Data
Radner, Ephraim, 1956–
    Hope among the fragments: the broken church and its engagement of Scripture / Ephraim
Radner.
        p.    cm.
    Includes bibliographical references and index.
    ISBN 1-58743-084-3(pbk.)
    1. Church. I. Title.
BV600.5.R34 2004
262′.001′1—dc22                                                                    2003025190

# Contents

# Acknowledgements

Many of the chapters in this book were initially used in conferences and papers for SEAD (an evolving acronym standing first for Scholarly Engagement with Anglican Doctrine and later for Society for Ecumenical Anglican Doctrine), an ecumenically expanding group of lay and ordained scholars within the Episcopal Church of the U.S.A. dedicated to theological reflection on the Church's faith and life. (SEAD has now merged with others to become the Anglican Communion Institute.) Some of these papers were subsequently published elsewhere: "Sublimity and Providence" in *Ex auditu* 82 (2003); "Apologetics and Unity" in *The Rule of Faith: Scripture, Canon, and Creed in a Critical Age* (ed. Ephraim Radner and George Sumner; Harrisburg, Pa.: Morehouse, 1998); and "Bad Bishops" in *Anglican Theological Review* 82.2 (2000).

Translations are my own, unless otherwise noted; scriptural translations, unless noted, are from the Revised Standard Version.

SEAD has represented a remarkable group of theologians, unique in the Church for their steady and consistent intellectual integrity and cultural discernment over the years. The organization's work often proves baffling to more established Church leaders of the right and left, whose commitment to programmatic strategies has a difficult time dealing with the temporal distensions of divine dislocation that the present era imposes upon faithful Christian speech and witness. SEAD has courageously, if with a struggle, accepted this burden. This volume is dedicated to the members of SEAD, especially to Profs. Christopher Seitz, R. R. Reno, Philip Turner, Kathryn Greene-McCreight, and George Sumner, all of

5

whom, in their prayer and work, patiently reflect the figure of hope the Church unceasingly, and often unknowingly, pleads to receive as its own; to the people of Ascension Episcopal Church, who have generously supported my writing. Finally, I also offer it in thanksgiving for my wife, the Rev. Annette Brownlee, guide and exemplar in Christ.

To all these I express gratitude; for all these I pray; with all these I unsteadily move forward. The time in which these reflections are being gathered is one of accumulating strain upon the very vision of hope that these chapters are designed to express, to the point that I even wonder if their purpose may not be somehow misguided or misperceived. The call to "stay put" for the sake of receiving—rather than demanding and enforcing—God's mercy within the churches of Christ's Church is not one I can assert with any other clarity than that of petition and pleading, nor with any other certainty than that of a trembling weakness. Even in this, however, may we apprehend some tracery of hope.

# Introduction

## *The Republic of Stones*

Robert Bellarmine, noted sixteenth-century Roman Catholic controversialist, once defined the Christian Church as an "assembly of persons as visible and as palpable as the Republic of Venice." He meant this as a challenge to his Protestant opponents, whose grappling with notions of election and "invisibility" seemed to subvert the call to historical order and the fact of temporal identity that Catholics wished to uphold. Protestants, for their part, wondered by what logic the body of Christ might suffer the same moral and spiritual assaults or corruptions as the Venetian state and still retain claim to the Holy Spirit's habitation. Republics—not to mention assemblies, councils, and curias—did not seem, at the time, terribly credible witnesses to the gospel.

But times change. And the allure of Venice, as it were, tended to exert renewed attraction, even and perhaps especially for Protestants. Missing the point of Bellarmine's call for linking Church and history in an essential way (the kind of link that would later give rise to dreaded theories of doctrinal development), particular and even arbitrary expressions of the pure Church have always snared the interest of reformed Christians rooting about Christian *invisibilia* for signs of faith. By critic John Ruskin's nineteenth-century era, "the stones of Venice," to keep with the image and to use the title of his most famous work, had become a marvelous quarry for uncovering nostalgic models of uncorrupted virtue. (Ruskin thought that Venetian gothic architectural style maintained the only ethically unsullied alternative to the grotesqueries of Victorian esthetic sensibilities.) So too in our own day the "great tradition," with its bag of historical treasures, has become a rallying cry for beleaguered Protestants unsure of how otherwise to defend against liberal emotivism except through the display of the cultural artifacts of an alternative integrity.

One of the great ironies of modernity, when it comes to the Church, is the way that Catholics and Protestants converged in a common descent into the sociological. The theology of the Church in our day has become a shared science of culture, examining the ways that not only Venice, but Corinth and Chicago, Ephesus and Lagos, Rome and Singapore have glittered and faded, worked miracles or dredged the gutter, excelled in cell-groups or skidded on skateboard ministry. To speak of the "the Church" today is to articulate the ultimate denoted reality. By "denoted" I mean something that can be pointed to, examined, analyzed, and wherever possible manipulated according to whatever current theories of cultural resistance or viability are at hand, all supposedly for the sake of God.

The logic of ecclesial "denotation" was invented largely to deal with the reality of Christians in conflict one with another, and the sixteenth century raised its application to a formal level of sophistication: miracles, confessions, martyrdoms, patterns of ordination and sacramental format, finally even the traces of historical accountability with their ebb and flow of membership, were all elevated into the signs or marks of the true Church.[1] The development by which ecclesial discernment as a form of theology quickly became one with the evolving practices of archeology, documentary analysis, and even sociology, while complex, represents one of the great and common transformations of Christian self-understanding in the last few centuries, whereby Zion and the world's cities found themselves conflated in ways even the sixteenth-century polemicists could not imagine. The measures of the Church are now all neatly traced according to quantifiable signs given up by each republic's records, from which Scripture itself is detached except as some justifying cachet to the deeper argument over the implication of demographic figures. Is the South taking over the North in its Christian vigor? What do the numbers show? Are conservative churches growing faster than liberal bodies, and is it based on moral demands or the dynamics of education? Do Gen-Xers and Bridgers respond to candles more than to

---

1. The main points of this argument over how ecclesial division gives rise to perverted "logics" of ecclesial self-understanding are discussed in my book *The End of the Church: A Pneumatology of Christian Division in the West* (Grand Rapids: Eerdmans, 1998).

videos? Catholic and Protestant alike now scrutinize these standards, and the wars not only among but also within denominations over tradition and innovation are supplied by a common arsenal of sociological markers whose scriptural character is simply absent.

Seeking some link between Holy Spirit and such historical referents is not particularly novel in Christian reflection. What is unprecedented today is the almost complete disavowal of that linkage's intrinsic obscurity—and with that repudiation a consequent flight from the Spirit's more intricate and shadowy temporal corridors by theological adepts and Church leaders. Everyone seems to know what the world's objects signify, what events add up to, how each affects the other, and therefore what and how the Church is doing within time and space; and if we do not quite know it yet, further analysis will yield the pertinent information.

The spiritual dangers of this grasping after ecclesial denotation are obvious, although seemingly ignored: when the reality and meaning of the Church are simply linked to the objective references of space and time, they become slaves to the standards by which these references are regularly, if usually unconsciously, analyzed by the cultural instruments of measurement—size, longevity, numerical expanse, ethnic representation, financial viability, and so on. If the Church's phenomenal history is coincident with its meaning, then it becomes the plaything of the historian's method, whatever it might be. And in our day, as one of C. P. Snow's characters in *The Light and the Dark* observes, when it comes to "history, success is the only virtue." It is a conviction bound to subvert faith in life itself and certainly the life of faith. The modern historical standards of successful survival tend to—and probably inevitably must—give rise to regular and inescapable waves of dismay over just that world of collected objects that these standards have set out to measure. Time has, after all, unveiled them as nothing more than a gathering of futility, consigned to death and vanity (Rom. 8:20) and incapable of yielding ultimately any virtue besides their own demise. Despair over this world has thereby ploddingly carried with it a sullen sibling: despair over the Church. And despair over the Church is the great vice of modern Christianity, even (and perhaps especially) when harnessed to strategies of calculated and frustrated renewal.

It is important to apprehend and name this linkage, especially because the linkage itself comes in the form of masquerade: often those most set upon the reform of the Church, those most given over to explicit acts of ecclesial expansion or restoration, those most driven by the press for the

Church's self-assertion in the world of eyes and ears, are those caught up in a sense of dismay and anxiety at the Church's desperate clinging to the edges of objective success. There are others, of course, whose discontent and worry have simply given them over to weariness itself, and despair is now but an open image of their unforgiving passage through the Church's years. Together, we represent the restless, often angered progeny of Christian aimlessness and fragmentation, looking for indicatives in a context where these are inevitably sworn over to vanity.

Still, we know of a better way. We have heard of it with our ears at least. If the medicine of despair is hope and if hope is given in Christ Jesus—for he himself is "our hope" (1 Tim. 1:1)—then ecclesial convalescence must somehow be located within the realm of his enunciation. So we remember, if only dimly.

It is clear to most of us, in any case, that Scripture's words move in a direction diametrically opposed to the pessimism of denotation's striving. But for its hopeful references to point to some alternative life for world and Church, the Bible cannot be read as a simple gloss upon the histories that our habits quantify. The logic of denotation by which the Church gradually subjected itself to the laws of physical entropy must also loose its hard grasp of Scripture's reading if we are to apprehend the freedom of God's promises. The skills involved in such liberated hearing of the word are long atrophied, however, largely because of the very life that the Church in its many churches has embraced in setting up multiplied ecclesial purposes one against the other within the world's evaluative arena.

It is the goal of this book simply to begin anew, even if timidly, the exercise of these wasted muscles by which the Scripture's spiritual meanings are moved toward the hope that undergirds the Church as God's vessel for our final life in him. The exercise is small and its purpose modest: press perception from the detonated Church toward something signified through other means, obliquely perhaps, clothed in multicolored garments, apprehended from afar and through various highways, folded into and itself unfolding the shape of objects and histories that the world's own being wraps around, measured only by the forms of Scripture, before all other worlds are seen. To understand the Church, there is nothing to scrutinize—and no hope by which to be grasped—before finding it first within the contours of the Scripture's world, a world that contains within itself all the stones of the globe and all the earth's republics.

The exercises presented here engage a variety of perceptions—how we look at church-shopping, bad bishops, disunity, sexuality, spiritual formation, and the like. But they are all designed to engender hope through honing the skills of seeing the Church as bound up with something other than the denoted objects of the world. And the skills of such seeing involve some basic postures toward the Scripture's way of speaking, some set of understandings of how the armature of its meaning functions not only within its own terms, but inclusively and exhaustively for the world itself. For the Church's hope depends upon the Scripture's speaking to us of hope's own reality and form, first and necessarily, in its own words and not in another's, a reality and form that is the Christ, Jesus of Nazareth, the Son of God—casting down stones one by one and building them up again in life (Mark 13:2; John 2:19–22; 1 Pet. 2:4–8).

## The Scriptural Figure of Hope

That Scripture does speak primarily of Christ is a traditional claim, and it is one not yet entirely forgotten by the churches. Still, the claim itself is so rich and so broad in what it brings into view of God that its very reiteration must itself form a necessary part of Scripture's own perpetual reading. As Origen does in his biblical commentaries, the repeated insistence upon the value of the spiritual sense that punctuates his actual reading of texts becomes itself the kernel of the evangelical message. For the claim that Christ Jesus is the primary referent of Scripture has some basic implications whose significance needs reaffirmation if the power of the claim is to maintain its sway over the world of our lives themselves.

In the first place, there is the whole matter of what scriptural words themselves are really talking about. To say that the Scriptures really speak of Christ implies that scriptural words themselves denote something other than their ostensive reference, but denote rather some form of Christ himself. In the second place, and conversely, there is the matter of what it means to apprehend some form of Christ within the words of Scripture. For here the implication is that, in addition to referring directly to God's own being, the form of Christ connotes the very things that speak of him—the Scriptures, the Church, and even the world in its own way.

The language of denotation, connotation, and form has a complex history in philosophy, logic, and semantics, though our use of these terms here is not meant to lead us into the realm of this knotted tradition. Rather, my application of these distinctions moves in a more common usage, if decidedly metaphysical, direction, responding to the questions not only of "what are we talking about?" but of "who is doing the talking?" when it comes to Scripture and the Church who reads and proclaims it.[2] We speak of things or signs or words as denoting something when they point to it clearly as their primary meaning. Connotation, by contrast, is a meaning only indirectly given *through* some object, sign, or word, a meaning hinted at perhaps, found with difficulty only after all the others, implied or imaged as a metaphor of hope.

And behind these signifying things, signs, or words lie the forms themselves, the matter that is used for carrying meaning and often representing meaning itself as references—the objects, material, sounds, and inner strivings of the heart that give and seek expression. The forms of the world, of things earthly and spiritual, can speak and be spoken of, can be indicated directly or indirectly, can be denoted with a shout or connoted through the complexities of height and breadth and depth. And thus the truth is clothed, and hope will come into our view.

If we take as a fundamental scriptural given that Christ stands as the original form, before all things and through whom all things are made, then we can organize the dynamics of denotation and connotation within creation around this reality. Form is that which is most real in terms of God's being and will. Creation comprehends a myriad of realities whose being depends on their formliness in relation to the will and being of God—they exist *for* God and *by* God, and hence their reality is always given in direct reference *to* God, by way of denotation. This relation of created grace, however, implies that God's own form, given in Christ, somehow gives rise to the expansive love that creates new forms in its own right. To apprehend God truly—which is to know Christ Jesus—is to perceive in and through him something of God's creatures, of their time, their shape, their acts and futures, their own purpose and meaning (John 1:17–18). To behold Christ is somehow to understand the truth of the world that is Christ's own. Thus, the forms of the created world are connoted by Christ. For instance, St. Paul speaks of human marriage as a mystery that somehow refers to Christ's form in relation to the Church (Eph. 5:32): in this relationship, human marriage denotes the form of Christ loving the Church; while Christ's love itself connotes human marriage. Finally, the created forms of the world themselves—in the case

---

2. Late medieval logicians developed the use of these terms in sophisticated ways, while their modern definition can be traced to the work in logic of J. S. Mill.

above, husband and wife, their bodies and lives—denote and connote other created forms, depending on their historical location.

That Christ *has* a form is stated by Scripture itself—the likeness and form of God (2 Cor. 4:4; Phil. 2:6; Col. 1:15) and the literal likeness and form of a human slave obedient to death on a cross (Rom. 8:3; Phil. 2:7). And this form, in its complexity and with all of its temporal contours and details, is taken first by God, before all else, and also given first by him. This form is what all truthful speech about God entails and to what the Scriptures first refer. It is also what therefore gives rise, in its own meaning, to the signs and forms of whatever would speak the truth and manifest it. Thus, the Scriptures—and the Church—denote primarily the form of Christ; and just that form of Christ connotes the Scripture's words and content and even the histories of the world and Church that seem so misleadingly, in our own day, to hold the fullness of their meaning only within themselves, like mute stones.

Much of what the Church has said about the spiritual and figural meaning of the Scriptures and of events of time is bound up with these implications. What refers first to Christ's form and is itself created for such reference must somehow speak through the voice of another; and all that it subsequently says about the world around us, about objects and moments and persons, is said only through that gift of a grace that allows objects and moments and persons themselves to speak of Christ, to become themselves indicators of the Spirit. What the Church calls a figure is nothing else than something that God makes for the sake of speaking about himself, even as that something ramifies its own references around itself, like a star in its illuminating and creative reach. Christ in his form—through whom and for whom all things are made (Col. 1:16)—created all things in their own proliferated forms and relationships to speak of himself—they denote the Lord, while they themselves are connoted by his own formly love.

How different is this way of understanding the world of human experience from our normal use of language! When we use human language, we assume that its primary purpose is to point to things, to refer to objects, and, if not objects themselves, then to refer to realms of meaning—thoughts, feelings, goals, attitudes—that are given shape by the referents that language indicates. Yet if language—even and especially the language of Scripture—is itself the object of God's creating hope in Christ, it is not first a referring tool, but itself a referent, something whose meaning is bound up primarily in Christ's giving himself and showing himself through its forms. The divine Word refers to the Scriptures and to the Church itself, not directly, but as a connoted meaning, something that comes with it, tied to its life somehow, as clothing, as resonance, as image and metaphor, as synecdoche, as the meaning in the world of the Word's own voice. When Christ is uttered by the Father and utters in himself for himself, then the Scriptures and the Church, his body, are heard.

St. Augustine points to this primary fact about the world's meaning in relationship to temporal reality and all that it contains: the events of salvation, he writes, are in themselves God's speech in history (*Epistle* 102.6.33). These include not only events and their players referred to by the Scriptures, but the Scriptures themselves, as objects of God's providential composition. And within Scripture's own referring reach, the whole world is found, not as a set of inert objects, but as meaningful referents and references, outlined in their divine significance. The world points to God directly, for God, in all his works, connotes himself through their denotative speech. For Augustine, this truth is given in the incarnation of the Word, whose being is the sign of God's interior essence and whose being in the world as Word made flesh, as speaker of words and as creator of new words and speakers, establishes the realm by which meaning and time are held together (cf. Augustine, *De doctrina* 2.2–3; 2.10.15; 3.9.13). As the word of God tabernacling in human life, Christ Jesus made the Father known within the world of created beings; yet in doing so, as their own creator, he continually makes possible and real the very forms of praise by which such knowledge finds its term. In the form of God, he denotes God; in the form of the slave, he connotes the servant's song of adoration, that is, the Scriptures and Church, which is his body.

## The Figural Tradition of the Church: The Hope of Providence

Both Scripture and Church together are therefore connoted by the form of Christ. This is a traditional assertion and one whose implications undergird the Christian hope. But it is also a difficult assertion to sustain in the face of the world's alternative systems of significance, where things are organized by the logic and the systems of direct and finally only functional reference. Hence, the scripturally enfigured meaning of the Church's life is rightly understood to be an ethical and ascetic concern, whose maintained apprehension represents the Church's hopeful testimony to its Lord. The traditional outlines of figural reality, as given in Christ, are therefore rehearsed in the manner of a virtuous discipline, something pursued as a means of being "at one" with the early Church's own embrace of authentic witness. Catholicity and apostolicity are in part given and manifested through this common rehearsal.

For instance, the unity of the Church's hope and testimony stands on the recognition that, as the end of the law (Rom. 10:4), Christ stands toward the whole of Israel's Scriptures as their fulfiller, the one who takes up each element, every iota in its details, and carries them in his person (Matt. 5:17–18). The Gospels' clear enunciation of Jesus' historical life as being contoured by this assumption of detail—"that the scriptures . . . might be fulfilled" (Matt. 26:56; Luke 4:21; 24:26–27)—underscores the way in which the whole of the Law and the Prophets was rightly understood as finding its primary referent in Jesus' own person (cf. the discussion of Moses and Elijah in Luke 9:30–31) and, in doing so, exposing its meaning as the bearer of historical form for the revelation of God's self-giving to the world of time.

The twin characteristics of ending (or perfecting) and fulfilling that the New Testament identifies as denoting the relationship of Christ to the Scriptures are described dynamically in terms of figure (referred to variously in the Greek as type, form, image, pattern, example; cf. Rom. 5:14; 8:29; 1 Cor. 10:6, 11; 15:49; Gal. 4:19; Phil. 2:6–7; 3:10; 1 Pet. 2:21). This Latin (and later English) word had a latitude of meaning that was designed to grasp a particular set of historical enactments that God created to accomplish the conformation of the world with his purposes in the incarnation, a set bounded by the locutions of Scripture itself. Building on these New Testament articulations of enfiguration, the early Church turned to Christ as the historical revelation both of what the Scriptures described in formal terms and as the referent of what it indicated as a historical future for the world.

It is true that by the seventeenth century a relatively limited and wooden method of typological exegesis had developed for relating Old and New Testament. But the method's original progenitors of the first Church saw before them not a system of emblematic correlation, but a vast arena of sought-after and discovered disclosures of God's work in drawing all things into Christ, through his subsuming of all scriptural forms in their reference to the world's history (Eph. 1:9–12). Both past and future, Jewish Israel and the Church refer or find their purposed form in the person of Christ Jesus, and the direction and character of this purpose is variously and repeatedly given over to discernment and adoration in the identification of scriptural figure within the world. On the one hand, the parameters of this figural discernment are given in the scriptural forms aimed at and embodied in Christ; on the other, these parameters embrace the infinity of God's creative acts within the universe. Christ Jesus as the "all in all" (Eph. 1:23) founds the Scriptures as bearing the breadth of articulated meaning for the world. His exhaustive embrace also founds the world, in its openness to such breadth, as belonging to God. And so the world finds its purposed self within the endless corridors of Scripture's figures, "unexplored and unsubdued," to use a phrase of Newman. The rigorous journey through this landscape was the central vocation, for instance, of Origen; yet it remains for the Church as a whole not only a vocation of hopeful recognition still unfulfilled, but, carelessly and thoughtlessly, no longer even pursued.

But *if* pursued, then receptive of all the promises by which the joyful peace of the Church's hopeful life within the world is governed. For if *in* Christ, then *of* God. That, at least, is the logic of the formal breadth of Scripture within the specifically Christian trinitarian assertion of the coming of Israel's Messiah as the incarnation of God's Son: the words of Scripture are the words of God, spoken by the Spirit (1 Tim. 4:1; John 6:63; Rev. 19:10). When Jesus refers to David's speech in Psalm 110 as "inspired by the Spirit" (Matt. 22:43–45), he dwells on the significance of particular words and pronouns and uses these particularities as clear statements regarding the historical reference of messianic prophetic fulfillments within God's cosmic plan. If the Scriptures are Christ's, then history as God's work is given in the form of the Scriptures. The words of Scripture, derived from the very interior reality of God's life (as Augustine insisted) and expressed by the Spirit in the form of the Son, constitute the language or grammar of history articulated in human terms.

The providential breadth of this claim regarding the words of Scriptures is temporally unlimited. Thus, when God "thinks" about human history, the forms of Scripture describe his divine ideas; when God "looks" at human history, he sees the forms of Scripture as the reflection of his will (Israel, David, Gomer, Ruth, etc.); when God "directs" human history, it moves in and into conformance with the forms of Scripture. And conversely, Scripture represents God's thinking, seeing, and moving with respect to creation, in all the creative complexity and depth that his utterly simple speech represents within the refracted understandings of the world. The hermeneutical implications of this providential breadth explain why its supporting interpretive tradition was never aggravated by the historical-critical conundra of textual and linguistic diversity within the scriptural corpus that have, by contrast, so flummoxed liberal and conservative biblical critics over the last two centuries. As Augustine implies, if scriptural form is given in a providential cast primarily, then the diversities that mark its various cultural receptions are not problems to be resolved by critical excisions, revisions, and reconstitutions, but are rightly viewed as themselves aspects of the historical force of a divine text asserting itself in time according to a creative will.[3] And critical wrestlings with a text are neither more nor less useful than their service to this will, whose formal clarity ever refers back to the scriptural forms themselves. The modern interpretive battle over Scripture's textual integrity is less about Scripture itself than it is about a common perplexity over the Church's vocation to be subject to the power of God within the breadth of Christ's rule. It is a perplexity that emerges from the violence lurking behind the functionalist and fragmenting denotative motive from the start, and its only opponent, practically speaking, is the deliberate discipline of a renewed perception of the Church's proper location within this history of scriptural form.

## The Figural Discipline of the Hopeful Church

For this, after all, is the issue at stake in assuming the stance of hope that constitutes the fruit of apprehending scriptural providence in the first place—a stance whose power to transform lives into the figure of God's redemptive will would place us in the form of Christ's own mind (Phil. 2:5–8). Such subjection to the subject servant, obedient to a deathly judgment because of the hope that was in him, is the very end of the Church's faithful self-perception within the unfolding of history's scriptural identity. All of Scripture—because all is Christ's—becomes the life of the Church, its form, its destiny, its meaning. And the proper way to look at the Church, in this providential context, is as a form-taker and form-giver within the breadth of Scripture itself, whose meaning is always receptive of the words that Christ himself enunciates within the echoing chambers of time's divinely collected objects.

Such a context of ecclesial life ought to attenuate radically the enormous anxieties that so consistently drive the Church and its members into historical spasms of desperation—anxieties over material stability and personal moral congruence and doctrinal coherence. While the concerns

---

3. This emerges in the early chapters of Augustine, *De doctrina christiana* 3.

themselves are usually well founded, their ability to engender decisions of disorder represents a failure of witness to the providential character of the Church's connoted life in Christ. It is *his* form that draws all forms of ecclesial existence into a unity of purpose. And both the singular nature of that form and its scriptural diversity of meaning, gathered together in his cross and resurrection, create the patience by which the Church's identity gains its integrity in suffering time and time's objects, rather than manipulating them.

In our day the realities of church disunity, of disputed moral disciplines or ecclesial decision-making, of confused scriptural readings or even missionary purposes, drive Christians into postures of competing aggressions and exhausted surrenders, as individuals and groups seek to reformulate and apply the criterion of quantified integrity to their common life and ministry. Yet as a connoted sign of Christ's own form, the Church cannot be an instrumental tool, but only a revelatory form of its own. The Church's witness of hope, and indeed the hopefulness of its promised future, is given in its disclosure of Christ in time; and Christian faithfulness is revealed in the subjection of life to this inescapable sway of the Church's disclosive work.

The chapters that follow seek to exercise this hope by confronting areas of ecclesial anxiety in a way that assumes such disclosive power. There is no free space in the midst of Christian struggle for individuals or groups to recreate anew the Church's form according to some aspect of the Scripture's application. If there is a whole Scripture, then in Christ, its whole embodiment in the connoted Church and world is guaranteed: the Church will be Israel in mercy and judgment; the Church will take the form of all the nations, in judgment and in mercy; the Church will die and rise in Christ, as mercy and judgment meet in him. As a result, there is no saving the Church, no discovering the Church afresh, no growing the Church or even tearing it down (Paul prescinds from both!). There is only living with, within, under, for, beside, and for the sake of the Church, for Jesus Christ has created us in and for this, and we cannot escape from this vocation and reality. Hence, it is sure; for he is faithful.

There is an urgent need to see this within the concrete forms and challenges of the Church's life, to press ceaselessly in this age for such seeing, from every vantage and in every posture. On this note, let me acknowledge two elements of this present volume's style. First, the perspectives given in this book's essays are often shaped in specifically Anglican terms. This is so because of the need to be particularistically moored in the life of a real church, visible stones and all, since such limitations are the material of providence, the only matter given over to be figurally molded. Furthermore, Anglicanism stands, I believe, as a peculiar exemplar of travail and of a historically marked vocation within the struggles of the Church's greater conformance won through and despite rebellion and resistance. But Anglicanism does not denote the Church as a whole; it is only one church among many.[4] Yet although not denotative of, Anglicanism is (as is every church in its own way) connotative of the Church as a whole (for Christ is embodied in us!). Thus, we find ourselves as churches, whoever we are, in each other's ecclesial agonies, and God proves his promised unity despite ourselves! In brief, the frequent bow to Anglicanism in these essays is a plea, derived not from denominational chauvinism, but from the realization that we are saved in history through our extradenominational figural recognitions. Let us look to one another. This is all the more so because, at present, Anglicanism itself is beset with travails that have reached, it seems, almost a zenith of destructive power, to the point that one wonders if, indeed, its ecclesial integrity can survive (let alone the persistence of its members, such as the present writer). It is only by such looking to each other, and within this mutual gaze by the discovery of the figural press of Christ's providential grasp, that we can, perhaps, discover the grace of transformative, because humiliating, perseverance.

Second, and in line with the above, the method of these essays is that of providential induction, the discernment of divine movement within the limitations of history's small and knotted contentions. Individuals, episodes, conversations, and distant pleadings from the past are laid out, not as some chain of reasoning, as much as the found objects turned up in a singular search that demand a faithful seeing. Providence is always circumstantial, and its arguments, drifting about the Scriptures as the Scripture's very and varied substance, are thus always discoveries, not strategies. This will perhaps irritate devotees of today's theological "power-point"; but God's forms are not purposefully displayed on reason's screen, they are embodied in the blurred corners of brute mortality.

If the way we talk reflects this fact, then form takes shape in our midst. What form? The rumble of stones hushes, not one left upon another (Mark 13:2). The Church, instead, emerges as the shadow cast by Christ,

4. I generally use lowercase "church" in referring to a fragmented denominational or local body that exists in the wake of the Church's division and as the figural detritus of Christ's sufferings; while uppercase "Church" refers to the unity of Christians referred to figuratively in Scripture as the object of Christ's continuous bodily destiny.

even while he strides across the world of his own making. It stands at the edges of his form, shimmering in some unimagined reach as his contours take the earth's objects into a movement of uncertain color, lit by the sun, marking the invention of time, inscribing the steps left behind for another to follow.

# Part 1

# The Merchants' Tears

*The Peace of the Church in the Marketplace of the World*

*And the merchants of the earth weep and mourn for*

*her, since no one buys her cargo any more.*

—Revelation 18:11

# 1

## Christian Unity
## in an Age
## of Church-Shopping

Some time ago, the congregation where I worked spent time in discussion about starting a new mission in the booming little town next door to us, a kind of suburb to our own city. In our commitment to ecumenism, however, we decided to see if we could do this with the local ELCA congregation, as a kind of joint new start, given the new relationship between our two denominations (however long it lasts). Among other things, we began scouting around for land. And while many parcels were available, most of them were not able to be zoned for churches. The rest we could not afford. At one point, we found a nice piece of property, however—well located, with beautiful views of the nearby mountains, not too expensive. Alas, the property sat right next to a small Missouri Synod Lutheran Church. I thought I had better go talk to them, so I made an appointment and met with their pastor and elders. "We'd rather you didn't move next door to us," they said. "Are you afraid that we might start competing against one another?" I asked. "Oh no, that's not the real problem. You see, we can't cooperate with you or with the ELCA Lutherans because we don't recognize you as orthodox Christians. And having these two churches right next to each other, both of which might have the word Lutheran in them, will be very confusing to people." "I suppose it might," I said. "But if we're a few blocks away, instead of next door, will that be less confusing?" The pastor answered, "Of course, it will be more as if people are just making a choice among options, and less as if we don't get along." Then he added, "Why push the issue?"

A good question. No one likes to think that Christians are actually, really, *rootedly* divided. If, on the other hand, we are simply picking what we like, just shopping, then the variety of choices appears reasonable, perhaps even exciting.

This is the era we have entered: an age of excitement amid choices. In beginning a reflection on the character of the Christian Church in this time, we should remember, however, that the generally religious context of church-shopping is not new. Rather it informs the soil out of which—and for some time away from which—the Christian community originally grew. To the extent that we have, as it were, returned to that earth—in the scriptural sense of mortality in the phrase *earth to earth*—we are also perhaps witnessing the decrepitude or senility of an aging organism. Or perhaps, it is just one of those opportunities that mask themselves as the blows of fate. In any case, it was St. Paul, after all, who entered into the heart of pagan religion and stood "in the market place" of Athens "every day with those who chanced to be there" (Acts 17:17), arguing with and meeting with, among many others, "Epicurean[s] and Stoic[s]." Onlookers observed that Paul was offering a new and foreign divinity (17:18, 21), and Paul himself later surveyed the variety of altars and putative gods that the Athenians displayed, took his place beside them, and hawked his own alternative (17:22–28)—as yet "unknown," perhaps, but surely better than all the rest.

Lucian, a second-century Roman satirist, wrote a colorful dialogue entitled *Philosophies for Sale*. In it, he gives his own take on the kind of scene that Paul entered upon, one apparently more common than the now-exalted episode in Acts might lead us to suppose. In Lucian's skit, Zeus and Hermes organize the sale in a market of some Greek city in the east. Zeus oversees the affair and directs his helper: "Arrange the benches . . . bring on the 'ways of life' [the 'philosophies']. . . you Hermes, be crier and call them together." And so Hermes begins: "Under the blessing of Heaven, let the buyers now appear at the sales-room. We shall put up for sale philosophies of every type and all manner of creeds; and if anyone is unable to pay cash, he is to name a surety and pay next year! Now, which one do you want to bring on first?" Zeus replies: "This fellow with the long hair . . . he seems to be someone of distinction." "You Pythagorean, come forward and let yourself be looked over by the company." "Hawk him now!" barks out Zeus; and Hermes bellows forth: "The noblest of philosophies for sale, the most distinguished! Who'll buy? Who wants to be more than man? Who wants to apprehend the music of the spheres and to be born again?"[1]

To be "born again" is an interesting promise in this religious potpourri. Still, if Christianity began with Paul in the marketplace, it did not stay there long. For in the scenes that Lucian and other Roman commentators paint for us, Christians rarely if ever appear.[2] By the time that Celsus is disparaging common Christian evangelists in the later second century, these tricksters for Christ whom he derides move stealthily in private, not in the public square, preying on the ill and the bedridden, the poor, and the ill-educated in their homes and workplaces (cf. Origen, *Contra Celsum* 3.53, 55). It is not so much public snake oil that they are selling in competition with the priests of Cybele and the votaries of Mithras that elicits Celsus's scorn; he attacks, instead, the Christian propensity to infiltrate and convince the credulous, their quiet development of an underground current that, gathering insidious force, moves against the stream of the civic culture as a whole. Indeed, it is their *distance from* the market altogether that sows Celsus's great unease.

Celsus had a point, of course. What refuses competition, what seeks not a share of the market, but the whole of life, is absolutely dangerous to the carefully orchestrated framework and balance of a diverse empire. To compete openly is to establish diversity as harmless; but to overcome competition is to own the world. And so the triumph of the Christian Church is celebrated by Lactantius in the early fourth century as the means by which Paul's marketplace is finally set in order, synthesized, and closed. Philosophical sects, Lactantius proclaims, "arm themselves for battle, neither knowing what they ought to defend nor what to refute; and [they] make attacks everywhere, without distinction, upon all things which are brought forward by those who disagree with them," canceling each other out in the process, multiplying their partial truths, and wallowing in the downward spiral of their own extinction. For the whole truth, Lactantius emphasizes, not the bits and pieces of the marketplace of

1. Translation cited in Robert L. Wilken, *The Christians as the Romans Saw Them* (New Haven: Yale University Press, 1984), 74–75.

2. Cf. Ramsay MacMullen, *Christianizing the Roman Empire* (New Haven: Yale University Press, 1984), chap. 4.

religions and ideas, is given by God alone—given by God and embodied in the Christian Church. Are the pagans so foolish as to miss the fact that truth is uniform and therefore that competing truths are but the signs of either ignorance or vice?[3]

Lest we think of Lactantius as but the first in that long line of hegemonic apologists for imperial Christianity—and he wrote during the years of Constantinian transition—we should recall, however, that his own vision of the uniformity of truth was marked by a remarkable diversity, doctrinally speaking. His own writings would probably not have withstood the theological inquisition of a furious post-Nicene debate, so full are they of elements of reflection and interest, borrowed from marginal thinkers, gnostics, and dreamers. Rather, he is an example of a deeper quest, at the end of pagan dominance, witnessed to by many in the ancient world—a quest for an underlying peace within the larger universe of competing spirits and metaphysical attitudes. Peace was sought so profoundly because the experienced outcome of demonic competition was the dissolution and destruction of the human spirit in the face of worldly pain and ultimate death. Who could survive, if there were no place to stand?

The genre of conversion stories from the early Church, which some call "disappointment with philosophy" tales, had begun already in Justin, who recounts his conversion almost as a retracing in his own intellectual life of the steps of Paul around the Areopagus. The genre's popularity and repetition attests to the sense of hopelessness among many for whom the Church's gospel brought deliverance, by moving people into some kind of steadfast wholeness.[4] While high-minded pagan philosophers like Porphyry could label Christianity as a religion that appealed only to the "sick-minded" and frightened, the need for some kind of liberation from the welter of competing and disabled claims of the Hellenistic pantheon was apparently widespread among the population, educated or not.

And so Lactantius's affirmation of the truth's uniformity in Christ was less a totalizing imprisonment for the timid than it was the establishment of a secure space that could encompass and integrate the feeble puniness of multiplied and mutually henpecked paganisms: all that is partial among the philosophies is here brought together and made one. Far from excluding anything, the unifying vision of the one truth offered

3. Lactantius, *Divine Institutes* 7.7 (trans. W. Fletcher; Ante-Nicene Fathers 7; repr. Peabody, Mass.: Hendrickson, 1994), 204.

4. Cf. A. D. Nock, *Conversion* (Oxford: Oxford University Press, 1933), 107–8, 255–71; E. R. Dodds, *Pagan and Christian in an Age of Anxiety* (New York: Norton, 1970), chap. 4.

by the Church brings peace to the vying and stunting rivalries of the religious market. And in this space, for people like Lactantius, reigned a remarkable freedom to think, explore, and live out a diversity of opinion that today's beleaguered and hence defensive denominational watchdogs would barely imagine possible for the righteous.

To speak of truth's secure space—that is, of a Church whose own shape figures the uniformity (if complexity) of the truth's embrace—is to offer an alternative to the market of religions. This would be an alternative, not in form of slavery to emancipation, but in the form of peace to warfare and thus of the possibility for free inquiry to the imposition of intellectual desperation. This is one of the great sociological paradoxes—at least paradoxical to contemporary liberals—touching upon religious liberty: such liberty's most fruitful form (as opposed to its most desiccated diversity) emerged more often in contexts of secure establishment than in environments of overthrown restraint. This, at least, is one of the results of more recent, if revisionist, research into the dynamics, for instance, of toleration in medieval Europe, a place where Enlightenment caricature too long veiled the openness of the former in order to distract from the cruel impatience of the latter.[5] Speculative interest in Islamic scholarship and wisdom was more prevalent in the twelfth century among Westerners than it is now in the twenty-first! And for all of its limitations and occasional precariousness, Jewish existence in Christian Europe through much of the Middle Ages was far more secure than when the sixteenth century forced new ideas regarding toleration. Indeed, some recent scholars go so far as to suggest that it was in part the erosion of medieval ecclesial authority during the late medieval period in favor of secular powers that spurred the rise of anti-Semitic violence in that period and on into the sixteenth century.[6] (The link between uniform religious environments and toleration can be observed, sociologically, in certain other religious establishments, like medieval Islam.) The truth's secure space of the Church provided, one might say, a kind of peaceable landscape across which the community's long march into unenforced discernment was guaranteed a safe passage and where no one would be obliged to lose their shirt in the course of endless and inevitable bargainings for the soul.

5. Cf. Cary J. Nederman, "Discourses and Contexts of Tolerance in Medieval Europe," in *Beyond the Persecuting Society: Religious Toleration before the Enlightenment* (ed. John C. Laursen and Cary J. Nederman; Philadelphia: University of Pennsylvania Press, 1998), 13–24. Many of the essays in this groundbreaking book deserve careful attention.

6. Ibid., 21.

But if the Church's very being came to embody the end of religious markets—at least historically—how could it find itself today morphing into the market itself? An article in a church magazine announces, "'Playful' Approach to Marketing Draws Many Newcomers to Chicago-Area Parish." The approach in question involves the sending out of thousands of flyers every few months, the last of which, the writer reports, has "generated a tempest in a teapot." For "the first [flyer] said in a bold headline, 'The best Catholic church in town is . . .'; the second said, 'The best Protestant church in town is. . . .' Open either flyer, and you get the answer: 'St. Nicholas [Episcopal Church].'" This is the church that, in the rector's words, "blends the catholic liturgy with the 'feisty democratic spirit of Protestantism.'" Playful, surely. But although the pastors of Queen of the Rosary Roman Catholic Church and of Elk Grove Presbyterian Church claimed there were no hard feelings, not all their congregants apparently agreed. The phone lines buzzed with complaints, as did area newspapers, something St. Nicholas's rector apparently saw as "good for business."[7] This is not exactly the Thirty Years' War; it is, rather, something far more evolved: the hawking, not of the truth directly, but of its space, its space now subdivided into lots and acreage, where the differences lie in the amenities and the views. But without a landscape, where shall the truth be found? Unless, of course, it has long since left the precincts.

The transformation of the Church from market-slayer into the marketplace itself is a complex one, historically.[8] So-called convergence theories, which relate social change to mainly economic transformation, have their own thoughts on the matter, as do recent students of population and climatological shifts. But most researchers continue to place a decisive dividing line somewhere in the sixteenth century, no matter the contested question of genealogy. Certainly, the sixteenth century represents a popular-religious watershed. Sociologist Peter Berger describes the experiential contours of this dividing line as distinguishing, on the pre-sixteenth-century side, a world of religious fate in which one woke up always to the givenness of one's religion (and work and play for that matter) that had been granted, in all its forms and meanings, solely and immemorially by the community.[9] Whereas, Berger writes, on the post-

7. *The Living Church* (Aug. 26, 2001): 9.
8. For a contemporary display of postmodern analysis of "market religion," see Lieven Boeve, "Market and Religion in Postmodern Culture," *Theology* 102 (Jan./Feb. 1999): 28–36. The difference of Boeve's theological approach with that of this volume will be obvious.
9. Peter L. Berger, The Heretical Imperative: Contemporary Possibilities of Religious Affirmation (Garden City, N.Y.: Doubleday, 1979), 11–15 and passim.

sixteenth-century side of the line, there was quite clearly (if not always consistently) a world now shot through with choice, perhaps not always individual choices initially, but at least communal choices for religion in general (and more and more for work and play as well) and, increasingly, choices for the kinds of forms that would grant religion its individual and communal meanings. There was now the possibility that one could not only choose the form of one's Christian belief, but even invent a form of worship (or rediscover it from Scripture, as self-justification might put it) or create the structure of a church or the shape of catechesis. Whatever diversities existed previously, all this was astonishingly new.

And so, by the end of the sixteenth century, we see French Catholic Pierre Charron reflecting for the first time on the social forces that might lead a person to be a Catholic or a Protestant or a Jew or a Muslim—why is a man or woman one rather than the other? This was a set of questions that, bound up with the presuppositions that allow for the discipline of the sociology of religion in the first place, is possible only in a divided space wherein truth's tether has been cut loose.[10] Where to land, if land at all, or how to land if we will land as one? The philosophical problems inherent in this opening to social relativity were just being broached; but the questions themselves could be asked only by someone forced to choose between options. As economists say, competition derives from the rivalry between real choices. And the reality here was the division of the Western Church. Whatever the causes of this division, its very social *fact* altered, quite literally and altogether, the landscape of truth itself.

This being said, I must emphasize that it was not until the mid-to-late seventeenth century that the crossing of the line, from fate to choice if you will, was seen as problematic to anyone. This needs to be noted because the actual Christian ideology of truth-as-uniform was not abandoned simply because of the Reformation (and this is important to remember as we reflect below on specific denominational, in this case Anglican, identity and possibilities). As is well known, Reformers by and large understood themselves to be driven by this vision of the uniform truth; so too the political press of the period was for an ever wider territory in which to establish a given confession. Just because so many *different* groups were wrong about the gospel did not mean that there was not one group—one's own!—that grasped it perfectly.

Even the moderates on the scene of religious controversy did not immediately give up on the notion of a unitary truth within a secure

10. See Charron's *De la sagesse* (1601), vol. 1.

landscape. Contemporary scholars of religious diversity, for instance, make the distinction between toleration as a search for concordant truth and toleration as true pluralism. Pluralistic toleration appears only in the eighteenth century. For through at least much of the seventeenth century, the most irenic and forbearing Christian leaders of separated churches—and there were not many—held on to the possibility of religious peace mainly through a hope that patience and leniency would allow such interchange between separated parties as to bring all to a common confession of the truth and to a unity of ecclesial purpose (usually centered in their own institution). This acceptance of temporary diversity for the sake of eventual uniform truth drove, for instance, the most liberal of the Roman Catholic reformers of the sixteenth century (e.g., Cardinal Pole in England) and later Catholic and Protestant irenicists in the seventeenth century (e.g., Cassander and Leibniz).[11]

By the late seventeenth century, however, the face of toleration itself changed. On the one hand, we find religious polemicists finally wondering aloud and at length as to the negative religious meaning of division as an ongoing phenomenon. The grand argument of Bishop Bossuet of Meaux on the "variations of Protestantism" stands as a large question mark on the religious value of social fissiparousness, given in the breakup of the Latin Church.[12] Bossuet, in brief, argued for the denigration of Protestantism in toto from the fact of its inherent tendency to fragment itself into more and more diverse and separated groups, a tendency that he took as an a priori contradiction of the gospel. Despite its partisan approach and its still-standard anti-Protestant polemic, the basic issues that this kind of reflection initiated still lie at the root of modern research into the phenomenon of secularization: does the division of the Christian Church, its establishment of territorial distinctions and enmities, and its final press toward the recognition of entrenched diversity imply an inevitable weakening of the Christian faith itself?[13] Many sociologists believe, happily or regretfully, that it must.

But the concerns of people like Bossuet were only the negative reaction to a far more powerful and growing shift *away* from any vestigial notion

11. Cf. Mario Turchetti, "Religious Concord and Political Tolerance in Sixteenth- and Seventeenth-Century France," *Sixteenth Century Journal* 22 (1991): 15–25.

12. *Histoire des variations des églises protestantes* (1688).

13. This question has marked the framework for much of Peter Berger's later work. But it also lies behind much empirical research, such as that by Steven Bruce. Secularization theory, of course, does not confine itself to the question of pluralism and tends to make use of various forms of convergence theory. Cf. the well-known study of Canada and the United States by David Martin, *A General Theory of Secularization* (New York: Harper & Row, 1978).

of uniform truth altogether. It was a movement that led, rather, to the embrace of religious choice, whose alluring attractions had been released already a century or more before and were steadily gaining adherents. That is to say, warnings about the religious dangers of division were but a sign that such division was finally being popularly accepted as a way of life itself—a new philosophy, one might say. And liberal spirits, in the proper use of the term, were now those who were moving away from any expectation of concordancy toward the establishment of a true pluralistic realm of toleration. And one might ask what it was that, by the end of the seventeenth century, had turned division, with its connotations of a fall from grace, into something more positive, something to be welcomed, into full-fledged pluralism? A single ingredient, I believe: the protracted experience of violence.

Violence—real, social, enveloping, and seemingly without end, from the early sixteenth century to the mid-seventeenth century—the violence of Germany, of Holland and Flanders, of France and Switzerland, of the Thirty Years' War, of England and its civil wars leading to *the* Civil War and Commonwealth anarchy. Violence that, for all of its diverse causes and ends, was always called by its participants and sufferers "religious war" and about which, finally, even poets and painters came wearily to describe its pointlessness. Violence—and violence alone—becomes the primary catalyst for toleration. *Les malheurs de la guerre* (The miseries of war) was the title that Nicholas Callot gave to his horrific series of pictorial engravings of northern France's devastation in the first part of the seventeenth century, as Catholic and Protestant armies raged back and forth through its helpless villages and towns, destroying up to a third or more of its population. And widely published images like his became the frame of reference for a tired acquiescence to religious diversity and then a final embrace of what the sixteenth century had so vigorously scattered. The result was that scattering itself becomes truth enough, just enough truth to keep the peace.

I shall offer as clear an assertion as I can in this regard: the "new market," the *marché neuf* that is the *forum redivivum* of Christendom, brought back 1,300 years after Lactantius seemingly bid it farewell, is truly something new. In the wake of ecclesial division and of the fears of its unrestrained violence, the religious market of modernity turns out to be but the sublimation of the Church's own unresolved furies and hatreds among its members, now cast into a world of enforced diversities. Let us note what the modern hero of the market (though he did not use the word), Adam Smith, says of the optimum relation between church and commonwealth:

> The interested and active zeal of religious teachers can be dangerous and troublesome only where there is either but one sect tolerated in the society, or where the whole of a large society is divided into two or three great sects; the teachers of each acting by concert, and under a regular discipline and subordination. But that zeal must be altogether innocent where the society is divided into two or three hundred, or perhaps into as many thousand small sects, of which no one could be considerable enough to disturb the public tranquility. The teachers of each sect, seeing themselves surrounded on all sides with more adversaries than friends, would be obliged to learn that candour and moderation which is so seldom to be found among the teachers of those great sects. (*The Wealth of Nations* 5.1.3)

Those who think division in its small beginnings is but a small sin must remember Jesus' words about anger and the murderous endings of name-calling (Matt. 5:22). Smith, after all, has seen both where it must lead and why it must lead there, when once the cat of Christian rivalry is out of the bag: Thousands upon thousands of sects, he tells us, will keep the cover on the roiled passions of religious men and women; more and more division will, of itself, neutralize the violence of its origins. This is the recipe not only for a new market but for a new world.

The new market and the new world contain, of course, many of the same dilemmas as in the pagan marketplaces of old: which path, for instance, among the thousands, ought one to take for life's sake? Christianity had, since Lucian's time, raised the stakes considerably—a "way of life" had become "the way to eternal life." And from Donne to Chillingworth, for instance, we find by the seventeenth century a reprise of the "disappointment with philosophy" genre of conversion story, now transposed into confessional journeys, in which salvation becomes the prize for the *right choice of church*. Should it be Calvinist? or Roman? or Anglican? Many accounts of this "journey of choice" survive from the early seventeenth century. But a profound change has overcome the search since the era of Hellenistic agony: now peace, peace from the competing claims, not of *daimones* or spirits, but of Christian communities themselves, is an offer taken away from the truth's space and indeed from truth itself and given over to the individual. If the Church (and, in a sense, the state as well) cannot guard the peace . . . then who can? Only individuals; individuals, in our acts of decision-making. And it should come as no surprise that such decisions could no longer, on their own, bear the weight of a singular eternity. Thus we find that salvation itself, the truth eternally asserted and grasped, is removed to a realm accessible to all chosen paths of personal conscience and civic respect.

The most famous (though hardly the first) theorist of this personalization and individualization of the Church's truth is John Locke.[14] His first *Letter concerning Toleration* (written in 1685), appearing just after the Glorious Revolution that maintained a Protestant monarchy in the wake of James II's openings to Catholicism, lays out the principles of what would, in fact, become the denominationalism of modern America and later Europe. Locke's *Letter,* influenced by his contacts in the Netherlands and coming in the long and disruptive wake of the disastrous English Civil War, seeks out a kind of rationalist scriptural minimalism, devoid of the Bible's historical train, whose theological value he will later encode in his classic treatise entitled *The Reasonableness of Christianity* (1695). The latter could be described as an outline for a religion of tolerance. His synthetic argument, in these two essays, runs something like this: Scripture itself, in the form of the New Testament, offers no command beyond the moral law of charity and self-restraint, pursued without coercion and thus with a sincere conscience. Beyond this, Scripture tells us nothing about ecclesial polity, and the question of the true church is left ambiguously untouched by the sacred writers. Since the Christian churches are in fact divided, Locke says, and since Scripture offers us no clues as to what church to choose, it is only God who can tell which group is right or wrong, based on the character of their moral integrity. This being the case, both Christian and civil duty combine in demanding mutual toleration among sects, since only such toleration can protect the individual conscience from constraint and provide a civic space for the exercise of good works.

It is interesting to consider that, if any social order or philosophy were able to offer a guarantee for salvation, it would surely be this proposal of Locke's. This is so because, in making his plea for toleration as pluralism, Locke asserts three central theological axioms that mark an identity

14. Despite Locke's modern fame, it is now generally acknowledged that his thinking on toleration was largely dependent on writers known to him during his stay in Holland and France, especially Huguenot exile Pierre Bayle. Bayle, in fact, had both a wider vision of toleration, as including Catholics and atheists (unlike Locke), but also was among the first to argue at length that toleration could not include permission for the "intolerant"—an ethical move with much appeal today (cf. the premises of the late Dutch politician Pym Fortuyn, who argued that, for example, Moslem immigrants undermined the tolerant bases of Dutch society through their exclusivistic religion and hence their entry into Europe should be limited).

between the tolerant society and the actual *receipt* of the kingdom of God—and hence place salvation easily with the reach of purely social arrangements. First, he redefines the Christian church as a voluntary society, thus making its character based not on its witness, its "oneness, holiness, catholicity, and apostolicity," let alone on its historical relationship with Christ Jesus, but on the Church's relation of freedom to the individual and in its harmlessness toward the commonwealth. Second, in doing so Locke quite explicitly excludes from the Church's essential character any reality that could go beyond its being such a benign vessel for individual conscience. Third, he transposes the peace given by the embrace of God's truth within a broad landscape of historical experience, into the sense of ease with which the individual, in this or that situation, pursues his or her efforts at honest goodness. The more smoothly run the gears of choice that take an individual in and out of a church, the more clearly society and its churches have established a realm of unencumbered sincerity. And thus, the more firmly salvation becomes a possession of the community as a whole.

We can see, by implication, how church-shopping could become, in itself, a *religious* virtue and how a participating individual might claim a more certain religious future for being such an unencumbered chooser among churches. Whether people today actually *feel* more virtuous for being such a chooser, and a frequent one, is a question for which there is not yet decisive data. But that such choosing has become something in our culture that we conspire to uphold seems irrefutable: we think our society is better for it, and that value is one whose cherishing itself informs our vision of the universe.

Indeed, the moral imperative that Locke felt to excise from truth itself "the historicity of the Christian spirit," in Erich Voegelin's characterization of his purpose, set the stage for the invention of such a new vision, even a new religion, unburdened by the past, by the divine weight of communities, by the embrace of a world, by the power of time and of providence.[15] Choose whatever path you wish; choose over and over again; just do it genuinely! With true pluralism, according to this vision, comes true safety, and the question of salvation is resized to fit this security (a movement, we should note, that reverses the direction of the early Christian response to the marketplace). We should note how Adam Smith observes that the competition of sects, in addition to establishing a dynamic of weakened

15. See Voegelin's incisive comments on Locke in Voegelin's *Collected Works* (Columbia: University of Missouri Press, 1998), 24.173–75.

(and thus socially unthreatening) religion, would have the effect of alter-
ing that religion itself (whatever it is) for the *better:*

> The teachers of each little sect [which Smith had encouraged to multiply
> into the "thousands"], finding themselves almost alone, would be obliged
> to respect those of almost every other sect, and the concessions which
> they would mutually find it both convenient and agreeable to make to
> one another, might in time probably reduce the doctrine of the greater
> part of them to that pure and rational religion, free from every mixture
> of absurdity, imposture, or fanaticism, such as wise men have in all ages
> of the world wished to see established. (*The Wealth of Nations* 5.1.3)

Religion is made better, Smith argues, simply because, through the
process of competition among small groups, religious choices themselves
become less threateningly interesting. What is the best Protestant church
in town? What is the best Catholic church in town? With enough benign
movement in and out, who really cares? To be sure, differences are not
ironed out, and theological particularities continue to give color to the
thousands of sects that toleration is designed to encourage for the sake
of defanging the venomous beast of faith. These differences have become
the staple of comparative church historians and ecumenical *causeries.*
Not to mention savvy marketers.

But what kinds of differences exactly? As Benjamin Hoadly, Anglican
Bishop of Bangor and ardent follower of Locke's religious theories, put it
at the beginning of the eighteenth century: in a tolerant society, it is clear
that "Christ's kingdom is not of this world." In the notorious sermon that
bore this title, Hoadly points out that a spiritual kingdom or Church is
the only one possible for a pluralistic community and that if churches
were to have any particular character outside of doing good, it could
touch upon only otherworldly—that is to say, socially irrelevant—matters. We might draw the implications of this, and test them against the
kaleidoscope of contemporary Christian traditions, as we call them today:
what marks one church as different from another? Musical sensibilities?
Communal warmth? Cultural creativity? Inner experience, mystical or
otherwise? Denominational profusion has centered, increasingly over
the years, on smaller and smaller slices of, thinner and thinner nuances
to an evanescent and disembodied realm of spirit, which, mercifully in
civic terms, offers little disturbance to a sometimes fragile social body.
Is it any wonder that even so central a term as "conversion," which for
hundreds of years designated a submission of spirit *and* body to the

visible worship of the one true God, should now point to a publicly inaccessible realm of interior decision? The modern church-shopper has, as it were, all choices available to him or her but one: the Church Catholic and its gospel.

It is not by accident that Locke and his ilk valued toleration for all sects but one: the Roman Catholics (Locke also distrusted atheists as lacking a basis for keeping oaths). There were political reasons for this, of course. But logically and theologically as well, this exclusion was perfectly natural: Catholics were the one church, at the time anyway, whose insistence on visible community as the necessary shape or form of the truth's life simply could not fit in with the new religion of the market. And it was logical too that the vestige of Catholicity that establishment Anglicanism still grasped became the strategic aim of liberal leaders, like Hoadly, to dissolve. It was a dissolution carried out over two centuries in England and with a single blow in the American Revolution. It is worth taking a moment to look at this Anglican tradition more particularly in its historical evolution, just because of its odd relationship with uniformity and diversity that so well displays some of the dynamics and tensions of the Church's transformation in modernity.

We can use as an example Herbert Thorndike, a seventeenth-century Catholic-Anglican theologian. To study Thorndike is to observe how great is the distance crossed into modernity that we have observed among Western churches—and also how awkwardly Anglicanism needed to be dragged along, a kind of stubborn reminder of the way things have changed for Christian ecclesial sensibility since the early days of arguing against pagans. Thorndike was one of the thousands of Anglican clergy who suffered bodily in the course of the civil war. His reaction to this personal violence, however, was curiously counter to the search for peace through divisions' embrace that Locke envisioned. In 1659, he published one of the greatest theological works of the English Church, *An Epilogue to the Tragedy of the Church of England,* a massive and contorted masterwork that sought to reflect on the possibility of ecclesial life in the wake of its assault by inter-Christian warfare and division. But Thorndike looks at the ruins of English Christendom, and instead of seeing the need to step to the side of ecclesial claims, he gazes at the rubble with a renewed sense of the *necessity* of establishment uniformity.

Where Locke releases the individual from history, Thorndike insists that there is no individual *apart* from history's matter—to reinvent the church or simplify it into renewal is, for him, a contradiction in terms.

Where Locke seeks to create salvific fulfillment in the multiplied choices of individuals, Thorndike locates salvation's approach only within a rich process of *communal* formation, wherein an individual's choices emerge only out of a *common* process—that there could be such a thing as a Christian who had not been soaked in the fullness of the Church's life and tradition was for him another contradiction. Where Locke makes the truth withdraw to the diverse shapes that can match sincerity of effort, Thorndike insists that the truth must envelop all particularities; it must bring its *own* particular shapes and forms—in Christ's life, in Scripture, in the rule of faith, in the tradition of the saints—to bear upon every facet of human life and ecclesial pretension, in order to bring all things into coherence with itself.[16]

Thorndike represented, to be sure, a certain kind of reactionary, but one with staying power in Anglicanism and to some degree in other atavistic Catholic sects. In the face of the acknowledged reality of division, his response was hardly to run away, but deliberately to run backward, into the energies of the established past, in order to find the breadth of history's power—the Holy Spirit, that is, who leads into all truth—with which to confront the present. *Reculer pour mieux sauter* (step back, in order better to leap ahead).

But both Thorndike and Locke were Anglicans and, if extreme in a sense, faithful Anglicans nonetheless. Thorndike's deeply sensitive concerns that the Christian faith itself be sustained by the kind of community that offers it the necessary space (and thus encompassing structures of order and teaching) for its shared nurture represent an awakened awareness of the gospel's own inner dynamic and embodied hold. His is a search for the "old peace." At the same time, however, Locke's defense of pluralism in the wake of Christian violence hardly constituted unfaithfulness, and his commitment as a Christian within the church to finding a way to revision a society in which divided Christians might live together peaceably should not be construed as an abject failure of nerve. His is a grasp at the "new peace." To fall into the field between these two historically realistic outlooks is simply to try and steady oneself on the impossible footing of "exemplary" Anglicanism (read "evolved" or "modern Catholicism") itself, straddled between its establishment impulses and its increasingly developed denominational context, wherein

16. Much of Thorndike's ecclesiological principles are explained in chaps. 1–4 and 21–29 of book 1 of the *Epilogue*, entitled "Of the Principles of Christian Truth."

the new religion of tolerance represents, after all, a welcome pressure for a certain kind of peace.

But what peace exactly? This is the great challenge of the present: peace where there is no peace. For much of what I am explicating, with this woefully twisted survey of the movement out of the market into the very shape of the market, is that this impossible footing is properly a symbol of modern Christianity as a whole. It is a symbol, in the burdens of this movement, that the seeming deformation of the Christian gospel that pluralism has engendered proceeds, with some weary self-awareness, from the same dark hole out of which Christian violence has burst, and this violence itself marks the contours of the pit in which division found its legs and crawled out. But so too is this movement away from the market into actually *being* the market, in its uneasy conscience and residual grasp of the gospel's infinite claims, a symbol of the still inescapable call to the Church to follow a Lord whose well-defined path and whose tangible gifts both embrace and overcome the power of this hole, far deeper than this or that social outcome, and of its darkness, wide enough to constitute our fallen character. With the bequest of our established claims and their mitigation by the increasingly pluralistic politics of our deeds, Anglicanism's impossible footing represents only the necessary possibility of being rediscovered by our Lord in *his* peace—a hoped-for act that all the Church awaits.

It is to this act, an act of alien peacemaking, to the divine opportunities of staying put on such a strange footing as this, that we should turn our attention. For there remains much for us to discover by dwelling in the unresolved betweenness of establishment and pluralism; much for us to be redeemed through, by standing in the new market, not rich enough to buy the lot, nor even to participate; but quite broke indeed, and content, even peaceful, with our impoverishment.

# 2

## The Virtues
## of Staying Put

What posture does the market's beggar take? Here we are encouraged to burrow for a few surprises. Right after the terrible events of September 11, 2001, priests and ministers were asked to open the churches and step into the empty pulpits and, somehow, "be there" with something that made sense. Nothing on television made sense, of course, but many clergy were thought to be ready, standing by, as it were, with wisdom, comfort, and hope at hand for all. Some, like me, were as confused and as ill prepared as anyone else. In retrospect, these were draining days simply on the level of expectations. I heard an older priest at the time, however, say this to his fellow clergy: "It's confusing and frightening; but it's not complicated. We know what to do." He then quoted Philippians 4:9: "'What you have learned and received and heard and seen in me, do; and the God of peace will be with you.' Continue to do what you have always done. That is what brings God's peace to the people who will seek you out or simply drift in. It's what they finally want; and it's what you have to offer." Do what you have always done.

The phenomenon of the religious market, including the church-shopping of the modern Christian, has to do with a certain search for peace. We can point, in summary of our last chapter, to two different realms of peace that the Christian Church now finds itself lying between. The first is the old peace, the peace of the first Church of old, the Church of the pagan empire, which grew up in contrast to the competing claims of the religious marketplace of Hellenism. In the face of the spiritually depleting struggle for allegiance that competing pagan religions and philosophies demanded, the Christian Church both pointed to and embodied a space of encompassing truth, whose very uniformity provided a stable place in which the individual might move with a surprising freedom of inquiry and discovery. We could describe this kind of peace in terms of a landscape for the truth, that is, of a vast area marked out by tangible objects and elements and historical and communal traditions whose collective reality designated the figure of the Church itself, in its unity and catholicity (even apostolicity). The Church itself, in its breadth, historical density, and embrace, *was* this landscape of the truth, and that very identity provided the peace in which a significant or fruitful flourishing was possible.

The second realm of peace is that which was pried loose from established Christianity, bit by bit, following the Church's western fragmentation in the sixteenth century. This is the new peace of multiplicity, of churches in their thousands, as Adam Smith says, vying for adherents among each other and thereby neutralizing the dangers unleashed by the fanaticism of internecine Christian battle. This modern realm of peace, which we call Christian pluralism, seeks to control religious passions by individualizing them and limiting them to the small choices that single men and women make, over and over again, regarding their Christian social location. Instead of being a large landscape of peace, filled with the Church's varied objects, the new peace of pluralism is defined by a welter of objects without a land, objects that individuals themselves collect as they choose and then buy and sell to others or simply discard. And thus, although the peace is kept in this new pluralistic realm, the character of Christianity, at least as compared to its origins, has been profoundly transformed back into the spiritual uncertainties of the very market that the gospel originally overcame.

The historical path that led from one realm of peace to another, I argue, was the reality of violence, and terrible violence at that, enacted by Christians one against another (not to mention against non-Christians in the newly expanded world of intercontinental traffic). And that violence was itself but the particular and enveloping form of a sin that has lurked for centuries in the heart of Jesus' followers, perhaps simply in their as-yet-untransfigured humanity, a sin that has surely roamed the truth's landscape all along and whose grasp upon the act of Christian division in the sixteenth century announced a new stage in its power. And this violence and its undergirding sin remain but the underside to the peace of the present, a present whose purpose is to confuse that sin, not to heal it.

A major question for the Christian of today, then, is how to stand in the midst of these two realms of peace, one of which has slipped away and been rendered socially impotent, the other of which is inadequately reactive, and woefully so, to the deformations of soul that Christ's own healing seeks to overcome and indeed to the very articulation of what such healing could ever mean. How does one stand between these two realms, in a place where violence simmers and where profligate choices dance about the waiting embers? Is there a peace between these realms, a third peace that belongs, not to a disarmed past or to the confusion of an individual heart or to the power of the enemy who goes "to and fro on the earth" (Job 1:7), but to God alone? If there is, it is surely not one that we can construct ourselves. And the question for the Christian peace-seeker today, therefore, will center on how we are to receive what lies beyond our power to create. It is a very *practical* question, and we can approach with a practical mind.

I have suggested that we might attend for an answer to Catholic Christianity's own peculiar balancing—or perhaps impalement—upon the marking posts of these two other realms, given in Anglicanism's exemplary knottedness in its establishment tradition on the one side and in our modern denominational dynamics on the other, the two aspects that tear at our sense of purpose and vocation. Let us pursue this suggestion now.

We can begin by comparing two modern reactions to our present location. The first belongs to someone mentioned in the last chapter, sociologist Peter Berger. Berger devoted his productive and influential career to the study of religion, and he has done so as a man of personal faith. And, as much as anyone, he helped, in his works, to describe the felt-religious dilemmas brought on by religious pluralism. How does he make sense of this for himself? Berger's answer is clear: one must avoid falling into the camp of either the "thugs" or the "wimps," as he puts it—the fanatics and the complete relativists.[1] First, then, resist a false embrace of the sectarian impulse—the easy retreat into the totalizing past of the church that (illusorily in our age) claims to be able to hold all truth apart from the depredations of a diverse world of choices. This, Berger, claims, is the thuggish path of fanaticism, and, in the tradition of Locke, he is adamant that such a path is ultimately destructive, a "crusade

1. Peter Berger, *A Far Glory: The Quest for Faith in an Age of Credulity* (New York: Doubleday, 1992), 18–21, 46, 75.

that ends up in a little ghetto" and that partakes of all the cruelties and shackles of both crusade and ghetto together. But the lapse into the arms of pluralism's secularizing bosom is no less to be avoided. That way lies the loss of transcendence and of a properly protected approach to God, wherein nothing is true and all things are right and where the resulting wimps float free from God altogether.

Berger's place "in between," he says, is the place staked out by the true liberal Protestant tradition, built upon the character of an Abraham or a Paul and revived in the masters of dislocated faith like Simone Weil.[2] It is the place of free choice for God, the place of the solitary believer, who seeks the heights of the divine from the principled posture of choice made eternal, the noble reach for a sovereign master, unbound to the assaults of the dirty banalities of communal pressures. Berger, to be sure, likes the accoutrements of traditional Christianity—the "poetic beauty" of the old Book of Common Prayer, for instance, now ignobly turned into the language of a mail-order catalogue to satisfy the banal lusts of the mob.[3] But that the Church should somehow render faith for an individual person, he finds abhorrent. The "subject of the first sentence of the Nicene Creed," Berger insists in a remarkable passage, is the "solitary 'I' . . . the 'I' over and beyond all collective or communal assignments—the 'I' alone with reality and alone with God."[4] It was the great gift of democratic pluralism to liberate this secure and believing ego. It resists the crowd's violence—as any good Lockean liberal must do. But it also resists a plunge into "anything goes," because it is some-how a noble ego, different from the complacent and corrupted pluralist masses. For Berger, then, church-shopping is not a sin; it is, rather, a deliberate and potentially virtuous trivialization of ecclesial meaning, which glories in the steely-eyed freedom of the lonely chooser.[5] Plural-ism is wonderful, so long as one has strong and discerning tastes and so controls one's own money.

One might properly ask if it really is possible to be such an ally of pluralist freedom while remaining impervious to the blandishments of the market. I rather think not, any more than university professors are less pliable to advertisers than others, so long as the packaging is sufficiently sophisticated. Mainline churches, like the Presbyterian and Episcopal churches in the

---

2. Cf. ibid., 20–21.

3. Ibid., 96.

4. Ibid., 103. The "solitary I" of the Nicene Creed's confession is, however, something that liturgical scholars have long pointed out as mistaken; the council wrote its creed in the first-person plural.

5. Cf. ibid., 180.

United States, have become exceedingly skilled at manipulating this reality, and we need to admit that such subtle niche marketing is hard to square with the acuity of Kierkegaardian individual resolve. But Berger's position is important to present, just because it *does* represent a principled position that is common enough among the classes that many modern denominations attract. We might observe, however, that just *because* the "soul in quest of transcendence" describes the very weariness that the ancient market could never overcome, it is hard to grasp the value of this deliberate regression. The sensitive and informed minds of antiquity, after all, were those whose intellectual and spiritual pilgrimages among the unstable offerings of Mediterranean religiosity finally exhausted themselves and turned happily to the exclusive clarity of the Church catholic's Christian gospel.

By way of contrast, let us take another modern—although from a previous century—John Henry Newman. In 1866 Newman appended a brief explanatory essay to a new French translation of his *Apologia*, which attempted to outline for his foreign (and ecclesiologically bewildered) readers something of the shape of the Church of England, which, of course, formed the context of this famous account of his religious journey into Catholicism. Among other quaint customs from across the Channel, Newman explains Anglicanism's three parties—liberals, evangelicals, and Tractarians—as all being at war with each other. His French audience, used to disdainful acceptance of Roman hegemony, would no doubt wonder at this display of intrachurch rivalry, so Newman goes on to explain one of the great mysteries of the Church of England's survival in the modern world:

> If the Anglican communion were composed solely of these three parties it could not exist. It would be broken up by its internal dissensions. But there is in its bosom a party more numerous by far than these three theological ones—a party which, created by the legal position of the Church, profiting by its riches and by the institutions of its creed, is the counter weight and the chain which secures the whole. It is the party of order, the party of Conservatives, or Tories as they have hitherto been called. It is not a religious party, not that it has not a great number of religious men in its ranks, but because its principles and its *mots d'ordre* are political or at least ecclesiastical rather than theological. Its members are neither *Tractarians,* nor *Evangelicals,* nor *Liberals;* or, if they are, it is in a very mild and very unaggressive form; because, in the eyes of the world their chief characteristic consists in their being advocates of *an Establishment* and of *the Establishment,* and they are more zealous for the preservation of a national Church than solicitous for

the beliefs which that national Church professes. . . . [This group] constitutes the mass of the Church.[6]

We have noted the establishment character of Anglicanism already, bequeathed to it by the Reformation's vestigial commitments to uniform truth. Unlike most other Protestant churches, however, the Church of England, as Newman rightly points out, held on to this vestige with far more vigor and passion than its Continental siblings in reform. Indeed, it turned the vestige into an ongoing character trait that proved unique among the pluralizing attitudes of other confessions. "Bishops, deans, chapters, clergy," in Newman's list—these were the great upholders of the establishment, and for all their untheological bent, they were not without doctrinal concerns. He continues:

> In the seventeenth century they professed the divine right of kings; they have ever since gloried in the doctrine: "The King is the head of the Church"; and their after-dinner toast: "The Church and the King" has been their formula of protestation for maintaining in the kingdom of England the theoretical predominance of the spiritual over the temporal. They have always testified an extreme aversion for what they term the power usurped by the Pope. Their chief theological dogma is that the Bible contains all necessary truths, and that every Christian is individually capable of discovering them there for his own use. They preach Christ as the only mediator, redemption by His death, the renewal of man by His Spirit, the necessity for good works. This great assembly of men, true representatives of that English common sense which is so famous for its good as for its evil consequences, mostly regard every kind of theology, every theological school, and in particular the three schools which we have tried to portray, with mistrust. In the seventeenth century they combated the Puritans; at the close of that century they combated the Latitudinarians; in the middle of the eighteenth century they combated the Methodists and the members of the Evangelical party; and in our own times they have made an energetic stand at first against the Tractarians and today against the Liberals.[7]

What exactly is this species of Christian that Newman disengages from the ecclesial soil of his homeland and upholds for view to the wider world as a remarkable survivor in the midst of ideological change

---

6. The appendix (in English) for the French translation of the *Apologia* is contained in the long introduction to the work by Wilfred Ward (London: Oxford University Press, 1913), xxv (emphasis original).

7. Ibid., xxvii.

and of the forces of increasing religious diversity? Newman himself speaks of this creature with a mixture of stunned and contemptuous admiration. One might call this specimen "the adjustable churchman"; that is to say, the Christian whose "church" represents the landscape of life itself, at one with country and countryside; the borders of which stand firm, whatever the admixtures in its midst; whose smallest customs hold together a culture of learning and questioning, thirsting and hoping, no matter the oddness of their ever-adjusting relations to the rest of the world.

Thus, Newman's enumeration of the establishment churchman's commitments holds the relationship of Church and nation (or "Church and King" as Newman describes its bibulous enunciation) at the top of the list, as somehow logically linked to the broad attitudes to Scripture and to Christ. It is a relationship, furthermore, that makes possible the shifting attitudes toward other parties in the church over time, now adopting a posture of liberalism toward the Puritans, now of conservatism toward the liberals, and so on. And to what does the churchman hold in the midst of these various historical eddies? The lively *shape* of the Church of England, its order, its prayer book, its embedded habits of worship, of authority, response, and relation.

Newman obviously found the whole thing far below the level of theological purity and virtue to which he himself aspired and that he thought the Christian Church ought to achieve. Establishment Christianity, he came to believe, was a hollow vessel without a lasting center. And the experience of American Episcopalianism after the Revolution would certainly sustain his fears: where, in the United States, the establishment was removed, and the broad commitments to, say, Bible and Christ were retained unbuttressed (as William White first proposed),[8] "adjustable" churchmen too easily become co-opted servants to the unending recreations of pluralist religion. Anglicanism refashioned for a pluralist setting, as the Episcopal Church proved to be, did not constitute, for Newman, a hope for the future.

But what counts as the establishment is more than the subservience of a church to a monarch or a parliament. As we know negatively from England's recent experience—not to mention Sweden's—the kind of co-

8. Cf. William White's 1782 *Case of the Episcopal Churches*, where the hope is evidently given that a "latitude of sentiment" (chap. 3) on matters of doctrine and morals will be held in check by a common taste in worship, despite the deliberate dismantling of establishment structures and their democratic alternatives put in place. White's proposal, of course, became the blueprint for the Episcopal Church's invention, the first Anglican Church to reorder itself explicitly for a pluralistic setting.

hesive continuity that Newman identified with the Church of England's character was not purely political but was informed more deeply by a host of actions and attitudes that more importantly allowed for the adjustments and survivals of Christian commitment within plural settings that themselves had overtaken the state. It is worth turning now to these actions and attitudes themselves.

In the seventeenth century, poet and priest George Herbert presented his own alternative to Roman satirist Lucian's market in a short (and posthumously published) treatise on the ideal witness of a "country parson." Herbert's alternative market centers on the life of this ideal parson's little rural parish. Its wares are the acts of the church, laid out on the same table every Sunday. Its customers are an unchanging group, the church's faithful and straying. And the profit made is whatever is useful to some man or woman from this consistent and unvarying stock:

The Country Parson, as soon as he awakes on Sunday morning, presently falls to work. And seems to himselfe so as a Market-man is, when the Market day comes. . . . His thoughts are full of making the best of the day, and contriving it to his best gaines. To this end, besides his ordinary prayers, he makes a peculiar one for a blessing on the exercises of the day. . . . This done, he sets himself to the Consideration of the duties of the day, and if there be any extraordinary addition to the customary exercises, either from the time of the year, or from the State, or from God by a child born, or dead, or any other accident, he contrives how and in what manner to induce it to the best advantage. Afterwards when the hour calls, with his family attending him, he goes to Church, at his first entrance *humbly adoring, and worshipping the invisible majesty.* . . . Then having read divine Service twice fully, and preached in the morning, and catechized in the afternoone, he thinks he hath in some measure, according to poor, and fraile man, discharged the publick duties of the Congregation. The rest of the day he spends either in reconciling neighbours that are at variance, or in visiting the sick, or in exhortations to some of his flock by themselves, whom his Sermons cannot, or doe not reach. . . . At night he thinks it a very fit time, both suitable to the joy of the day, and without hinderance to publick duties, either to entertaine some of his neighbours, or to be entertained of them, where he takes occasion to discourse *of such things as are both profitable, and pleasant, and to raise up their mindes to apprehend Gods good blessing to our Church, and State; that order is kept in the one, and peace in the other, without disturbance, or interruption of publick divine offices.* As he opened the day with prayer, so he closeth it, humbly beseeching the Almighty to pardon and accept our poor services, and to improve them, that we may grow therein, and that our feet may be like hindes feet ever climbing up higher, and higher unto him.[9]

Herbert's is a shop to which people return over and over again, despite its limited inventory. It does not advertise, it does not compete, it does not propagate its dealers. The center of its store is a tiny display of goods, pearls, one could say, that are proffered and handled day after day, again and again, the buyers returning, gazing, touching, taking up, and selling back, in a round whose recycled elements make the notion of a self-sustaining market a theory fulfilled. Herbert's church is a market, yes; but a market where buyer and seller turn out to be the same. A market where goods are thereby virtues, by definition transferred from one person to another and back again, through the process of a settled relation and influence.

What, after all, does the country parson, the "market-man," sell, according to Herbert? Regular prayer, the divine office, over and over, catechism, and visiting. Elsewhere in his little book Herbert elaborates these riches further: they include the Scripture at the center, the fathers, the buildings of the church, with all of their care and tender ornament, a sober life, the example of love and charity, the subjection of obedience and social responsibility vis-à-vis the Church and State, the embrace of order (of "old custom," as he puts it), and so on. Is it, then, a narrow and dowdy shop? Whatever we might think given the sheen of today's merchandise, Herbert uses exalted language to describe his small boutique. It is, he says in one place, the public square for a new "Socrates," where the truth is guarded and celebrated, yet all the while handled with an openness and discernment and depth that the empty pratings of the world could never wait long enough to entertain. "Patience and mortification," Herbert says, form the divine market-man's most precious wealth, wealth that makes all the rest amenable to this astounding "business."[10] Through his waiting and his discipline with tiny things, ecclesial and personal habits, what is small envelops the whole of existence.

What we have here is a radically odd adjustment to the market. And it is one based on this sense that the shape of the Church's life, in all of its detailed and customary texture, is astonishingly rich, too rich to grasp at once, too broad to embrace in a moment, too great to dismiss before a lifetime. Only the *time* of exploration, only the destiny of an ongoing commerce amid its many pieces, could ever adequately discover its value.

9. George Herbert, *A Priest to the Temple; or, A Countrey Parson* (1652; repr. London: Mowbray, 1915), chap. 8: "The Parson on Sundays" (emphasis original).

10. Cf. ibid., chap. 3, and elsewhere, chaps. 5, 8, 12–14, 19, 21, 24, 30, 35.

So, what Newman saw as a shallow malleability, Herbert's market-man signals to be the business of profundity.

One of the major struggles of Anglicanism—even more so in our day, obviously—was to follow this signal. To jump forward a century after Herbert, we might listen to Bishop Butler: "The Form of Religion may indeed be where there is little of the Thing itself; but the Thing itself cannot be preserved amongst mankind without the Form. And this Form, frequently occurring in some instance or other of it, will be a frequent admonition to bad men to repent, and to good men to grow better; and also be the means of their doing so." Joseph Butler, known for his great defense of Christianity against the deists entitled *Analogy of Religion* (1736), placed this remark at the center of his 1751 charge to the clergy shortly before his death in the diocese of Durham.[11] Little had changed in the kinds of wares that the church hands round to Butler's parishioners in the century since Herbert's manual. The form of religion that Butler elaborates in his charge contains the same divine office, the same catechism, visitations, sober living, and so on, as the country parson valued.

But Butler writes in a new era on the far side of the rise of toleration and its creeping alteration to Christianity. He therefore frames his remarks to his clergy in a special context: how to minister in the face of unbelief that is actually encasing a once-Christian culture. His main strategic answer is this: Do not waste your time arguing, but instead carry on with your appointed rounds. The reasonable weight of Christianity, Butler insists, can be grasped only on the basis of "a long series of things, one preparatory to and confirming another, from the very beginning of the world to the present time." Without such a working framework of time's extent, there is nothing helpful to say to unbelievers and skeptics; and who, today, wishes to stand still long enough to listen to such an argument, built upon the "ages of ages"? The culture has shrunk itself to a scale incapable of grasping God's history.

Rather, Butler tells his clergy, the greatest gift you have for this unbelieving culture and thinning cultural Christianity are the forms of your church's common life, forms that, he admits, can often seem empty. Still, he says, the "reality and power" of these forms' content, as he describes it, assert themselves through the imposition of the forms themselves, the only means by which *over time* the divine reasonableness of a gospel that embraces time itself can ever touch a person. The incessant round of the Church's life and forms—the great and perhaps only value that establish-

11. Contained in *The Works of Joseph Butler* (London: Macmillan, 1900), 1.287–301.

ment can give the Church—is the only apologetics, the only advertising, the only marketing, that will ever begin to match the breadth of a truth whose hold is history itself. That is explicitly *why* Butler spends his charge detailing for his clergy the duties of divine office, catechism, and visiting: these habits alone, astoundingly, can embrace the universe.

Butler is, of course, the quintessential churchman, that kind of person whom Newman admired (and Newman, it seems, read Butler with care), but also the kind of Christian that Newman finally rejected as the product of a civil, not a truly evangelical, religion.[12] But being a churchman, as even Newman realized, involved a certain character and a certain take on the place of the Christian gospel itself within the realm of an increasingly pluralist culture. In the late Middle Ages, the term *churchmanly* originally pointed to the moral qualities of priests—their chastity, their charity, their prayerfulness. By the late seventeenth and eighteenth centuries, however, these virtues had been transferred to the establishment itself. And the word *churchman* had come to designate specifically *any* upholder of the established church, including Presbyterians in Scotland. But that a churchmanly character should become an establishment character was not a religiously vain thing, as Newman charged. Rather it represented a powerful truth, in Butler's terms, according to which the ordered and patient life of the established church had now become the only vital context of the Christian virtues themselves.

The contrast with Newman is worth emphasizing. Those who see Newman as a nineteenth-century product of Christian pluralism are correct, in my mind. For who but a "solitary believer," in Berger's phrase, cast among the market's customers, could have chosen Catholic*ism*, like Newman, with the gusto of a Red Sox fan or an American political conventioneer, whatever the careful theological arguments formulated on the choice's behalf? And in this, Newman helped invent the public shape of conversion to a *product* for which Christian culture was now ready and that has itself now produced a long tradition, far less threatening, to be sure, than confessional persecution. But, spread among evangelicals and Catholics together, this conversionary invention tended to undermine the virtues of Christian time that probably alone are able to resist the demeaning of evangelical hope that pluralist religion entails.

12. Butler, we remember, was bishop of Bristol during John Wesley's initial preaching tours, and he told the ardent revivalist that "the pretending to extraordinary revelations and gifts of the Holy Spirit" is a "horrid thing—a very horrid thing." Wesley recounts his conversation with the bishop in his diary for August 1739. See *Works of Joseph Butler*, 1.xvi.

Still, what of Newman's critique, however modern it might be? Take away the husk of establishment itself, and does any kernel reasonably remain? Newman's fear was that there would be none at all. And, as we noted, American Anglicanism may seem to prove Newman right. But that is only so long as we accept the premise that establishment Christianity is an empty form and that forms themselves are devoid of essential Christian meaning. Here is precisely where Butler was trying to point us in a different direction. We do not have time in our own hands—time to make the changes we need to make in order to convert cultures, historical diseases, and so on—but God does. We do not have the power any longer to embrace a culture as a whole with our religion and so, in a deliberate squeeze, to transform it—but God does. We do not have the focused Spirit to quench the passions of human hatred that poison even the heart of religion—but God does. What we have are the forms, Butler insisted, that tie themselves to God's time and to God's power and to God's transformation. We have such forms, and whoever we are, and to whatever church we belong, we can submit to them.

Perhaps, then, this should be the focus for an ardent reflection in our day: the third peace of the Church, lying between the peace of the market's absorption by the Church and the peace of the market's embrace of the Church over violence, is the peace of formal waiting. Do what you have learned to do, as St. Paul says in Philippians 4:9: *stay put.* So that time, which belongs to God, can make its argument in a place where history has been sucked dry and where the forms of communal life remain the only cord that ties an individual to the power of a message rooted in God's history. Such a peace as this is built up amid the ecclesial structures of virtue themselves, now cut loose from civil coercion, to be sure—"disestablished"—yet still unwilling to undo the pressures of its inner forms.

Berger's "solitary believer" deliberately resists these pressures and chooses nobly. But there is a sense in which forgoing choice altogether and simply submitting to shapes given by the church represents itself a divine movement of redemption. W. H. Vanstone uses the term *exposure* to describe how God, in Christ, opened himself to the shapes of the world, how God stood within them, received them. On the one hand, this kind of exposure depends on the divine willingness to allow incarnate form simply to take its place within the world's many other forms; on the other hand, this taking of place, this staying put, is the basis of divine patience, a waiting that is love itself, suffering even as it redeems.[13] So the peace of waiting, then, is

---

13. Cf. W. H. Vanstone, *The Stature of Waiting* (New York: Seabury, 1983), 94–100.

bound up with the patience of offering and receiving the forms of one's life from the hands of God's providence. This, surely, must be the case for the Church as much as for its Lord.

Of course, one must have a church to do this, and that church must *have* a form. And many Christians today, on the left and right and even middle of the theological spectrum, have already given up such value claims. If there is a threat to the very possibility of Christian peace today, it comes from the assault on, as it were, formalism itself as a basis for Christian life. To forgo choice is something that takes place wherever we are, and it submits us to the forms of such a discovered place. If we are shopping, it will mean stopping even at one spot and staying the movement on; if we are struggling against the place of our childhood, it will mean ceasing to struggle there; if we are warring or wilting in the denomination of our discontent, it will mean allowing what chafes to be cherished. But assuming there *is* a church where today we stand, sit, rage, or wrestle—whatever church it is—and that this church does have a form, then the ecclesial structures of virtue through which the long waiting for the gospel's reassertion in an alien culture can take flesh are precisely those that can mitigate the market of individual choice in favor of the internal market of communal self-referral, in Herbert's vision. In a world where the Church is no longer one, where markets proliferate and the Church is made invisible amid the welter of these choices, the uniformity of truth will emerge perhaps in a peculiar way, simply as the *subjection to form itself,* the vehicle for time's renewal, each fractured church's historical weight and worry. Unity will be freed as we carry division upon our bent backs, the figure of consignment to partiality the transforming image of redemption. A strange vision of ecumenism, to be sure. But the "Israel of God" is one where peace "bear[s]" on its "body the marks of Jesus" (Gal. 6:16–17).

As a prod to reflection, here is a simple list of a few of the kinds of "ecclesial structures of virtue," the forms to which we might seek subjection. Every denomination has their equivalent, although here my focus lies upon the forms that are tied to Anglicanism, this model of the unworkable—and hence thoroughly honest!—modern church.

To begin, we might think in terms of those aspects of our formal life that emerge into visibility when we distance ourselves from the choice-making elements of pluralist virtue. To subject ourselves to the forms of the Church's life is also to forgo such choices as much as possible. (Clergy and other church leaders, more than anyone, have this responsibility and opportunity to forgo choice concretely.) Thus, in the context of worship,

Anglicanism's prayer books (increasingly attractive to other struggling de-nominations and pilloried by the market culture), their prescript forms (to use the Puritan negative), the lectionaried Scripture (assuming its demanding breadth), the unswerving order of its application in time and season, and the refusal to edit scriptural claims according to any intellectual principle—these represent, within the modern setting, a realm of commu-nal exposure to the word, in the posture of patience, whose shape, purely and in its unmanipulating deliberateness, prepares, almost like an act of weeding, a landscape in which truth one day must make its dwelling.

After the rounds of our worship, consider next the set polity of our various traditions—and again I think particularly of Anglican polity. For we might even extend this distancing from choice to our deliberative lives. The proroguing (or indefinite adjournment) of the Church of England's convocation for almost 150 years beginning in the early eighteenth cen-tury may well, retrospectively, have proved a stay *against* secularization, rather than the spiritually stultifying force it was for so long thought to be. Without legislative debate and the demand to choose and vote for the shape of the Church's life, it is interesting to note the ways in which the forms of the Church of England's habits became the soil for creative growth, not its suffocating grave. How we might dispense with our voting assemblies today is a purely strategic question appropriate to another realm of investigation—although the question merits hopeful fantasies. But the point is that when the choices of the present are banished, the choices of the *past* become freed for our primary attention, only because they are left to constitute the forms of the present most clearly. And to live with past choices is a mark of waiting, filled with all the fruit that scriptural and Christian tradition ascribe to such patience.[14] Further, the form of life that is willing to do this is one that cracks open the Christian heart to the forms of God's own coming.

With respect to the Church's teaching, we can return to a theme on which we touched in the previous chapter: it is historically the case that the creative powers of the Church's spiritual life were often unleashed within a context of freeing the past, through, one might say, a moratorium on the choices of the present. However one judges the final outcome to Wesley's reformation in the mid-eighteenth century, the most potent source of his renewal derived from the energies given by the disenfranchised es-tablishment of his generation's Church, energies set loose for historically

14. A good overview of these traditionally located fruits is given in David Baily Harned, *Patience: How We Wait upon the World* (Cambridge, Mass.: Cowley, 1997).

retrospective exploration. The limits eventually crossed by a Wesley are pertinently marked, in contrast and two centuries earlier, by Erasmus, who was explicit in his defense against Luther of the Church's formalism as being the vehicle for rediscovering the abundance of the past and of its choices. Erasmus, more than any other, wedded noninquisitorial inquiry to the steadiness of ecclesial form, achieving (at least ideally) a marriage of Church and peaceableness that has stood for centuries as one of the few alternatives to the Great Divide of sixteenth-century Christianity.[15] Choose, but always choose backward.

If American Anglicanism marks a failure in disestablishment, it is a relatively gradual one, dating less from its foundation as an independent church than from its evolving disdain for formalizing past choices. And it is only recently, in fact, that this disdain has risen to the level of ideology. To be sure, Episcopalianism's founding exclusion of doctrinal articulation from the Church's "storehouse of forms" proved a singular and original misstep. In this light, it is necessary to emphasize that any "Erasmian discipline" must engage not simply habits of scholarly delight, but the ecclesial habits that permit doctrinal forms to exercise creative pressures on any communal discourse: what used to be guarded as formularies that shaped—and also freed—the church consistently throughout the centuries. As the term itself expresses, a formulary provides the form within which a broad range of speech can be enunciated, not in contention but in variegated peace. And if this is so, far from setting communities one against another, formularies are well suited for the patience of a disabled and divided Church, which awaits its redemption as a *gratia aliena*. Indeed, doctrinal formularies, in their clarity and simplicity, need to be embraced anew, though perhaps without the anathemas that attached to their ignorers.

Finally, to be thrown back upon past choices, devoid of expectations for daily overthrowing of present forms, is also to be thrust up against the human embodiments of the Church's life, stripped of their ideological masks—that is, the people of God who make up the body of Christ. When choice is removed, we are faced with demands of life together, in all of its moral burdens: bishops, superintendents, colleagues, wardens, boards, vestries, leaders, followers, the sick, the crazed, the ill willed, and the joyous. They are what is left when there is no future strategy to hide them behind. And, of course, it is only here, within such a body of egregiously present members, that the true life of the Church as Christ's own takes flesh, in

15. See the essays by James D. Tracy and Hilmar M. Pabel in *Erasmus' Vision of the Church* (ed. H. M. Pabel; Kirksville, Mo.: Sixteenth Century Journal, 1995).

the demand for and inculcation of the somatic virtues that Jesus shares
with us, pictured in something like Romans 12: affection, honor, zeal, service, joy, hope, patience, compassion, constancy, forgiveness, generosity,
hospitality, suffering. There are no choices around these things; only the
inescapability of the divinely given.

To think, to inquire, to argue even, to serve, to worship, to pray, to weep, to
give of oneself—that is, to do business, to be the Christian market-man—all
within the bounds of the given is certainly an odd exhortation to offer leaders
for whom denominational and church consultants constantly urge action
outside the box. But we should listen to the call, because submission to the
given, to the forms of the church, is a transformative practice, it is gracious,
it is something wherein a great promise is made: "What you have learned
and received and heard and seen in me, do . . . *and the God of peace will be
with you*" (Phil. 4:9 [emphasis added]). Submission to form, or obedience
itself, constitutes the hope that overleaps the boundaries of the present.[16]
Overleaps them in the patience of God's self-exposure to the world of our
own division and violence. "Continue to do what you have always done."

Of course, people will also continue to choose. And there is no method
capable of either keeping people in a given church or dissolving the lines
between churches. The thirty thousand or more Christian denominations
of the world, however much a few here and there may try to cooperate,
remain an image of grotesque capitulation to the sinfulness of human
rebellion, and any method we follow can be tied only to the overcoming of
human sin itself. Shopping will, in any case and in the face of sin, continue
to prove a more attractive alternative to violence. But those Christians and
churches who stay put, despite their continued ties to this reality, will also
be suffering a different service, a better service, the service of time. And
such a service will bear its fruit. For the uniformity of truth, which the
Christian gospel affirms, asserts itself from within time and as time's own
vessel. More than anything, the Christian faith is marked by a peculiar relationship with providence. It is a relationship, primarily, oriented toward
a divine shape given to history, in the flesh of Jesus Christ. But it is also
a relationship with providence that, as a result, submits to forms, not to
futures. As Church and truth embrace, they will do so through this gate.
Our age is no different than any other in this fact. Only let our Christian
lives display such contentedness and peace as this, and the comings and
goings of a restless, rootless age may themselves one day be stilled beneath
the cooling shadow of the world's originating forms.

16. Cf. Glenn Tinder, *The Fabric of Hope: An Essay* (Grand Rapids: Eerdmans, 1999), 147–50.

# 3

# The Peace
# of the Church
# and the Providence
# of God

## The Problem of Providence

It is more than a statement of optimistic fatalism to say that providence will be the maker of our peace and of the Church's peace in particular. In the last chapter, I wrote of our call, in this age more than in any other, to maintain the forms of our common life, forms whose clothing marks the virtues of divine time. It is worth taking a moment, now, to reflect on how this service and this time—the divine shape given to history in the flesh of Jesus Christ—actually represents a substantive truth on its own terms, an announcement from God given into the midst of human life, that is a gospel, and not merely an attitude adopted in the face of confusion. Discerning such a gospel, to be sure, is a struggle and leads into the hard wrestling with the angel of history, into the Church's coming-to-terms with the agony of its birthright, wrested from the world's order. For to wait with God is truly, finally, to be free from sin itself. And since we do not claim "that [we] have already obtained this or [are] already perfect" (Phil. 3:12), today it seems we wait only as we suffer.

The very notion of providence is today, after all, little more than a pious anachronism, usually noted only contrastively by critics of its once formidable chauvinistic power to justify empire—from Bossuet to the American frontier—now reduced somehow to comforting the pointlessly afflicted. Novelist Richard Hellenga, for instance, devoted a long and often bitter narrative to this kind of modernistic commentary, using as his baseline the famous phrase, often sentimentalized by the resigned, that Dante wrote of God, when he said: *e 'n la sua volontade è nostra pace* (in his will is our peace).[1] That oneness with God's will is the perfection of life had become, by the end of the nineteenth century (no more!), almost a truism of the spiritual tradition. But is God's will to be equated simply with "what is"? The modern struggle for discernment might be epitomized in the Ignatian exercises, invented to traverse the sixteenth century's swamps of ecclesial discrimination. But as the necessary discipline attached to peace, they are, along with the era stretching to our present, but a reflection of the burden that competing truths have planted on the shoulders of the spirit. "What is" itself is open to dispute, and even the shape of fate appears to be muddled. Thus, the forms of the Church's historical life demand precise identification, or at least a way of being seen, if they are to bear the specific peace of providence. They must be something more than the arbitrary retrospect of a distracted gaze, but rather must form the deliberative shape of a creative purpose.

Dante himself described this will of God as a kind of sea, in and against which all creation moves, as if borne on waves and currents, washed against flotsam and shores, lifted and cast down in foam and surges, calms and breezes, whose pull and demand are inescapable and minutely determinative. Unless the Christian Church can confront these dynamics as the specific forms of God's steadfast love, unless they can be articulated as such, prayed over in fear, and praised in release, unless the forms of the Church's life as passed on are *in fact* the forms of God's willfulness in constraining history, then the sea is a sheer abyss and not a glorious embrace. In Christian terms, providence must have a form. And the form of providence—the way that God's will in time is seen—must hold an identity that stands before the onlooker speaks, that calls forth speech itself, that creates the space wherein desire takes its words, that creates love by loving first, and so transcends the whipped and beaten charity of *amor fati.*

1. Richard Hellenga, *The Fall of a Sparrow: A Novel* (New York: Scribner, 1997), quoting *Paradiso* 3.85.

## Adjusting Providence to the Market's Churches:
## The Case of Newman

So, providence must have a form. But whose form shall it be? Let us turn again to our friend Newman, whose genius was, in part, to live and apprehend the breadth of the modern church's interior and diseased dilemmas, embodied almost as it were in his own person. From the beginning of his serious theological writing, Newman sought to find his peace within the Church and to do so through some articulation of the Church's peace within its history. Already in his 1833 *Arians of the Fourth Century,* he identified this peace with the coherence of the Church's teaching through time, something that required what he later came to explore in terms of the "development of doctrine," the historical and unsystematic outworking through providence's hand, of the intellectual expression of that full truth held in the bosom of the Church since the apostles' time. The logic of Newman's insight need not be faulted (more on this in a moment). But the service to which he put it held a decidedly modern cast, that is, within the market's competitive hawking of wares, to defend the truth and rightness of a given church over and against others—first the so-called Anglican *via media* and later the exclusive legitimacy of the Roman Catholic Church. Newman's argument regarding the unfolding of dogma was over and over made a justification that *this* church deserves my allegiance (and yours) because, in and over time, its shape coheres with the pattern of God's truth. Development was an apologetic assertion that a given church reflected God's temporal choices. And thus, the form of providence lay in the form of this particular church, assumed and given within history.

What is interesting for our purposes is that this way of looking at providential form, generally, was not all that different from attitudes held by Newman's explicit opponents, the liberals of the Church of England. Newman had always lamented the Protestant appeal to a wooden conception of *sola scriptura,* since he saw this as an inevitable handing over of revelation to the individual conscience, something that led necessarily to the multiplication of opinions, assumed truths, sects, and finally a culture of relativized and relativistic assertions and doubts.[2] Yet the liberals also justified this ecclesial culture of religious relativism through appeal to the outworking of providence. When, for instance, Newman crossed swords with Renn Dickson Hampden at Oxford in 1834 over the admission of

2. Cf. John Newman's *Via Media* (London: Longmans, 1890), 1.26–30, 239.

dissenters to the university, at issue was Hampden's argument that the historical division of the Church into distinct communions logically requires the rise of discordant opinions; but if the Church is one as we claim, Hampden went on, this can only mean that the unity of the Church by definition tolerates the greatest disagreement imaginable. Hampden's assertion—still central to liberal appeals to diversity, if today buttressed by a critical historical progressivism—was founded on the assumption that ecclesial division itself was a providential act and therefore that the present shape of the church in disagreement represented the form of providence itself.[3] The difference with Newman here lay in which church's historical form providential identity had deigned to reside.

No one should confuse the theologian Newman with the logician Hampden, however, and herein lies the problem: in raising the question of "whose church?" the underlying principle is exposed as being that of *adjusting* providence to the shape of the church itself—someone's particular church anyway—and the sense of arbitrary self-pleading by particular adherents as they claim providence as theirs begins to make itself felt. The *ad hominem*—or better, *ad ecclesiam*—character of providential reasoning to which this leads can be seen in Newman's postconversion 1850 *Lectures on Certain Difficulties Felt by Anglicans in Catholic Teaching Considered.* In these highly readable essays, Newman skewers all non-Catholic churches on a set of criteria drawn from the providential history of Roman Catholicism—its prevailing struggle against heresy over the years, its persistence in nurturing the saints, its steadiness of doctrinal formulation, and so on. The lectures' engaging wit, however, fails to mask the argument's underlying *petitio principii:* just whose history holds the form of providence's positive claim? How would Roman Catholicism look if the argument's participants were simply turned around and it were held up against the formal standards of, say, Monophysite historical experience?

Many a half-hearted ecumenical discussion ends in just these sorts of irresolvable self-justifying providential applications. They derive, after all, from the modern Church's self-distribution in the market, much as we have been observing. And the forms of the ecclesial market, if providence were to don them together, would appear fairly incongruous as garments. Who would not wonder, then, if providence, as we have seen

3. Cf. Thomas Charles Hummel, "The Nature and Authority of Christian Doctrine: The Debate between Renn Hampden and John Henry Newman" (doctoral dissertation, Vanderbilt University, 1981), and the many discussions of this notorious controversy in accounts of the period; e.g., Meriol Trevor, *Newman's Journey* (London: Collins, 1974), 64–65.

in these last centuries, were simply mocked for its rude clothing and sent out the door? Certainly, it is the beggar of the present age.

## The Vision of Prophetic Form: Tract 83

Newman, however, could also perceive other options to this self-adjustment of providence to the forms of the church. What if, for instance, the market itself were but a small reflection of some larger form of providence? What if the Church, in all its vagaries even, instead of distributing forms, were the recipient of them? Toward the end of his Anglican period, Newman raised this possibility, only to let it drop later in the face of a logic of separation whose power he seemed almost incapable of resisting. But at least for a moment, pressed by his studies of the early Church to question the self-justifying claims of the Church of England, he still sought to find in it some divine purpose that could get beyond the simple choice between truth and apostasy, even while acknowledging the claims of both as explicators of the Christian life and community. For this he turned to Scripture, seeking for it a more determining historical role than he otherwise and generally felt comfortable in accepting.

Tract 83, which Newman wrote in 1838, constitutes a clear example of the "road not taken" in this regard. And although he thought well enough of it to republish it later, the essay has never gained a foothold in the literary *cursus* of either the Oxford Movement or Newman's own writings. In large measure this is because of its ostensive form and topic: four sermons on the antichrist, based on texts from 2 Thessalonians, 1 John, Revelation, and Daniel. These were and remain unattractive objects of reflection, certainly for Anglicans and Roman Catholics. Newman's purpose in these sermons was threefold: to record elements of patristic exposition for this set of prophecies; thereby to encourage a contemporary attitude and discipline of apprehending figural resonances within the historical life of the church; and finally to suggest a formal explication for the Church's present experience and so expose a vocation to its members.

As for the first, Newman recognized in Tract 83 that the details of any interpretation of biblical prophecy cannot be asserted as infallible; still, where the fathers tend to agree, given their clearer grasp of the apostolic core of the faith, we should pay attention. In any case, the early Church's attempts to parse the scriptural references to the coming of the antichrist, to his wiles and ways, are useful to us in keeping us tethered to the real history of the world in which we are placed, a world where actual cities and empires, politicians and cultures, teachings and actions, have meanings that are tied to the providential purposes of God as betokened in Scripture.

If this is so, Newman went on to stress, we must in our own day remember, second, "that we are still under what may be called a miraculous system . . . [where] our present state is a portion of a providential course, which began in miracle, and, at least at the end of the world, if not before, will end in miracle. . . . An Antichrist, whoever and whatever he be, is to come; marvels are to come; the old Roman Empire is not extinct; . . . the contest of good and evil is not ended" (sermon 2). Whether this or that historical event represents some exact fulfillment of prophecy is not important to Newman. Rather, that this or that event be seen by us as a part of providence's structure described by Scripture, that it find a place, even if it be not the only or the exact place, within the figures by which Scripture calibrates the world's providential course, that today be a portion of the prophetic store of Scripture's exposition of time—all this is necessary to grasp if we are to apprehend our stake in God's saving power and will. Salvation is somehow tied, in Newman's argument here, to seeking out and discovering the shape of scriptural prophecy as taking us into its own form; for salvation, viewed historically, is just this act of being taken in through the act of grace.

Finally, being so taken into the unfolding of time's frame in scriptural terms and hearing the prophecy spoken into one's own history is to respond to the call that God brings with this. Newman had no interest in determining whether the apostasy of the present age and culture "is to give birth to Antichrist, or whether he is still to be delayed," for "we cannot know" such distinctions before the fact. "But at any rate this Apostasy, and all its tokens, and instruments, are of the Evil One and savour of death"; and our faithful posture in its face is given in the forms of the prophecies of antichrist in their indeterminate array (sermon 1). The prophecies point us to our vocations in the present, precisely in their historical ambiguities, for they hover over us as ever-imminent endings. At every moment they cause "the shadows to move" by unveiling the pressing conformances that stand between us and Scripture's foretellings. Commenting, for instance, on political events in northern Europe in relation to Italy and the Vatican, Newman brings to bear the images of Gog and Magog in Ezekiel and Revelation:

Now, I do not mean that as to the present time, we see how this is to be accomplished in its fulness, after the pattern of the Shadows which have gone before. But this much we see—we see that in matter of fact the nations of the North are gathering strength, and beginning to frown over the seat of the Roman Empire. . . . Here then we have a sign of Antichrist's appearance—I do not say of his instant coming, or his certain coming, for it may after all be but a type or shadow of things far future; still, so far as it goes, it is a preparation, a warning, a call to sober thought. (sermon 4)

The sober thought that Newman had in mind here is simple enough, and with it he ends his essay: repentance of heart, the battle against pride, the call to generosity, and the particular care to guard the faith in the face of an eroding religious culture of disdain. Stand firm, he counsels, much as Jesus and the Scriptures counsel; no more than that.

There is much here that coincides with comments I have already made regarding the virtues of staying put. Newman, however, specifically locates the force of this counsel: it emerges from a particular understanding of and lived relationship within providence, whose form is given explicitly in the figures of Scripture. That is the entire thrust of his prophetic exposition. And included in these forms, of course, are the very elements of the Church's life that demand his counseled discipline, elements figured in the Church's prophesied disarray. For the market itself, Newman ends by asserting, stands as a type or shadow of a vast unfolding of history's subsumed flesh in Scripture's form:

Satan may adopt the more alarming weapons of deceit—he may hide himself—he may attempt to seduce us in little things, and so to move the Christians, not all at once, but by little and little from their true position. We know he has done much in this way in the course of the last few centuries. It is his policy to split us up and divide us, to dislodge us gradually from off our rock of strength. And if there is to be a persecution, perhaps it will be then; then, perhaps, when we are all of us in all parts of Christendom so divided, and so reduced, so full of schism, so close upon heresy. When we have cast ourselves upon the world, and depend for protection upon it, and have given up our independence and our strength, then he may burst upon us in fury, as far as God allows him. (sermon 4)

As if to clinch the point, Newman appended a postscript to the tract, quoting from a letter by eighteenth-century high-church bishop Samuel Horsley that the "times of the Antichrist" must needs coincide with the proliferation and indifferent toleration of Christian sectaries and plural religions within the world.

It is critical to see how Newman here took a stand deliberately outside the market's logic of adjusted providence. The Church's history, for all the effort in scrutinizing it entailed by the prophetic interpretation of apocalyptic texts, does not itself exert a pressure or demand upon the providential course—the miraculous system—that Newman asserts continues for our era too. Rather, this history is given over to the scriptural forms of the biblical text, and in this dedicating and dedicated act their own meaning within that course is uncovered. And precisely by eschewing an insistence upon temporal exactitude in the fulfillment of prophetic detail—something that Newman believed is ruled out from the start by the very nature of prophecy—he deliberately elides the forms of Scripture and providence together. Thereby, the Church itself is freed to be judged, conformed, and redeemed as an object of grace, rather than as its arbiter. And in Newman's argument, its historical vocation is given—because wholly lodged in the Scripture's own voice—in terms it cannot manipulate.

### The Scriptural Breadth of Providence

Was this an attitude too hard to sustain? The hopefulness of its promise, as Newman saw it, was perhaps overwhelmed by the visionary threats contained in Tract 83's apocalyptic expositions. And these are not the stuff of an accessible peace, especially in an era, like the mid-nineteenth century, still immersed both in the impetus toward and in the fear of ecclesial violence. But I should add that Newman never quite gave up on this understanding of providence as scriptural form, despite later lapsing into the Catholic side of the market's clamor. Among the most persuasive passages in his famous *Essay on the Development of Christian Doctrine* (1845)—itself an apologia for Roman Catholicism's providential favor—are those in which he locates development within the character of the scriptural text itself.

It would be tempting to read Newman here as viewing the biblical revelation in terms of some intellectual outworking of an idea suited to the exigencies of time (as he does when he elaborates his main theory within the context of the Church's postapostolic teaching). The Old Testament, in this latter context, would then be seen as a set of divine teachings accommodated to the more primitive demands of culture and history, yet open to explication, elaboration, outworking suitable to the evolving demands of subsequent times. But Newman, ever sensitive to liberalism's devaluation of the past just on these terms, perceives the inner relations of the biblical texts more subtly and sees their development more as the formal resonance of scriptural figure within the providential history of the biblical narrative. The "ever new, yet ever old" of divine revelation, as he puts it in *Essay on the Development of Christian Doctrine,* is not simply some progressive movement forward built on the past. Development, if we can apply the word to revelation, is a "structure so unsystematic and various ... that ... it cannot, as it were, be mapped, or its contents catalogued"; applied to the Bible, it takes its form in "an unexplored and unsubdued land" given over to an unexhausted diligence of study whose goal is to find history's ever-changing landscape already described in the forms of Scripture's unexpected figural alignments. Rigorously understood as this unsystematic cataloguing of discoveries of figural research within the mines of the Bible—the human display of providence's gracious artifacts of historical recognition—doctrinal development more strictly speaking would not have taken on the temper of apologetic hostility that it did as Newman turned from devotion to applying developmental logic as an act of ecclesial demarcation.

In any case, Newman's singular if passing articulation of a providence whose forms are Scripture's and not first the Church's gives an answer to the kinds of questions that the notion of an ecclesial peace must pose, if such peace is to embrace the unresolved destructions of the Church's own repressed violence: Is the shape of the Church's life actually directed by God? Is it so directed, and in such a way, that this shape is accountable, in history, for its own derivation in human sin, and in its distinctives accountable to the one truth of God? The answer given in the propheticism of Newman's Tract 83 is this: if the form of providence is Scripture's own, then we can and must posit the bare forms of Scripture as themselves the historical shape of the Church. From this assertion, we can move on to say that the peaceful gaze is that which takes in this one reality: *the Church of Christ looks like the Scriptures that it reads.* Not at one time only nor of a part only, but at all times and of all parts, ever "unexplored and unsubdued ..., with heights and valleys, forests and streams, on the right and left of our path and close about us, full of concealed wonders and choice treasures."

Without a sense of this breadth and inexhaustible richness of Scripture's figural world, there would be little reality upon which to base such a claim that providence's forms are Scripture's own, even as they are taken up by and given over to the Church. But with this sense in place, we can see how the will of God—*la sua volontade*—is sufficient both to draw the Church into its embrace and to do so with the deliberation of a grace capable of containing even the fallen aspects of the Church's time, as it is sustained for its redemption. This sense itself was not new with Newman, of course. It represents a long-standing attitude, nourished theologically in the Church from St. Paul through Justin and Irenaeus, flourishing in the intellectual devotions of Augustine and Gregory the Great. And within this tradition, the sense of breadth that in particular informs the coincidence of providential form and scriptural figure as the Church's peace-maker takes in a wide range of realities: the breadth of Christ's fulfillment of Scripture as he brings to their term every jot and tittle of the law, the breadth of the words themselves as God's ordering word, spoken by the Spirit as an act of creative grace in each and every instance, and the breadth of the Church's assumption of these ordering forms as itself the body of the word spoken in history and shared with the one by whom all things are created.[4]

It is Scripture's breadth, granted to the Church, that is, after all, the stumbling block that confronts those looking to carve out a secure space amid competing claims. Newman himself, as we have seen, could not hold on to this destiny and finally sought to turn it on its head. To be sure, that there is some comprehensive and stable structure to the truth—a uniformity that properly refers to the divine grasp of wholeness, of the "all in all"—cannot be denied without denying the very nature of God. But the mystery of providence (Rom. 11:25, 33–36) is given in the historical constraints upon its final articulation in human terms, except they be those of Scripture's forms. In historical experience—that is, as a phenomenon within the world—the Church represents an *array* of scriptural forms, each under a sober judgment, each with a calling, and each on its way toward a perfect conformance with Christ, whose fullness alone can integrate the seeming diversities these forms embody. What the Church is, formally speaking at any given time, is discerned as a figure of vocational penitence and hope that points to and is taken up by Jesus.

4. See my discussion of figural reference in the introduction above.

## The Providential Shapes of the Church's Life and Speech

To adjust the Church to such a scriptural providence, of course, must undercut the simplistic notions of development, let alone of progress, that have been taken from Newman's unintentional lapse into the structures of modernity shared with his liberal opponents. If ecclesial or doctrinal development means anything, it can only be in terms of some abstraction projected into a divine prerogative inaccessible to historical reason. Scriptural form, by contrast, is certainly given a kind of horizon of direction—something toward which Newman properly groped in his discussion of the antichrist; but this final form is received only as a multiplicity aiming at Christ's embrace. Phenomenologically—to offer an alternative to Newman's list of seven providential "notes of genuine development"—the historical indicators of the Church's life will therefore embrace at different times growth and decline, faith and faithlessness, endings and disappearances, beginnings and novelties, revolutions and conflagrations, anticipations and despairs, truths and lies. None of these have any intrinsic explanatory power for the whole, of course, except as each is discerned to indicate a form that can be received as Christ's form, received and submitted to, yearned after and bowed before.

Even if we confine ourselves to Newman's purely doctrinal perspective, theology in this light takes its own form in history as the garb hanging upon the greater forms of Scripture at any given time, and not as some growing stream of directionally evolving material. Theology's criterion of appropriateness will vary according to secondary phenomena imposed by the habits of learning and writing of an era and space; but ultimately they can be judged only according to their revelatory power vis-à-vis the Church's vocational direction toward scriptural form itself. Doctrine's consistent truth over time will emerge in the way that the Church's articulate reflections are able to maintain the power of scriptural form to disclose history itself. And thus, doctrinal truth is properly judged by its *usefulness*—hence doctrine's moral ground and ethics' basic doctrinal purpose—in maintaining the structures and postures (the forms) both of the Church's scriptural apprehension and of its malleability in the face of God's power to transform it into the clarity of his scriptural will.

This ascetic foundation to articulated Christian truth is critical to bear in mind if we are to grasp how there could be an alternative to the combative discourse of division that uses doctrinal debate to mask the deep-seated violence of the Christian heart still beating through the rhythms of time. Recent scholarly insistence on the fundamental narrative character of the Bible reminds us of the basic historicality of Scripture's self-assertion, but also misses the important way this functions. Though it has a projected temporal ending, the story of Scripture has no directional map that could point to a determined phenomenological trajectory to its forms toward that end. Jesus warns his disciples against marking ahead of time the day of the end and tells them rather to watch (Mark 13:32–37), a practice given in the shadow of his own life, death, and resurrection, forms whose figure alone provides temporal determinants to the Church's history and within which the actual end stands as one form from among many.

Newman's struggle to describe how the "antichrist is now," while also refusing to fix its perfected work for the Church, indicates the temporal paradox of such figural providentialism in elucidating the contours of ecclesial destiny. But just because of this paradox, it is possible to speak of the Church's disordered character of existence, to speak of the Church and also at the same time of the churches in their wounded and wounding division, to speak of the sins and of the failures of the true Church. Because its historical identity is governed by scriptural forms that emerge variously from within the realm of Israel's and Christ's existence, their procession from a divine will can and must include the figures of sin and redemption, penitence and hope. And their temporal structure has no predictable pattern except to the degree that the Church discerns their figural appositeness as God's own instrument of conformance at any given moment—the grace of temporal creation and redemption itself—and accepts them as such in humility. Within this expansive sea of transfiguration, providence stands as the explicit divine enunciation of apposite figural reality, and faithfulness stands as the Church's reception of this reality as its own.

The Church longs for the clarity of its life before God; it is thrust back continually toward a realization of its deserved distance; it reaches out after its vocation to acknowledge the turbulence of this demanded history: "Thou hast said, 'Seek ye my face.' / My heart says to thee, / 'Thy face, LORD, do I seek.' / Hide not thy face from me. / Turn not thy servant away in anger" (Ps. 27:8–9). Yet finally, it recognizes its Lord close by as it apprehends the glory of each moment of conformance, the figural abundance that in Jesus' life is made the Church's: "And we all, with unveiled face, beholding the glory of the Lord, are being changed into his likeness from one degree of glory to another. . . . For while we live we are always being given up to death for Jesus' sake" (2 Cor. 3:18; 4:11). *La sua volontade è nostra pace*—it is the Church's claim to peace embraced through discernment and subjection before a Scripture ever unveiled in the forms of Christ.

Early church writers on the topic of providence seemed to understand this relationship. The very concept, for John Chrysostom and even more for Theodoret of Cyrus, pointed to the way in which the world's forms—in nature and historical experience—had been brought by God into conformance with the shapes of Christ's own temporal incarnation (cf. discourse 10 of Theodoret's *On Divine Providence*). Within this act is disclosed the fullness of God's care for the world—a meaning almost synonymous with providence itself. The Church's vocation, in response, lies in entering into this act of seeing, through Christ's forms, the depth of this divine love within every aspect of the world's set and giving itself over to its formative sway. The correlative duty, according to Salvian (cf. his *De gubernatione dei*), lies in the Church's willingness to bump up against the subjective unattractiveness of these forms, acknowledging its own willful rejection of their meaning, and to suffer the weight of this incongruity as it effectively forces itself upon and thereby changes its historical condition. Plumbing the life and forms of Israel's sin and beholding its own image reflected back becomes the passage of the Church's redemptive penitence through time. The body of Christ floats in the sea of the Old Testament's embodiment of the Savior: "His will is our peace; this is the sea / whereunto all things fare that it creates or nature furnishes."[5]

## The Market and the Providence of Peace

The market itself stands as an elaborate avoidance of this vocation, a deliberated obscuring of providence itself. Its own figural location, in Matthew 11:16–19, represents the refusal to discern at all, for fear of discernment's call: "But to what shall I compare this generation? It is like children sitting in the market places and calling to their playmates, 'We piped to you, and you did not dance; we wailed, and you did not mourn.'" Neither heeding John (who "came neither eating nor drinking, and they say, 'He has a demon'") nor embracing the Son of Man (who "came eating and drinking, and they say, 'Behold, a glutton and a drunkard, a friend

5. Dante, *Paradiso* 3.85–86 (trans. Dorothy Sayers; Harmondsworth: Penguin, 1962).

of tax collectors and sinners!'"), the children of the market cannot bear
the demands of distinguishing the dispensations of their time. *This* time,
the time that takes the Baptist up and follows on his heels, the time of
one form that follows another, the apposite time of the Church, is one
form they cannot comprehend and order on their own. Although their
choices turn about the divergent tunes they whistle, although they dance
and cry out to one another at their whim, *in fact* the market children have
nowhere else to go, to play, until they are girded by another and led away
(John 21:18). And where would they be led? First to John, then to Jesus;
first to repentance, then to the cross. And then—with form following
and building upon form—then by the Spirit. "Peace be with you," the
Son of Man will say next; "receive the Holy Spirit" (20:19–22).

But who should know the Spirit's peace, except by the dispensations
of God's providence, by the will of repentance and sacrifice? God's
providence is the maker of the Church's peace, not as the inevitable and
overpowering force of fate, but as the form of Christ Jesus, given, ordered,
and thus astonishing. Whether playing as now or following as one day it
will, the Church will finally hear and see, look upon and handle, purify
and hope, one form calling to another (Ps. 42:7); finally, "be like him"
(1 John 1:1; 3:2).

That Newman's propheticism should so cautiously (and briefly) attempt to engage the force of providence for a confused Church is hardly
surprising, for providence framed in Scripture's forms is both affront to
and unmasker of the Church's dividing violence. Providence is therefore ever the insistent and unwelcome guest at the ecclesial banquet,
whom in the end Newman himself could not tolerate, heir as he was to
a certain conceptual etiquette that had no protocol by which to submit
to the ecclesial invitation to "take the lowest place" (Luke 14:7–14). By
the seventeenth century, the theological notion of providence had been
refashioned by the market so that its self-assertion (real though it was!)
was permissible only in the most unobtrusive ways around the table: in
nature unchurched and in the individual soul left to grasp that nature
unattached. The Church's providential time, for those who still struggled
with this reality, lay exiled somewhere in the creases of its defense of
these two antiorganizational realms.

"You never enjoy the world aright, till the Sea itself floweth in your
veins," wrote seventeenth-century Anglican theologian and poet Thomas
Traherne. The sea, in this context, seems to envelop only the glorious
forms of the created world. (It was predictable that Traherne's redis-

covery in the twentieth century coincided with a renewed and nostalgic postindustrial attention to the gifts of nature.) And Traherne goes on to say, "You never enjoy the World aright, till you see all things in it so perfectly yours, that you cannot desire them any other way; and till you are convinced that all things serve you best in their proper places."[6] Does providence here designate the celebration of the gift that is the world itself, in its pristine natural contours? Then the Church's time is a time of return, of reform at least, perhaps even of battling the depredations of a false civilization for the sake of still-well-ordered Eden. The modern desire to find a home in this world coincides with a deep-seated need to make that home unthreatening, to discover in its corners a peace inherent with our birth into its confusing arms.

It is not surprising either, then, that contemporary spirituality has joined the naturally domestic with the historically benign. Thus, modern providence became the kind of happy resignation that Christians have read into late-seventeenth-century French Jesuit Jean-Pierre de Caussade, whose posthumous collation of letters now known as *Abandonment to Divine Providence* has achieved a classic status. Each moment given sacramental weight by de Caussade turns into the canonizing of the individual's wondrous self-reflection: "O bread of angels, heavenly manna, pearl of the Gospels, sacrament of the present moment! . . . What God arranges for us to experience at each moment is the best and holiest thing that could happen to us."[7] Only look to the details of what befalls you in order to see the face of God. (But do not look at the Church!)

It is true that readers of this emerging modern spiritual tradition have forgotten the public and scriptural framework of its original providential concerns. For both Traherne and de Caussade, each in their own way intentional retirees, like Herbert, from the market of their religious culture, reembraced providentialism as a spiritual reflection on the character of the Christian life given over to the forms of *God's*—neither uniquely nature's nor the individual's—history. Nature's word is given its integrity of articulation only in the divine word spoken to the Church, the whole providence of God's will given flesh only in the universe's scriptured forms. The sea of time, for these reticent modern questioners of the market, constitutes the vast waters of these forms given for the life of conformance to God's own image at each moment, the "dark drops in an

---

6. Thomas Traherne, *Centuries of Meditations* 1.29, 38 (London: Dobell, 1935).

7. Jean-Pierre de Caussade, *Abandonment to Divine Providence* 1.2, 4 (trans. John Beevers; Garden City, N.Y.: Doubleday, 1975).

ocean" of divine self-giving in history.[8] Here then is the Church's time: a passage marked by the moistened droplets falling from each figure of the Lord into which its baptized calling leads (Mark 10:38–39).

But neither Traherne nor de Caussade could express this scriptural context clearly; they strained at it, yet increasingly relaxed themselves into the quieter realms of the descripturalized countryside of paradise and the place-markings of the individual's minutes ticking past the formless eons, precincts still frequented by the churches' modern transients. The providence of Christ's exhaustive forms, their breadth pulling at the Church's skin and bone, was consigned to be a night vision, taken from the closet only occasionally in the moments of passion such as Newman felt during those few years of agony caught between a chastened Canterbury and confident Rome. The market has no staying power: beware and rejoice.

For prophecies are no less powerful for their stealth, bound up for the time of waiting and hoping (Isa. 8:16–22). Providence takes these fastened forms and uses them, one by one, even in these hollow years. It is its genius to work while it seems to sleep, to convert while it seems to ignore, to call while it seems to be mute. And its peace awaits the waking, however quiet they may be, who look, who read and mark, who take stock of who they have become and are becoming, whose forms are found riveted to their future, beyond all barter and betrayal.

It may seem incongruous to call the bewildered and unnoticed populace and pastors of beleaguered churches to adopt the wild postures of a Habakkuk: stake out towers, stand, watch, wait (Hab. 2:1–4), as if the great signs and skies, the lights and thunderings that the heavenly temple come to earth shall cast, are somehow given over to *their*— our—years and times (3:2–16); as if the forms of *their*—our—small prayers and catechisms, praises and patience, should open up to glory; as if the remnants of the Church scattered on the market square should still be lifted up, cradled, and cherished by providence. But we, who seem to stand still at the end of this busy day, if we read "the vision," if we finger its forms as they promise their molding of our history into the shapes of his image, if we cherish them as we are cherished by them—we will surely run (2:2), freely and joyfully bringing, merely as we stay, messages of peace, even the gospel of peace (Nah. 1:15; Isa. 40:9; Rom. 10:15).

___

8. This is the burden of the Third Century of Traherne's *Meditations*, especially its second half on the Psalms and the Church. De Caussade, for his part, consistently links every individual moment with the shadows of Scripture's reflection of God's hidden wisdom, itself the sea that mirrors God's mysterious gift of time; see *Abandonment to Divine Providence* 2.4.

If a contradiction seems to be involved in seeking the peace of the fragmented Church through a willingness to stay put within the confines of
the fragments themselves, it is only the contradiction of the unrepentant.
The market calls for choice; but if that choice is choice's refusal, made in
the midst of incompletion and discontinuity, then choosing itself becomes
an unveiling. We stop so that we can be seen; we forbear movement for
the sake of thought; we halt in order to be sobered. The power of God
is not thereby circumscribed. For providence renders the world through
the always muted tones of its temporal instrument. Yet they can be heard
in vibrancy when they are carefully attended. And so the silences of the
Church too will become sonorous when we become still, and choice is
quieted. There at last emerge the forms of our destiny, and hence the grace
of our hope.

## The Providential Form of the Present: A Short Figural Envoi to the Church

What sober image looms? Staying put instead of choosing must seem
to most a willful blindness to the world's energetic directions and to the
Church's heady rush amid the mix. Let us end upon the practical note
of answering discernment's call to sober thought, to penitence and hope,
by simply holding these reflections to their final account, not of some
theological history and imaginative induction, but of the figures by which
providence must mold our hearts.

Newman's own mistake in face of the violence of the market was, in a
sense, to throw himself into its own turbulent eddies. Instead of asking
"where shall I go?"—the modern question of the bewildered Christian
that was once the question of only the perplexed pagan—we should be
asking "where does providence set us down?" If still children of the market,
even while searching for the meaning of Jesus' prayer to the Father for
unity, then we must see how Jesus strode across the *agora* and where his
passage led. Watch there, and follow. There is still unity of hope for us,
but it is given in a peculiar communion, a wasted gathering of penitents,
of Lazaruses, whose choices turn out to be wounds licked by the dogs,
whose dried-up abandonment of choice leaves only the accepted reality
of having been set outside the palace's door, whose dwelling is among the
outcast. Pope John Paul II, reiterating a favorite vision he holds, sent a
message of congratulation on February 27, 2003, to the new Archbishop
of Canterbury, Rowan Williams, still praying for unity but casting its

coming as only a "gift of the Holy Spirit." But the Spirit unveils the form
of Christ, and this is precisely the set of history's drama. In the title of
one eighteenth-century meditation on Christian unity, this is the form
of "Jesus Christ, anathematized and excommunicated." *Pneuma* and
providence have a similar object in their grasp.[9]

As we ponder the strains on the continued integrity of the various
Christian churches, from within and without, we should see how providence itself has made of the logical contradiction that is "broken communion" an impossibility now overcome—and rightly and imperatively
overcome—by abiding with Christ himself within the communion of
brokenness. The only place in Scripture, after all, where the body of Christ
is explicitly described as broken is on the cross, that is, as the actual body
of Jesus. This is significant, because it means that the place in which to
look for the figural or providential context of the Church's fracturing is in
the passion of Christ and all that it, and it alone, represents and fulfills.

Thus, the passion and embodied fulfillment in the flesh of Jesus deserve
our final word with respect to the question of unity in the Church, of its
oneness, its uniformity, its single place of staying, its peace. "Here might
I stay and sing no story so divine," in the words of Samuel Crossman's
hymn. We can end this reflection with a meditation on the forms of just
this place of rest: Israel, exile, excommunication, communion.

As providential form, first and foremost, we need to see the body's
summary end as reflected in Jesus' own summary referent, which is the
people of Israel. The fractured body of the New Testament Messiah fulfills the historical and popular narrative of Israel in the Old Testament,
and this is where our main ecclesiological context must be explored in
terms of institutional models.[10] Indeed, the main ecclesial reference to
the Christian Church in the New Testament that makes this context explicit is given in the term *dispersion* (*diaspora*) in 1 Peter 1:1 (cf. James
1:1), a reference that both plants the Church within the narrative of the
passion and shows its institutional history to be that of the Jewish exile.
The question of communion in the fractured Church of the market,
then, is properly framed within the terms of the *galuth* (exile) of Israel,
following the temple's destruction, among the nations.

9. *Jésus-Christ sous l'anatheme et sous l'excommunication* (Amsterdam, 1731), perhaps written by
Abbé Gudvert. See the discussion in my *Spirit and Nature: The Saint-Médard Miracles in 18th-Century
Jansenism* (New York: Herder & Herder/Crossroad, 2002), 284–95.

10. This is one of the main arguments of my *End of the Church: A Pneumatology of Christian Division
in the West* (Grand Rapids: Eerdmans, 1998).

And does this not make sense when compared with other possible scriptural contexts often used in the midst of ecclesial conflict, for example, the violent sifting of choice by Moses and Phineas ("who is on the Lord's side?") in the desert on the way to Canaan (an exodus theme) and the antiapostate call and slaughter of Elijah's challenge to the prophets of Baal? The exilic context makes sense because it is tied most explicitly to the passion itself, the pure figure of the broken body, which is ramified, even in the New Testament, through references to the destruction of Jerusalem and its temple and linked, prophetically, with the exilic figure of Jeremiah. *Here* we can see the providential course that still is ours, indeed is the current of our very life.

Israel's exile provides a number of providential parameters that ought properly to be applied to our choice of leaving choice behind. Because exile is divinely ordained, it is also rightly borne in patience. The brokenness of the body of Israel is experienced not as a search for the true remnant, but as a suffered condition that embraces the whole of the people. Jeremiah 29's letter to the exiles represents the posture of brokenness here, and that turns the whole category of communion among members of the people into a single acceptance of a common staying put among foreigners. Verbs like *separate, go out, come in*—the actions of exodus and cleansing—are not a part of such exilic brokenness. In ecclesial terms, dispersion renders the people's marks of identity less geographic and local than elements of character. Communion in brokenness is a matter of the contacts of virtue and not of the contacts of flesh and institution. And thus, communion and brokenness cannot be antithetical.

This is emphasized through the singular ethical sign of exile: judgment is individual, no longer corporate. The famous prophecy of Jeremiah (31:29) and Ezekiel (18:2)—that "the fathers have eaten sour grapes, and the children's teeth are set on edge"—is now subsumed into a new covenant of personal responsibility and is the great moral transformation of exile: each shall bear his or her own sins (Gal. 6:5). The passion of Jesus shows us what this means in terms of history, an unveiling of the whole character of exile until then grasped only under the sign of the servant Israel: that we are not responsible for the sins of others, only that we suffer *for the sake of* the sins of others. And St. Paul lifts this up as well, in the enigmatic Colossians 1:24, a mystery now fulfilled in Christ Jesus and enacted in the Church.

Ecclesial communion, in this context, is not and cannot be a matter of institutional sanctions and permissions, but can take place only through the individual "for-the-sake-of"-ness by which exile is borne at all. Churches cannot properly put other churches out of communion with themselves, except according to worldly strictures, because true communion—if providence is to have its say!—is in any case a matter of mutual suffering and is thus, paradoxically, embraced in its fullness precisely when communion's brokenness is purely suffered. As long as individuals within separated churches suffer the brokenness of the body experienced among churches, it makes no sense to speak of broken communion among larger churches, but only of institutional willfulness and disdain. These are the choices of the market children. It is not possible any longer—if ever it was—for one church to place another outside of its communion, except in the most superficial of ways, the course of which itself implies a "kicking against the pricks" that exile rejects—though, of course, such kicking itself contains the abrasive press of providence as well.

In fact, there is within exile little method for explicating institutional correctness and sifting from among those parties that deserve our money and respect. Exile itself is a condition of shepherdlessness, even though shepherds be of good and bad ilk. The exilic promise of God's own shepherding, given in Jeremiah and Ezekiel, is matched in the human experience of confused shepherds among the people (Zech. 9–13), wherein good shepherds are distinguished only retrospectively through "the wounds [they] received in the house of [their] friends" (13:6) and are otherwise incapable of leading any more effectively than the evil shepherds. Exile is given and lifted by God alone. Exile renders pastoral distinctions blurred, and the question of judgment rightly falls, in the figure of Jesus, amid the mass of mutual distaste, wherein true evils are lost among the severally blind. Communion, in this context, cannot be based on the packaged glitter given to pastoral links of institutional integrity.

From every side, the providential form of exile is the narrative in which we find ourselves. Within it, all characters can remain defined only by their "withinness"; and to step outside the form is to reject the body altogether. The challenge, for every person and party, is to remain within the place they are set, staying put while remaining Christian or, at least, finding their Christianness in remaining within. *The Jews are Jews in Babylon, not in Samaria.* That is a crucial affirmation, because Jesus is Savior of the world by remaining in Jerusalem, not by going among the Gentiles. The Church of Christ remains the Church by remaining with the Church (though this Church "remained-within" may well appear no Church at all).

A sobering thought: if these forms can be assumed in our individual and common lives, if they can be described and commended, then "communion in brokenness" will prove the figure of Christ, rather than "broken communion" proving a human figure of speech that has no referring power beyond the constricted self. If or when? For who will determine the shape of remaining? Who will tell us and show us? Who will call the shepherds back from their flailing? Who will have the courage to remain, as at Golgotha, where only scattering comes from the mouths of the faithful and only silent women prove sturdy? If someone will tell us what it means to remain, instead of this incessant clamor to escape and buy and choose, then we will have found the patience to be the Church—the task of theology, the task of leadership, the task of prayer, the task of living and dying and of living again.

The communion of the church, as we have it in our control, is already broken; it has been broken for many centuries; its fragments are no longer amenable to further breakage. One cannot excommunicate the already excommunicated. The Christian world is populated by the excommunicated. Who is a Christian today, but one who is also an excommunicate? What we today call a communion within the Church, among any set of churches, is really the linkage of what is already broken, the gathering up and the holding together of what is already torn apart. What we call a communion today is only—but significantly and all-importantly—the communion of brokennesses. If a church, because of communion's long condition of being broken, cannot claim integrity, then it cannot withhold a communion it does not have. A divided church has no communion to withhold. It has no more choices. The fundamental call among churches today, any churches, can only be to abide mutually each other's brokenness.

To what does unity or communion, in the end, refer? We must readjust our thinking on this matter: with regard to the baptisms performed by heretics, Cyprian's exclusivist claim was overcome, and baptism, even heretical baptism, stuck. In fact, its sticking has proved intractable to the church's efforts at self-division. We stick to each other, we stick to each other's failures and apostasies. And although we have rebelled against such sticking and denied it outright, we cannot repair what God has refused to break, except insofar as God himself is broken. This breaking is the market's task; yet in casting lots and gathering goods at the foot of the cross, it is also bought by God and taken into his store. The communion of brokenness is what God does with the rebels and the deniers and the helpless. It is to our inescapable judgment that what we do with God is to drive him from our midst in the form of our brothers and sisters. Charity itself is now excommunicated. What time is this? What providential form? To join what we have made of God and to join what he has made of us. "Let us go forth to him outside the camp" (Heb. 13:13), "for he is our peace . . . through the cross" (Eph. 2:14, 16).

# Part 2

# The Scriptural Search

*Reading the Bible as an Act of Grace*

*They received the word with all eagerness,*

*examining the scriptures daily to see if these*

*things were so.*

—Acts 17:11

# 4

# The Faith
# of Reading

*Keble and Scriptural Interpretation*

Having discussed in the introduction and part 1 of this volume the providential core of figural interpretation of Scripture—and the figural core of providence—we should also attempt to place the fate of this reading within a providential outline as well. After all, we are currently seeing a vigorous revival of interest in patristic exegesis. And, no doubt, a number of scholarly and cultural strands have come together to moor this singular renaissance—academic developments in biblical hermeneutics, historical research into the early Church, literary theory and cultural poetics, sociological investigation, reactionary retrieval, the search of spiritualities, and, yes (ironically), the market of religious publications, always taking the pulse of such interests and ever ready to stoke their desire.

But one element glaringly lacking in this revival is any focused theological discussion of the character and significance of patristic exegetical practice, precisely in its figurative orientation. Period studies of one or another ancient writer are (and have been, in fact, for some time) plentiful; but there has been little attempt at formulating normative judgments of, or uncovering consistent fundamentals within, the figural interpretive views of the fathers. The best treatments, in this respect, remain those of an earlier generation, by Daniélou and De Lubac, for instance, whose approach to their sources remains, however, for many contemporary scholars, disturbingly ahistorical.

Of course, there is no accepted standard for what should count as a historically valid evaluation or appropriation of patristic exegetical practices and insights. What does even the past, in such matters, mean for a present to whom a figurative apprehension of a biblical personage, event, or object seems *intrinsically* unnatural, foreign, and perhaps even dangerously ideological? It is not clear, for example, what De Lubac really meant by lifting up the integrity of an interpretive vision that could see Abraham's willing sacrifice of Isaac as enclosing a startlingly bright vision of Jesus' toweringly humble love.

In this regard, John Keble's 1840 essay *On the Mysticism Attributed to the Early Fathers of the Church* maintains a still unusual place.[1] Keble wrote this piece as Tract 89 of "Tracts for the Times," that series of provocative dispatches by the group of scholars, including Pusey and the still-Anglican Newman, that gave its name to the Oxford Movement. As an attempted exposition of the principles governing patristic figurative exegesis of the Scriptures, Keble's work was among the first, and in some respects still the last, to examine the question, not only of what the fathers were about in their exegetical practice, but how their purely theological—and theologically utterly orthodox—concerns were somehow tied to their scriptural readings in a persistently pertinent way.

Keble himself was not without precursors in his interest in the theology of scriptural figuration. Perhaps his most notable progenitor in this regard was William Jones of Nayland, whose 1786 *Lectures on the Figurative Language of the Holy Scripture* represents a surer and clearer example of the living practice of such exegetical attitudes. But Jones had no interest in exploring the tradition, as did Keble, though this focus hardly gained the latter much readership. Keble's essay was quickly tarred with the "antiquarian" label and has since, in any case, been marginalized as a secondary work by a second-rate mind. Nor is the essay easy to read today. Its unsystematic character mimics (all too well) the character of patristic exegetical theory and practice, and Keble apparently brought

---

1. All Keble quotations in this chapter are cited from John Keble, *On the Mysticism Attributed to the Early Fathers of the Church* (Tracts for the Times 89; Oxford: Parker, 1868). R. R. Reno has also noted Keble's contemporary pertinence as an explicator of patristic figurative exegesis, in his *In the Ruins of the Church* (Grand Rapids: Brazos Press, 2002), 198 and 165–81.

it to an abrupt conclusion only partway through his proposed outline, because it had grown too long by half, and he himself had lost interest in steadying its coherence with a developed ending.

But Tract 89 bears careful attention today all the same. In an era of flailing attempts at reclaiming biblical authority for the Church and desperate measures at maintaining the pace of scholarly novelty within biblical and theological disciplines, Keble's examination of patristic figurative exegesis represents not simply a challenge on behalf of a potentially useful or corrective early tradition, but hangs over our restorative and self-advancing concerns the basic question as to our capacity to read Scripture at all.

One way of looking at Keble's goal in this work, beyond his offering some simple defense of antiquity, is as an attempt to uncover the theological conditions underlying the vital use of figural exegesis as a whole. In doing this, Keble tried to show the utter orthodoxy of patristic practice—orthodoxy, that is, according to traditional Protestant attitudes—even while exposing the de facto repudiation of these standard commitments on the part of those (Protestant) critics of early Christian figuration: "On the whole, the discrepancies between the two ages [ours and the fathers'], occasioning the imputation of Mysticism to the ancients, are far beyond being accounted for by local, accidental, or temporary circumstances; they must be referred to some difference in first principles." If contemporary denigrators of patristic exegesis are genuine in their rejection of such ways of reading Scripture, it can only be, Keble hints, because they do not *believe* what the ancient Christians believed.

So does Keble charge his analysis. And given the stakes he raises over the issue of exegetical form—the relative historical character of our faith—we too are invited to examine the theological conditions of figurative exegesis that he outlines as a window onto our current theocultural capacities for reading Scripture. Keble offers, at the outset of his essay, four principles lying behind the fathers' reading of the Bible: (1) they shared a basic conviction about the divinely generative breadth of Scripture; (2) they assumed a providential ordering of human life "national and individual" by God; (3) the saints and theologians of the early Church included the whole natural world within such providential reach; and (4) underlying all these assumptions was the perfective or ascetical character of interpretive practice, which formed both the context and the goal of Scripture's reading in general. Let me now outline each of these conditions as Keble discursively addresses them.

First, Keble is at his most exact in citing the widespread antipathy of modern theologians toward the patristic relish for finding allegories in Scripture that are not explicitly sanctioned by Scripture. The antipathy that Keble identifies derives from traditional Protestant exegetical principles, ones that exclude any figurative interpretations except those already performed by the biblical writers. For instance, St. Paul *does* use the allegory of Hagar and Sarah in Galatians, and he applies it as such to a discussion of the letter and spirit, law and gospel. But according to the typical Protestant hermeneutics that Keble addresses, other readings of Old Testament personages as figures of Christian truths or other historical events are strictly ruled out.

Patristic exegesis, then—apart from certain literalist heroes like John Chrysostom—must strike the modern mind as "far-fetched and extravagant," Keble observes, based as it is on "irrelevant or insignificant details of language or history." Indeed, figurative exegesis strikes a sensibility long nurtured on the thin gruel of literal explications as an affront to "common sense and practical utility" (what Keble calls the "idols of this age"), because it seems untethered to a common and universally accessible reason that can limit the reach of scriptural texts to agreed-upon usage.

For his own part, Keble sees this constricted sensibility as almost a denial of what is in fact the divinely inspired character of the Scriptures. Nowhere can he openly make this claim, which questions the basic Christian commitments of established leaders of his day. But, in his long and rambling discussion of Origen, for instance, Keble consistently comes back to the insistence on the plenary reach of the Bible's inspired nature that Origen claimed and to the way the multilayered "triple sense" that Origen explored was in fact an assertion of Scripture's divine authorship, not its subversion. In large measure, Keble seems to say, this is because a divine word can reveal its origin and character only through its disclosure of a breadth of signification that expresses the reach of divine power at work through human history and the natural world itself, not to mention the many levels of the human soul's health and disease. If Scripture, in any given text, *cannot* give up to the faithful reader a range of figurative meanings that apply to history, nature, and spirit, this is to limit its connection with the God that Christians claim to be its author, the author of the world in which they live and move.

Keble's argument with regard to his second principle is a familiar one of experiential analogy; and, given the looseness of such analogical arguments, it does not hold up as a necessary conclusion. Still, it is coherent with his other claims about the conditions for patristic figuration, and such coherence is at the root of analogical reasoning in the Butlerian tradition in which he writes. The breadth of Scripture's allusive character, according to Keble, fits well with the more basic patristic conviction of God's providential ordering of human history, both national and individual. Indeed, the category of divine providence stands at the center of Keble's defense of the fathers and represents his argument at its most robust and obvious.

Mystical interpretation, according to Keble, was possible and in fact necessary for the fathers insofar as they were convinced that human history was a chain or tissue of designed affinities, miraculously ordered by God to refer, in their larger shape, to the divine purpose revealed in Scripture itself. Events and characters from Abraham to Moses do their work and suffer their fates not only as isolated figures on the historical stage that has, as a later act, the life, death, and resurrection of Jesus; rather, their historical narratives exist through a divine *intention* that grounds their fundamental meaning solely in the forms of this later act and person.

The essentially creative force of divine providence in constructing these historical meanings and holding them together—giving birth to the particular persons for the sake of larger temporal displays of meaning—is, for Keble, the very reason why Scripture itself can exist at all. Keble is hardly naïve in his assumptions about subjective context, however. He makes no claims that Abraham or Isaac knew or were conscious of the figural significance of their lives and acts. Nor, for that matter, does Keble insist that particular interpreters from different ages must invariably perceive the same breadth of figural interpenetration among events of the past. Divine providence has force as a conceived reality only to the degree that such humanly subjective consciousness not function as a criterion for meaning, but exist as a subordinate phenomenon whose exercise itself comes into play only as God chooses to use it. Intentionality, for Keble, is primarily a divine attribute with respect to the significance of the biblical narrative. And the Scriptures, in their figurative depth and diversity, fulfill their divine revelatory function insofar as God uses the text's disclosiveness variably in conjunction with providentially directed interpreters.

This is why the variety of patristic figurative applications is not a problem for Keble, but rather a sign of divine directive in the process itself. Rules and systems of exegesis—a "hieroglyphical alphabet" such as might be used by rationalistic cabbalists—are not discernible by Keble among the fathers. They would, in any case, be properly absent from a providentially orchestrated history, whose providentially recorded narratives are themselves providentially applied by Christians whose spirits, minds, and ministries respond in faith to the complexity of contexts reflective of God's plan for the Church and the world.

The plan itself, of course, has as its source, center, and term the incarnation and redemptive acts of Jesus, the Christ. And this generative focus precludes, assuming its assertion in a given interpretive act, any destructive deviation from the real meaning of Scripture's texts. Keble is adamant that the fathers' figurative exegesis by and large worked within such a christological assertion with such consistency that any personal diversity in interpretive application could redound only to the privilege of christological glorification toward which, as everyone agreed, all of creation and human life was geared. The trinitarian and christologically oriented rule of faith, to which Keble sees the fathers tethered, defines the very shape of the providence by which the Scriptures have any divine meaning at all. But because such a rule—comprising, for instance, the historical shapes of the Apostles' Creed—grounds the very temporal (and literal) integrity of Scripture's referents, those referents, in all their discrete historical being, must also have their own origins and purposes, as well as their basic significations, oriented toward the forms of Jesus' divinely incarnate life. What Scripture describes, in every detail, exists only because of the historical truths of Christ.

Third, the central role of accepted providential activity that Keble claimed lay at the root of patristic figurative exegesis was certainly something his Protestant opponents were unlikely to question. How could they, without openly defying the basic Christian conviction of Jesus' messiahship, which even Lockean liberals had made a buttress of their gospel? And with this conviction firmly erected, the far more debatable primitive exegetical practice of extending figuration to the natural world was provided by Keble with an accepted logical ground. More than simply artifacts from the early Church, Keble was well aware that naturalistic figures—whereby birds and trees and planets were read as signifying aspects of the Christian gospel like the cross or the resurrection or the Church itself—struck his contemporaries as typically medieval and therefore popish. But the movement "from allegorizing the word of God, to spiritualizing His works" was, within the logic of the "discernible links in the providential chain" that constituted the Scripture's human history, a reasonable passage given the common created origins of word and work together.

The concern to stress naturalistic figuration may strike contemporary readers as tangential to Keble's basic concern with scriptural exegesis per se. Finding an image of the cross in a blade of grass was at best a quaint pastime. But Keble writes out of a particular tradition, tied, for instance, to Jones's even more insistent concern with this area of figuration fifty years earlier. It was a tradition that had returned to spiritual interpretations of the Bible in large measure out of a deliberate desire to reclaim God's nearness within the midst of a dedivinized secular universe, popularly engrained in the wake of deistic and scientifically empiricist enculturation. Not only was naturalistic figuration logically dependent upon the basic Christian axiom of scriptural providentialism, but its assertion acted as a singularly striking defense of such divine activity, in that it flew in the face of so many of the era's unexamined secularizing presuppositions. To collect the world's objects within the sphere of the gospel's forms, to identify the very colors of a harlot's wardrobe—that is, Rahab's scarlet thread in St. Clement's reading—as only part even of nature's hues ordered by the Holy Spirit to the proclamation of the Savior's redemptive blood, to gather the impressions of a sensible universe into the godly realm of scriptural signification, this was to repopulate daily life, and the shapes of an otherwise rapidly dissected natural environment, with at least the traces of divine personality; it was to elevate a philosophically or commercially degraded cosmos into a renewed vessel of adoration. The romantics' parallel revolt pales in comparison with the moral grandeur and doxological depth of Jones's vision and Keble's extension of it to the early Church.

Finally, this evangelistic undercurrent in Keble's argument is, of course, only that. The ease with which the fathers were able to elide Scripture, human history, and the natural world is more evidently, in Keble's mind, a sign of their more acute spiritual condition than anything else. And hence, the distance between the present age and theirs in exegetical taste is a token of something far more significant religiously than cultural habits of perception. Rather, the fathers understood that such habits both were founded on commitments to holy living and were themselves exhibitive of such habits' realization. Thus, the perfective character of patristic exegetical practice lies as the root experiential condition for figural apprehension. If the world itself speaks of God's love in Jesus Christ, if its corners and edges and even central heft all conjoin in a varied and coherent explication of the Scriptures' enunciated story of redemption, even though their visible form remains their own, then the parabolic call to see and hear must be met by a disposition bound to readied eyes and ears (Matt. 13:13–17).

Keble, following Jones, and for that matter simply rearticulating a basic patristic assumption most fully enunciated in Origen, plays off the Pauline description of the true reading of Scripture as a spiritual apprehension grounded in the disposition of faith and discipleship (2 Cor. 3:12–4:12). For Paul, the veil that obscures the true referent of Christ within the Old Testament is removed only in the Lord, within a process of sanctification that itself mirrors the form of Jesus' death (4:10). And so Keble affirms the fathers' essential practice of "fasting, and prayer, and scrupulous self-denial, and all the ways by which the flesh is tamed to the Spirit" as the form by which one can sanctify oneself and "draw near, with Moses, to the darkness where God is," and so see God in the "study of the Bible."

That "it [is] an awful thing to open" a Bible—as awesome a thing as entering the presence of the Holy, in that one confronts the reality of the "Personal Word . . . every where in the written Word"—was clearly a principle bound to rankle the sentiments of those defenders of the perspicuous clarity of scriptural texts—not to mention the hopes of present-day Gideonites. This is especially so if the scriptural Holy One demands a responsive holiness of intent and life in order to be received and its power for truth to be discerned. Right dispositions for the reading of Scripture, of course, were always prerequisites for understanding in the minds of Protestant, especially Puritan, divines. But the kinds of sanctifying practices that Keble identified from the fathers as necessary to spiritual reading were so patently tied to Roman Catholic devotion as to offend even the most morally scrupulous of Reformed sensibilities.

Keble's strategy here, as with the other elements of his analysis, was to lay bare any implied alternative to such sanctifying preparations as would logically require a complete demystifying and rationalizing of Scripture. In this case, Keble evidently felt that his argument would require Protestant minds to shy away from their anti-Roman prejudices, for the sake of maintaining some semblance of orthodox substance. Or, for lack of such modesty, they would at least be forced to confess their hypocrisy in still laying claim to any orthodoxy in the first place. Indeed, one way of describing Keble's larger rhetorical maneuver in Tract 89 is to see it as a trap for exposing Protestant apostasy vis-à-vis Scripture as a whole: antimysticism, or the scriptural constrictions of a popularly assumed anti-Catholicism, must surely end by subverting any deeper sustaining theistic premises one might otherwise continue to presume. If, that is, the breadth of divine providence is such as orthodoxy claims and has always claimed, then the shape of the Scriptures and their relationship to the larger world, its history, and the moral form of its readers must be congruent, in a basic way, with patristic exegetical practice. If that practice is genuinely rejected, so too must be any pretence to holding orthodox theistic convictions.

In some sense, Keble's intuition here has been confirmed by the evolution of much modern fundamental theology. One way of describing this evolution is to say that in the 150 years since Keble's tract we have carried through with the integration of antitheistic premises into our theological discourse, having a deliberate intent to unseat traditional *scriptural* commitments that appear incompatible with pluralistic realities. The process, in fact, began long before Keble's day, and his understanding of its dynamic was hardly novel among orthodox thinkers. The particularities, historical exclusions, distinctive judgments, and realistic forms of the Church's traditional reading of Scripture's referents were, already by the late seventeenth century's experience with religious conflict, so threatening to the social necessity of civically protected religious pluralism that the reach of any divine order that might found such particular scriptural forms could be seen only as deserving of a special anathema. Keble wrote in an era already well advanced, in which the Scriptures needed to be neutralized, and a gradual method of detheizing the scripturally integrated world was experienced as a compelling moral duty. We live in a time where the advance has further progressed. From deism through German idealism to contemporary pan-pneumatisms of some feminist and revisionist theologies, the direction and purpose has been constant. If the providentialist outlook is now more overtly denigrated than in Keble's time, its repugnance has had a long preparative gestation amid the sharpening distaste with Scripture's particularist claims.

Some will doubtless feel, however, that this direction and purpose need not be shared in order still to set aside the actual exegetical practices of the fathers. The sense of hermeneutic anachronism is not necessarily a sign of a degraded theological culture. Surely, we might wonder, Abraham and Isaac can be extracted from the gospel accounts and returned to their Hebraic context without thereby subverting that gospel? And here is where a rigorous reflection on Keble's argument needs to begin among self-styled Christians of whatever theological stripe: are the theistic premises that Keble identifies *necessarily* and *logically* tied to the figurative discipline?

This question goes beyond Keble's own topical argument, which was perhaps less concerned with patristic figuration in itself than with its usefulness as a mirror to his own theological culture. In our day, in any case, figurative exegesis is less a practice of disease than it is an interesting option among imaginative tropes, though without unavoidable demand—a curiosity, though without homiletical plausibility. So the question is raised: Can one hold to the breadth of Scripture's revelatory reach, bow to the creative sovereignty of God within our temporal lives, embrace the coherent character of nature's divinely transparent sheaths, and run after the transforming allure of the purified soul—can one inhabit this vision of the world *without* traversing Scripture's figurated terrain?

An answer to this kind of question is not easily offered. This is so in large part because the Christian Church's contemporary language about God is fraught with so many murky confusions, a mixture of bequests from both the tradition and its assailants, that have been distressingly ill digested before being passed on into the general soil of our common speech. The very developments referred to earlier in biblical hermeneutics, historical research into the early Church, blossoming literary theory and cultural poetics, sophisticated and speculative sociological investigations, reactionary retrievals and yearnings, the search of spiritualities old and new, and even the unslaked market of religious publications—none of these and other contributory currents to the jumbled flow of our present theological reflections are susceptible to clear evaluation as valid determinants of the limits of our scriptural apprehensions, for their genetic interactions and the intents of their reception and deployment lie beyond the capacities of current scientific analysis.

What is obvious is that—despite the philosophical responses that have been given aplenty to rationalist disavowals of providentialist theistic frameworks or of personalist articulations of divine-human relations or of the seemingly elitist rewards of self-abnegation in favor of divine reception, responses given with crisp aplomb from Butler to Swinburne—even moderate theological voices today are uneasy with the kind of talk that would actually say outright that the forms of the world are ordered to an expression coherent with the shape of both Pentateuch and gospel. Few, certainly, even among more conservative Christians, could openly agree with Keble's brilliant contemporary, H. L. Mansel, in his relentlessly post-Kantian conclusion that the scriptural language of the incarnation and its prophetic contours is not only potentially meaningful, but *exhaustively* so from the standpoint of a *rational* believer, and hence compellingly hegemonic in its exposition of the cosmos and its Maker. Philosophy has rarely changed minds, let alone hearts. And for lack of such a willingness to pursue intuited premises to their end—a lack whose abortive power remains historically and sociologically mysterious—it remains difficult to know how to test Keble's thesis. That is, figurative exegesis will and must remain in our day at best a curiosity or a spiritual consumable.

To be sure, there remain nagging questions about generally accepted presuppositions that the Christian Church continues to uphold, if often without much enthusiasm: the unity of the two Testaments, the overriding character of the incarnation as a rule of faith, even the necessity of some predisposition for Scripture's fruitful reading. Just as we may feel a hovering sense of these presuppositions' continued importance without knowing quite where they ought to lead us concretely in our exegetical practice, we may also remain obscurely distrustful of Keble's insistence on their vital place within a tight-knit scheme of mystical appropriations of Scripture's spirit. Could he be right? Is the methodologically constricted manner in which we read the Bible, the approach that must at best tie itself in hermeneutical knots in order to look at Abraham's willing sacrifice of Isaac as enclosing a startlingly bright vision of Jesus' toweringly humble love, only to end wearily by consigning such glimpses to the faded library of historical exegesis—could such constricted reading simply be a sign that our faith in God has faded too?

"Nevertheless, when the Son of man comes, will he find faith on earth?" (Luke 18:8); or will he not rather discover a love grown cold (Matt. 24:12)? Keble's opening query about the "discrepancies between the two ages," that of the fathers and our own in the matter of scriptural mysticism, might, as he put it, be resolved into "some difference in first principles"; it might even be answered with the strong judgment "that the ancients may have been in the right, and we in the wrong" about such intellectual groundings. But the drift of his arguments, perhaps despite himself, with their repeated references to the world of wonder and astonished humility inhabited by the fathers in their entry into the Scriptures, their delighted and driven discoveries of a creation enmeshed in Jesus' forms and words, themselves terms of the prophets' languages and gestures, their eager subjection of mind, body, and spirit to the climate of this strangely knotted universe—Keble cannot seem to help himself in pointing to a veil let down before the eyes of the present church. And who shall remove such a veil as this?

There is a final sense that Keble seems to hold, then, that what is at stake in the question of figural reading is not simply one of hermeneutical method or even of cultural expectation or for that matter of orthodox doctrine in itself—as if the problem here is resolvable through some intentional effort at cognitive reform. And it is just this sense that most firmly underscores the naturalness with which Keble himself had imbibed the figuralist vision. For in the end, the mysticism of the fathers was grounded on the vital apprehension of God's sovereign and intricate sway over the all world's forms—physical, psychic, and literary together. There is nothing methodological or narrowly theological about figuralism's deployment at all; rather, it marked the enunciation of the world's reality. And thus, its obscurement itself clings to the shapes of providence and, in secrecy, continues to assert its truth unwaveringly. Why can we no longer see as the fathers saw? The answer to such a question, Keble indicates, is given in the power of the thing seen, whose force and beauty emerges in blindness and sight together (Isa. 6:9–10; Mark 4:12–20) because it is the very fact of God's judgment and mercy given in the shapes of the creation. In this, Keble seems to turn back to the words of his movement-launching 1833 sermon on national apostasy, whose vision of England and the English church's figural attachment to Israel's exilic fate represents a foundational mystical construal of his era's meaning. Like Bishop George Berkeley a century before him in his famous 1732 sermon before the Society for the Propagation of the Gospel, Keble reiterated the Irish bishop's trembling query—"may we not therefore suppose a similar treatment of the Jewish and Christian Church?"—and pronounced the supposition true, not as a passing analogy, but as the necessary glory built into God's historical creativity

It is not a question, then, *if* a veil is laid before the eyes of this age's Church. There must be, if the Church is to be the Church of Scripture's world. And its lifting ought to shape our prayer. Our prayer, of course, is rightly formed by one whose forms insert themselves into our stutterings just in those places where Scripture proves itself, not simply an object for our understanding, but a force that overwhelms it.

# 5

# Sublimity
# and Providence

*Figural Reading as a Spiritual Discipline*

T he sweetest and most sublime occupation for a theologian is to search for Jesus Christ amid the sacred books [of Scripture]."

Taking my cue from this sentence, written by a now-obscure theologian of the early modern period, I want to reflect on what I believe to be the central truth about the relation between spiritual formation and the Bible, especially in our day. Particularly in light of the question that Keble left us—that is, the question of our waiting in the face of our understanding's redemption—we ought to be prodded at least toward some tentative steps of inquisitive petition: How shall we hear? How shall our churches listen and begin to hear anew? And the key truth about the relation between the spirit's education and the Scripture's own power to educate is, I believe, the following: our spirits are formed by the reading of Scripture, more than by anything else, and this reading is the particular discipline of hearing the whole Bible, Old and New Testaments together, speak of Christ Jesus. I mean this as specifically as possible: if we cannot search for—and somehow come to find—Jesus in Genesis and Acts *together,* in Leviticus and Philemon, in 1 Samuel and

Jude, in Job, the Psalms, Nahum, and in Revelation, *and with the same particularity* as in the Gospels, then we have not yet opened ourselves to the forming of our spirits by the Holy Spirit of God, the author of life and word together.

I state nothing novel here. Only what the tradition has long since stated clearly, that the *way* we read Scripture is itself the form of our life:

> So long as [a person] cleaves to the letter [of Scripture], his inner hunger for spiritual knowledge will not be satisfied; for he has condemned himself like the wily serpent to feed on the earth—that is, on the outward or literal form—of Scripture (cf. Gen. 3:14), and does not, as a true disciple of Christ, feed on heaven—that is, on the spirit and soul of Scripture, in other words, on celestial and angelic bread. I mean that he does not feed through Christ on the spiritual contemplation and knowledge of the Scriptures, which God gives unstintingly to those who love Him. . . .
>
> And this in its turn is followed by a complete ignorance of the deification given by grace according to the new mystery.[1]

We live in an era, of course, when the category of spiritual reading of Scripture is hardly unexamined, not only by scholars, but through the popularization of books on *lectio divina* and the like. Yet, for all that, the kind of Scripture reading that is focused on the discovery of Christ within *all* the Scriptures remains decidedly rejected as a legitimate, let alone absolutely necessary practice for serious Christians. The reasons for this are complex, as noted in the last chapter. But a major one is surely our peculiar sense of what history is and how what history is must limit our reading of Scripture. St. Gregory the Great, for instance, writes that "we must hold on to the historical truth [of Scripture] with respect to the past, without thereby destroying its prophetic sense with respect to the future—for if the virtuous powers of the saints were not authentic they are nothing at all; and if they do not enclose some mystery, they are very little at all" (*Moralia* 35.20.48). Yet when Gregory speaks of scriptural history and factuality in these terms, we moderns, on the right and left of the theological spectrum, seem incapable of giving such claims a free pass. Our concerns with the constraining force of historical reference derive variously from our worries about ethical focus, about doctrinal openness, and about scientific integrity. And in the face of these concerns, the more important claim—that the health

1. Maximus the Confessor, "Various Texts on Theology," Fifth Century §35 and §31, in *The Philokalia* (trans. G. E. H. Palmer, P. Sherrard, and K. Ware; London: Faber & Faber, 1981), 2.267–69.

and shape of our spirits depends absolutely upon seeking and finding Christ in *all* the Scriptures—must seem whimsical, however intriguing. We are dealing, then, with more than cultural distances, but with our inability to comprehend God and our own time in a certain way, a way that, for centuries, was thought to bring life.

"The sweetest and most sublime occupation for a theologian is to search for Jesus Christ amid the sacred books [of Scripture]." I want to reflect on this phrase, because I think it is aimed at the very crux of this incapacity. It speaks of the fruit of overcoming it, and it confronts its contemporary power directly, with a specifically Christian vision of God's life that was articulated into the midst precisely of our own situation.

I quote the phrase from an author virtually unknown today, but celebrated in the early part of the eighteenth century, in both France and England. You cannot find him mentioned in the *Oxford Dictionary of the Christian Church,* but you will discover him cited, translated, and anthologized in many a Scripture commentary on both sides of the Channel through even the late nineteenth century. Jacques-Joseph Duguet (1649–1733), the author in question, was a devout Jansenist Catholic, who, in the latter seventeenth and during the early years of the eighteenth century, would lecture on various books of the Bible to packed halls of listeners in Paris. These long expository discussions of both Old and New Testament writings were later collected in print and proved among the most popular works of their kind in the course of that latter century.

"The sweetest and most sublime occupation for a theologian is to search for Jesus Christ amid the sacred books [of Scripture]." This particular sentence comes from the introduction to a small primer that Duguet wrote in 1716 entitled *Rules for Understanding the Sacred Scriptures.*[2] The rules in question, to which I shall return later, have to do almost exclusively with what we would today call typological or, more broadly, figurative ways of the reading the Bible. And Duguet explains his purpose in outlining this interpretive perspective as follows: "There is nothing truer than what we have learned from the apostle, Saint Paul, that Jesus Christ is the end of the law; that he is predicted and figured in the whole Old Testament; that the prophets had nothing but him in view; and that we do not understand the Scriptures that came before him, unless we discover him within them everywhere

---

2. Jacques-Joseph Duguet, *Règles pour l'intelligence des saintes écritures* (1716; repr. in *Scripturae sacrae cursus completus,* ed. J.-P. Migne; Paris: Garnier, 1877), 27.20.

and unless we are satisfied with only an interpretation that leads us to him."[3] And thus, to read the Scriptures truly, is to engage a "search for Jesus Christ" within them all.

Duguet calls this search a specifically theological task. But it is also a task that is, he says, "the sweetest and most sublime" of all. And this is where I want to begin a little digging. These are not idle adjectives, but carefully selected terms that, in themselves, point to an entire way of understanding the Christian life. To take the second qualifier first: in what way is the christologically figural reading of Scripture sublime in a theological sense? And to answer this, we need to take a moment to enter the spiritual search by way of the rhetoric of esthetics current in Duguet's world.

In speaking of the sublime, Duguet takes up a word that already by his day had elicited a special concern from artists and intellectuals. It was Duguet's Jansenist colleague, poet Nicolas Boileau, who gave to the reading public in 1674 the first modern translation of Longinus's first-century treatise on rhetoric usually called "On the Sublime."[4] And with this volume and subsequent commentary, an entire tradition of evolving esthetics was set in motion, pushing through the eighteenth century and into the developing self-consciousness of romantic writing and painting.[5] Longinus's own interest in this category of artistic expression only distantly resembled later conceptions of the sublime in terms of terror and awe at the infinite (cf. Burke and Coleridge). But his sense of a kind of writing that generally elevated the spirit to some higher plane of grandeur and nobility akin to a divine reality beyond simple human grasp stands at the base of his commendation of sublimity. (Longinus even cites the opening verses of Genesis in this regard, a classical reference to biblical literature that puzzles critics to this day.)[6]

3. Ibid., 15.

4. Cf. Longinus, *On Great Writing (On the Sublime)* (trans. G. M. A. Grube; Indianapolis: Hackett, 1991) (the brief introduction treats the vexed question of Longinus's identity); Nicolas Boileau-Despréaux, *Le traité du sublime*, published in 1674 as an appendix to his *Satires*, *Épîtres*, and *L'art poétique*. In 1694 he published a set of *Réflexions sur Longin*, containing discussions of an array of esthetic debates in which he was then involved, using Longinus as a springboard.

5. John Dennis is credited in the early eighteenth century with disseminating the French interest in "sublimity" among the English, which found classic definition in Edmund Burke's 1757 essay *An Enquiry into the Origin of Our Ideas on the Sublime and Beautiful*. S. H. Monk's *The Sublime: A Study of Critical Theories in 18th-Century England* (New York: Modern Language Association, 1935) remains the standard treatment of a topic that continues to attract enormous attention among literary critics and art historians.

6. Longinus, *On Great Writing*, 9.

Boileau, for his part, followed Longinus's general concern with elevation, although he stresses a more regulated means toward stylistic excellence. Sublime writing, for Boileau, was characterized by the harmony of order, coherence, and reason, where each element "is put in its proper place" and where "beginning and end respond to the middle" together.[7] Furthermore, Boileau was far more explicit in his linkage of form with formation. Longinus's interest in the careful use of figurated speech, for example, whether of metaphors or historical apostrophes (i.e., using an image of the past as if it were a living precedent for the present, bringing it to a new resonance of vital meaning), represents a necessary means by which this ordering of language and ideas moves us to a directed and passionate relationship with narrative reality.[8] There is an element of experiential ecstasy in Longinus's view that, properly, was noticed by the early romantics. In Boileau's view, however, such directed passions have value to the degree that they are ordered toward the morally edifying.[9] The transformative grandeur of sublimity, in other words, lies in its power to engage the virtuous, at once in terms of the poet's own productive character, the text's power, and the reader's receipt of its gifts. The virtues of the sublime, for Boileau, take flesh in the way that human passions are formed into the reasonable image of the divine. And the power of genuine artistic beauty is that it should lead toward docility with respect to the true.

When Duguet, therefore, writes that the "most *sublime* occupation for a theologian is to search for Jesus Christ amid the sacred books [of Scripture]," he injects into a particular form of study the power of a text to order the passions of the human soul into a receptive openness to God's own character. Reading the Bible a certain way changes the heart. And that Duguet links the sublime with the sweet—"the *sweetest* and most sublime occupation," as he puts it—underlines this claim most surely. For in choosing this next adjective, Duguet defines a divine rhetoric explicitly in terms of divine grace. Jansenist that he is, Duguet deliberately picks one of the most pregnant Augustinian terms, long associated with the Catholic debate over victorious grace, and tethers it to an interpretive scriptural discipline. As his argument with Pelagius expanded, Augustine began increasingly to elaborate upon an understanding of the grace of Christ, almost identified with the love embodied by the Holy Spirit,

---

7. Boileau-Despréaux, *L'art poétique*, 1.175–82; cf. Longinus, *On Great Writing*, 39.

8. Longinus, *On Great Writing*, chapters 16–32.

9. Boileau-Despréaux, *L'art poétique*, 4.85–145.

as something capable of metaphysically winning over the human will through a divine attraction:

> Let [the soul] flee by faith for refuge to the mercy of God, that He may give it what He commands, and may, by inspiring into it the sweetness of His grace through His Holy Spirit, cause the soul to delight more in what He teaches it, than it delights in what opposed His instruction. In this manner it is that the great abundance of His sweetness—that is, the law of faith—His love which is in our hearts, and shed abroad, is perfected in them that hope in Him.[10]

This sweetness of grace becomes, in Augustine's later writing, an irresistible force, a conquering and victorious power that overcomes the prideful lust of the fallen human heart with a contrary and greater attraction, persuasion, and delight (cf. Augustine's *Epistles of John* 26.4–8 and *On the Merits and Forgiveness of Sins* 2.19.32). Sweetness, in the Augustinian vocabulary of late-seventeenth-century theology, represents the very presence of God's grace to change and recreate the heart.

The sweetest and most sublime occupation, then, does not simply concern a form of pleasurable excitement, however noble. It is about exposure to divine presence, literally, through the instrumentality of an ordered text. Duguet's search for Christ in all the Scriptures is, he claims, a discipline in which a certain approach toward a text leads the reader into a realm in which the character of the author—God the poet, if you will—becomes the transformative subject or substance communicated—the grace embodied in Christ. *His* reason, *his* coherence and order, *his* balance and internal resonances, all given in the shape of the scriptural text—sublimity—become both the end and the means of human conformance to the truth—sweetness. The moral values of sublimity, taken in a purely literary sense, are transmuted into the very tools of conversion and, in Maximus's wording, deification of the human creature.

*But through the reading of Scripture* as a figurated text of Christ. This is Duguet's striking claim. That is, that it matters how we read; that there is something morally at stake, even spiritually at stake; that Scripture and the Holy Spirit's being are joined together in their redemptive work within the human heart. If there is order and coherence in the work and character of God, it must structure our own souls; and if this can happen, it is only because the world itself is structured by a scriptural

10. Augustine, *On the Spirit and the Letter* 51 (trans. Holmes). The notion of the "sweetness" of the Holy Spirit, tied to Rom. 5:5, is a favorite one in this and other books, like *On the Grace of Christ*.

history informed by the Holy Spirit. Scripture is designed to change us into God's image, given in Christ, through a key process of being taught in its reading in a particular way, a way that structures the working of our minds, our observant eyes, and our spirits.

Duguet claims that this way is the way of figural reading, of searching for Christ "amid the sacred books." The Scriptures themselves, written by a sublime author, reflect his order and coherence and unity amid diverse parts and periods. And they do so in the ways that reveal the echoes and shadows and figures of Christ, resonating within Old and New Testaments, thematically organizing, imagistically interconnecting, narrationally weaving a unified vision of God's being within the world that is perfectly given in the incarnation. And thus, to enter this orchestrated and divine reality is to be changed by an encounter with a grace that converts the intellectual and spiritual being of the reader. When in Leviticus 12, for instance, we hear of the laws governing the purification of women after childbirth, we are invited into a search for Christ amid the details of birth, blood, and sacrifice, whose traverse must inform the depths of our souls. Duguet himself commented on Leviticus, and, along with early Christian readers of the book like Origen, he was able to thread his way through the thickets of this text and discover Mary, her own conception of the Second Adam, the purifying blood of his life of sacrifice, given as the Lamb of God but received in the poverty of the indigent worshiper of the levitical text. Creation, fallenness, incarnation, humiliation, sacrifice, and finally divine love are all found to be bristling within these legal verses, disengaged only with the most patient and hopeful care.

Is there anything transformative about such a reading, in the sense of sweet sublimity? The question arises in our day especially, emerging from our culture's own deep suspicions over the potentially reactionary political and ethical burdens carried surreptitiously on the shoulders of revived ancient exegetical tropes. Duguet implicitly answers the question when he enumerates the virtues of figural reading in the rules that he offers in his hermeneutical primer. There are twelve of them, and though relatively unexceptional and unobtrusive as general guides to the discovery of figural texts within Scripture, they all speak to a certain kind of attention that must engage the active spirit of the reader in a disciplined way, that is, as an occupation whose fruits are both sweet and sublime.

The first is a self-evident rule of figural reading shared by Catholics and Protestants alike: "We must see Jesus everywhere that the apostles saw Him, as in Isaiah 7." It is worth noting, however, that what was once regarded as an obvious basis for accepting a figural reading—apostolic (or canonical) precedent—is today precisely a reason for its rejection, that is, as an intrinsically suspect product of cultural limitation and apostolic self-justification. "Of course," we are wont to exclaim, "the early church would wish to link Isaiah's words regarding 'Immanuel' with Jesus; but such retrospective verse-collage clearly goes to the side of Isaiah's own meaning." The practical demands of Duguet's first rule, then, are *in fact* particularly challenging, since they imply a deliberate setting aside of certain historical presumptions on our part and press into another mind-set, an apostolic one at that. And this, in fact, involves a search in its own right for both the form of apostolic character and an ongoing means of putting on this mind, a renewed mind (Rom. 12:2; Eph. 4:23), which represents a broad range of historically recreative tasks, all centered on learning with the apostles (Acts 2:42). The renaissance of biblical and patristic study that marked the milieu from which Duguet came was nothing other than one aspect to this effort at reading the Scriptures for the sake of Christ.

Another subset within Duguet's rules touches upon the ability to identify characteristics of Jesus that are peculiar to him—and to him in a special or supreme way. For example, when certain aspects of a text "can only fit with him," we must "see Jesus visible" therein (rule 2); or when they deal with august and magnificent elements otherwise incapable of immediate historical reference (rule 3); or when their narrative whole resonates with the grand themes of Jesus' own life (rule 8). The examples that Duguet gives for these interpretive parameters—Isaiah 9; 43:19; and the story of Joseph respectively—are all traditional christological figures within the history of the Church's biblical interpretation. But the practical aim for Duguet here is that the reader of the Scriptures be attuned—and seek such attunement—with the characters, themes, and spiritual impulsions within the text that all are linked with the power and form of Jesus' own life and reality, so that the visible figure of Christ might arise within a distant passage of its (God's) own accord.

Such attunement is practical and practiced; it is also the framework for intellectual conversion in the face of the Bible's words, which themselves are structured by the Holy Spirit's instrumentality. That Duguet uses adjectives like *magnificent* and *august* in this context places his discussion squarely within the lineage of literary sublimity; yet now transfixed upon the theological topic of the search for Christ, the recognizability of these characteristics of elevated passion are clearly understood as the interior apprehensions of virtuous capacities well immersed in the passion of and for Jesus himself. The practiced theologian searches for the magnificent and rejoices in it, just as Abraham rejoiced to see Jesus' own day (John 8:56), himself understanding that the joy of being caught up in God finds its fulfillment in God's own self-giving to the one in search for joy.

This sense of searching within the Scriptures for something that cannot so much be found but only given is present in several other rules, whose fundamental ground for the claim of Christ's visible presence throughout the whole of Scripture is given in God's sovereign ordering of the Bible according to his own creation and recreation of human history as a whole. In this light we are to see Duguet's direction that passages that do not fit with our rational expectations or that outstrip our "feeble reason" (rule 6, with the example of Abraham driving out Hagar) or that are "astounding" and "visibly mysterious" (rule 7, e.g., the whole narrative of Jacob) must somehow hide within themselves a mystery whose form is the figure of Christ. If these texts and the histories they enclose belong to God, then we must expect some basic obscurity in their composition and referent, an obscurity born of the profound mystery that is God's own life given in Christ and his cross. Conversely, when a passage is so "simple, natural, and easy" in its "interrelated parts," this too speaks of Christ (rule 10), for the order and coherence of a spiritual text can represent only God's being; and since it is a being whose historical exposure is given supremely in the dispensation of the incarnation and its life-making sacrifice, such seamless coherence must point to Christ as clearly as a text's assault upon our reason. The marks of sublimity must always be parsed by the acts of divine grace. And only thus is Scripture's reading sweet, like every word of God, in its offering of judgment and mercy (Ps. 19:10; Ezek. 3:3).

To search for Christ within these contexts, contexts of both disturbing mystery and astonishing coherence, demands therefore an ongoing submission to our own littleness, to the humility of creature before the generative power of an ordering yet uncomprehended Creator. The Bible is truly, in this respect, like the natural world and the shape of individual experience. The center of these "two books" must be presumed to reflect the very character of the revealed (and thus incarnate) God. Yet its apprehension arrives only temporally, and thus gradually, through the process of subjection, of giving oneself over to the humbling and exalting movements of divine providence within the world and within Scripture, the world's explicator, which is fraught with the image of Christ as its interior reason for being. Just as we daily pray in our own lives, the reading life of Scripture's study becomes but the obverse of that realization that experience—lived and studied—must engage the awesome searching of God within the depths of our own being (Ps. 139). If we cannot say, in the face of Scripture, "such knowledge is too wonderful for me" (139:6), we have not yet searched it as we ought.

Duguet's peculiar occupation gains its formative power, then, from its deliberate immersion in the perceived providential power of the triune God. The rules for reading Scripture figurally are aimed at guiding the Christian to treat the Bible in a way that is coherent with faith in this God's creative character and, in thus reading it, to become more and more pliant and receptive to its reality. Searching for Christ amid all the Scriptures is but another way, in relationship with the Bible, of describing how the human creature stands in the world with respect to God and is called to stand ever more firmly. To live in the world as it truly is—that is, as *God's* world, the God revealed in Christ—is to read Scripture in a figural way. Similarly, to read Scripture in a way that can uncover this God in all corners of its textual universe is to learn to live truly in this world, God's world, as it is.

The ascetic power of this approach to Scripture was, in Duguet's context, historically demonstrated in the drive to mission embodied by many of the most fervent of his Jansenist colleagues, like Deacon François de Paris, whose yearning to have a body that itself became tied to the figures of Scripture drove him into the slums of Paris in an ultimately exhausting struggle for humble service and turned upside down the religious culture of the capital during the early part of the eighteenth century. But de Paris's missionary appropriation of figural reading was, at base, no different from St. Francis's five hundred years earlier, and its origin in the ascetic posture of Duguet's form of reading was common enough in traditional circles of biblical theology. To turn to a writer more familiar to us, Pascal (1623–62), we can easily see the continuity between the latter's more conceptual outlook and Duguet's expository practice, precisely on the level of spiritual formation.[11] The Jansenist linkage between the two is direct, especially in the undergirding sense of God's historical providence that is common to the movement in its

11. Whether any of Pascal's writing on the Bible, in his fragmentary *Apology* for Christianity now known to us as the *Pensées* and perhaps circulated partially in manuscript copies among Jansenist circles, was in fact known to Duguet is uncertain.

approach to the Scripture. In his *Pensées,* Pascal devotes long sections to
the question of scriptural prophecy and figuration, something that has,
perhaps, puzzled modern readers more interested in his metaphysical
and existential vision. For Pascal, figuration lies at the root of the ordered
destiny of human life: nature is a figure of grace, the visible of the invisible in every respect; while grace, in its historical experience, is a figure
of glory, the full vision of God. At all levels, the Scriptures themselves
are figures of each. The vocation of the human creature is, quite literally,
to engage in a search amid this universe of multilayered signs, a search
whose goal is the gradual progress to divine sight and touch.[12]

The character of this search is described by Pascal in openly Augustinian terms, as the transformation from concupiscence to charity, the
letting go of creatures as the object of our loves and the apprehension
of God alone in their place. The reality of the cross, the humiliation of
God, represents the historical explication to this process of transformation. In a famous, if cryptic, fragment, Pascal writes: "*Figures.* The letter kills—Everything happened figuratively—Christ had to suffer—A
humiliated God—This is the cipher St. Paul gives us. Circumcision of
the heart, true fasting, true sacrifice, true temple; the prophets showed
that all this must be spiritual" (268; cf. 253). Here, clearly, the scriptural
figures point to a spiritual ascesis that is accomplished by grace through
the cross, even as it is appropriated historically by each individual through
some kind of temporal conformance to this reality.

But Pascal goes even further in identifying the specifically *scriptural*
search of identifying and understanding biblical figure as a key element
within the actual change from concupiscence to charity. His celebrated
discussion of the "hidden God" is, in fact, lodged within his attempt to
explain the character of scriptural figuration as a spiritual discipline.
Why, he asks over and over, did God not speak more clearly in his self-
revelation? Why are the Scriptures redolent in figural language? Why the
inherent obscurities to which this leads? Taking up Jesus' use of Isaiah
6:10, Pascal claims that the Bible as a whole is swathed in the semidarkness
and half-light of figures in order to humble and, if necessary, condemn
human beings who cannot give themselves over to the work of grace,
even and especially in the acts of reading and intellectually searching for
the truth. Figurative speech is itself an image of the cross, which can be

12. I use the Lafuma enumeration of the fragments, a translation of which is given by A. J. Krailsheimer
in his edition of the *Pensées* (London: Penguin, 1966). For the above, see fragments 275 and 503, among
others.

either a cause for stumbling or a means of life for the dying. Speaking of the scriptural prophecies and figures, he writes: "There is enough light to enlighten the elect and enough obscurity to humiliate them. There is enough obscurity to blind the reprobate and enough light to condemn them and deprive them of excuse" (236). The "humbling of pride" (234) becomes the context of faithful scriptural reading, which is a continual process of submitting oneself to the realities of crucified desire in the face of a humanly rejected divine love whose character upholds the universe.[13]

What Duguet outlines as practical interpretive parameters are therefore, within the perspective of this tradition, designed to inculcate habits of a recreated affection. This new love is born of tethering the mind and spirit to the form of the cross as it continually remolds the meanings of scriptural passages and images according to the comprehensive shape that God has given the world through his redemptive purpose. That the human heart should reflect the true shape of the world as God has created and directed its history is the very purpose of Scripture's reading. And the christologically figured folds of Scripture's exposition lie at the cusp of that desired mirroring of heart and world. Pascal the scientist, who grasped the awful implications for human experimental knowledge of an infinite universe—infinite in cosmic expanse and microcosmic matter—also saw these same implications as refractions of a truth unveiled by the Scriptures' own role in rational understanding: human thought, given over to the searching of the mysteries of the Bible's revelation of Christ in all its parts, represents our greatest dignity in relation to a world created by God (cf. 199).

It is worth raising the question now as to why or at least *how* contemporary habits of biblical reading have strayed so far from this vision. It cannot merely be because of the rise of some new scientific spirit and set of methods that, for instance, gradually demanded that we take scriptural reference as presuppositionally historical or ostensive and thus undermining its christological figuration, even while we investigate the accuracy of the purported reference itself. It is true that neither Pascal (who died too young) nor certainly Duguet had any interest in engaging the historical-critical problems that contemporaries like Spinoza or Richard Simon raised. What was the case is that the essentially figural approach to the Scriptures they adopted simply overleapt the critical

13. On the whole of this theme, see the important texts in "Section 18—Foundations," in ibid., 223–44.

concern with historical origins altogether, through its complete identification with a vision of providential order. That vision logically subsumed such concerns, even if they were voiced, because it resolved them in the overarching orchestration of details by God's orientation of scriptural specifics within the world's history according to divine will, whatever their referential status.

The critical methods of textual analysis and historical suspicion were, in any case, hardly foreign to these writers; indeed, the methods were seized upon, sharpened in sophisticated ways, and finally identified with the specifically *Jansenist* circles in which Pascal and Duguet moved. Duguet himself was a colleague of Simon in the French Oratory—an intellectual context for textual criticism—and was personally engaged in the kinds of study of positive theology that developed the critical apparatus that was later to uphold what we now call historical criticism. The point is this: the critical questioning of the Bible's historical reference was wholly uninteresting, once the conformance of world and Scripture to the reality that exhibited sweet sublimity—a reality wholly reflective of God's creative power over the shape of time and its artifacts—was apprehended. Not that such historical reference was doubted; only that the mechanism of its truthful affirmation was subsumed into the more miraculous and wondrous power of God's providence, a form of historical existence that presupposed the references intended by God as the substratum of all humanly accessible critical evidence.

It was not science itself that informed the disintegration of Scripture's figural reading, but a peculiar evolution of scientific reasoning. That modern historical criticism of the Bible was, in the nineteenth century, called scientific criticism is a product of what, retrospectively, can only be termed an anomalous view of science itself. Pascal, as we saw, viewed the character of the universe as revealed to human experimental inquiry to be an existential buttress to the spiritual demands of scriptural reading. And, in the seventeenth century and early eighteenth century, he was not alone in wedding such scientific insights with a moral embrace of scriptural depth. We could, as a marvelous example of this, take Robert Boyle (1627–91), innovating chemist and organizer of the Royal Society in 1662. Much more explicitly than Pascal, Boyle sought to explain the right relationship between Christian faith and experimental science, something he outlined in a host of writings. His attempt to lay out the basis upon which Scripture acts as the providential exponent of the world's divine order is given in the 1661 treatise *Some Considerations Touching the Style of the Holy Scriptures.* It is interesting to see how, from a religious—and non-Augustinian—culture widely different from the milieu of Duguet, Boyle can outline the same context of scriptural reading as a process of spiritual formation tied to the transformative power of God at work in the texts of world and Bible.

Boyle's treatise is deliberately designed to answer objections to the Scripture that may derive from the concerns of more scientifically or literarily oriented minds: for instance, that Scripture is obscure, unmethodical, incoherent, historically and culturally impertinent, and so on. Boyle's apologetic strategy in the face of almost all these objections is to describe how the analogy[14] with nature—a parallel creature of God—must lead us to expect of Scripture a similar depth, profundity, and mystery to the intricacies of the material universe before the limited searchings of human reason:

> This seemingly disjointed method of that Book is by many much caviled at; to which, were the supposal a truth, I might reply, that the Book of Grace doth but therein resemble the Book of Nature; wherein the Stars, (however astronomers have been pleas'd to form their constellations) are not more nicely or methodically plac'd than the passages of Scripture, that where there's nothing but choice flowers, in what order soever you find them, they will make a good posie: That it became not the majesty of God to suffer himself to be fetter'd to humane laws of method, which, devis'd only for your own narrow and low conceptions, would sometimes be improper for, and injurious to his.[15]

The scientist does not doubt some underlying coherence, though he can see none immediately. Instead, he searches for it tirelessly, pressing experiment upon expectation, uncovering each mystery and holding it up to view with a mind full of hope, unabated scrutiny, and wonder. The reader of Scripture can do no other. And doing no other, the reader of Scripture is caught up in a power that "discerns a close (though Mystick) connection" between the parts of a text whose shape and ends and means are Christ himself, in "tipic" or in "hidden" figure, "edited" and held together by an "omniscience [that] comprises and unites in one prospect all times and all events" in the set of redemptive form.[16] Ironically, Boyle's

14. Cf. Lotte Mulligan, "Robert Boyle, 'Right Reason,' and the Meaning of Metaphor," *Journal of the History of Ideas* 55 (April 1994): 235–57.

15. Robert Boyle, *Some Considerations Touching the Style of the Holy Scriptures* (4th ed.; London: n.p., 1675), 53–54.

16. Ibid., 73–76.

integration of creation's and Scripture's common providential base and order offered the scientist and exegete alike a realm of unconstrained openness in investigation, whose freedom of range and imagination stands in sharp contrast to the pinched and ideologically driven methods of contemporary practitioners in both disciplines. The wonder of God's being in the "two books," sprung from the fount that is Christ's centered figure in both, made seventeenth-century science and corners of the period's exegesis a well of common and variegated joy.

Working to the side of Boileau's moral esthetics, then, Boyle arrives at a similar place through his reflection on theological science: a discipline literally of the sublime as Boyle calls it, that forms human humility and astonished gratitude through an immersion in the figurated universe of scriptural questing.[17] And at the base of this shared commitment and promised receipt is an open yearning and pursuit for the apprehension of an utterly embracing and creatively ordering reality of God. The figurated breadth of the Scriptures *must* flow directly from the very nature of God's own gifts of creation and redemption, whose meaning structures the very world we touch within our temporal passage.

What links Duguet and Boyle in their self-giving to the figurated texts of Scripture is, in fact, a common (if very differently received)[18] presupposition of the providential and ordering powers of God, coherent with the physical and spiritual worlds of religion and science together. And this appreciation of a set of divinely ordered structures and connections is surely a good part of what was left behind by a cultural trajectory—including science and politics—that quickly moved in a direction other than Pascal's and Boyle's. It is the breakdown of this providential coherence that marks the debilitation of scriptural discipline within the churches of today, in which the impetus toward scriptural incoherence and historical deconstruction stands in sharp contrast to long-standing

17. Ibid., 26, 132–35.

18. Boyle's metaphysics were decidedly nominalist and voluntarist, rejecting notions of supranatural "substance" and "form" in favor of "direct" actions by God upon physical matter; while Duguet, through his patristic roots and his spiritual connection to Bérulle's Oratory, was more wedded (to the degree that these topics arose for him) to traditional Neoplatonic assumptions. However, this shows only that specific metaphysical theories are not the basic coinage that buys scriptural disciplines and that the history of modernity and hermeneutics is not fatally tied to some line of scientific evolution. On Boyle, see Margaret Osler, "The Intellectual Sources of Robert Boyle's Philosophy of Nature: Gassendi's Voluntarism and Boyle's Physico-Theological Project," in *Philosophy, Science, and Religion in England, 1640–1700* (ed. R. Kroll et al.; Cambridge: Cambridge University Press, 1992), 178–98. Also Amos Funkenstein, *Theology and the Scientific Imagination from the Middle Ages to the Seventeenth Century* (Princeton: Princeton University Press, 1986), 192–5 and 202–89 (on Providence).

Christian conviction that figural referents represent the necessary integration of biblical texts. Michael Buckley argues that the rise of atheism was tied to the early modern effort to practice natural theology as an apologetic art independent of Christology and spiritual discipline.[19] If this is true—and Buckley's argument is certainly open to debate—it is also the case that the Church's Christology devolved into the ramified pietisms of nineteenth- and twentieth-century moral spiritualities in part through the evisceration of natural theology as a pregnant context for scriptural reading. The "how" of the Bible's alienation from its reading in sweet sublimity is answered, in part, through the process by which God and world seem to have suffered mutual evacuations.

Is the process one of an evolution of ideas? Of material shifts in culture? Historians and sociologists can rightly examine this. *Theologically*, however, the question centers on blindness, the darkness of mind and futile thinking by which creation's tracing of God's reality is obscured (Rom. 1:18–32) and its glorious coincidence through God's single providence with the shape of the Scriptures (Ps. 19) is somehow lost to view through the mystery of human sin's own historical enfiguration. These, at least, are the terms in which Pascal articulated the historical situation in which we find ourselves. And not Pascal alone, of course: the tradition of the Scriptures' spiritual reading is founded on a sense that our very participation in its illumination is governed by the same providential ordering that its forms themselves present to the world. Thus, Maximus the Confessor, whom we cited earlier as an exemplar of this tradition, understands the very blindness of those who are not converted to the "mystery of new grace" as, on the one hand, a blindness that takes its form as a rejection of reading the Scripture spiritually and that also receives its historical explanatory force through its own adoption of some spiritual figure *from* Scripture, for example, the figure of Saul, in his descent into self-destructive madness, or of Jonah, in his rejection of God's mercy for the world.[20] Our lives, in corruption or in redemption, themselves conform to the figures of a Scripture whose shape mirrors the world of creation as God wills its purposeful consummation. This is the main reason that the reading of Scripture figurally unveils our very selves.

The demise of spiritual reading is thus itself a providential figure. And the arrest of this demise is not, therefore, a matter of engaging in

19. Michael J. Buckley, *At the Origins of Modern Atheism* (New Haven: Yale University Press, 1987), esp. chaps. 1, 6.

20. Maximus the Confessor, "Various Texts on Theology," in *The Philokalia*, 2.264, 269–70.

a conceptual battle over hermeneutics, as much as it is an awareness of our own place within this coherent order. It is interesting to observe how proponents of the Scripture's figural reading in the modern age—people like Duguet and later George Horne in England—saw their interpretive projects as part of a larger struggle against the spirit of their age, as an element in the formation of a kind of anticulture. Yet they realized, in the end, that this effort was intrinsically incapable of historical efficacy on its own.[21] Much like the call of John the Baptist, crying in the wilderness, the practice of figural reading was but the response to an acknowledged call to repentance, made in the midst of an otherwise teeming "brood of vipers."

To this day, we do not know the names of those soldiers who did as John asked them, or if they were many or few. And the figural connection between those who read and how they read is raised up to view, perhaps, only *as* the discipline of the few, the promise ever given for conversion. Furthermore, the figural reading of Scripture is for us as much as for others of the past a consistently conversionary task akin to the ascetics of repentance. Its forms in fact describe much of the tradition of spiritual formation from our past: the self-emptying, the opening, and the receiving—demanded by the search for Christ in every part of the Scriptures—are all necessary aspects of any vital existence in the Spirit. And while these actions and habits have always been tied to an array of formal disciplines and find their authoritative impetus in Scripture, they are actually themselves enactments of the ways that Scripture itself would mold our spirits into figures that inhabit its own referential spaces, wherein God's true being and truthful actions are described in their real purpose toward us.

To become what God says of us and how God speaks of us—conversion as conformance—is a mighty challenge to engage, even to long after, in an era where the forms themselves have been questioned and, in many cases, rendered suspect. Yet sublimity and sweetness are not themselves mere cultural attitudes or artifacts. They represent the gifts shared from

21. Horne's *Commentary on the Book of Psalms* (1771) has happily been reprinted (Audubon, N.J.: Old Paths, 1997). His preface to this work contains probably the most succinct description of figurative reading in modern English. This essay also contains a subtext, muted in comparison with many of Horne's other writings, of struggle against prevailing cultural rejections of the approach. Tellingly, Horne's most cited sources within the course of the commentary itself are, on the one hand, Bossuet, that most extreme seventeenth-century defender of divine providence, and Robert Lowth, instigator of the application of the esthetics of sublimity to the Scriptures. On Horne's cultural "battle," see Nigel Alston, "Horne and Heterodoxy: The Defense of Anglican Beliefs in the late Enlightenment," *English Historical Review* 108 (Oct. 1993): 895–919.

God's nature, since they describe the work of divine grace in the soul
as it moves through time. To remove the Scriptures themselves as the
discardable vessel of these gifts is to wish that time itself were no longer
the skin of our transformation, an almost gnostic yearning for release
from a world that is felt to be cut loose from God. To the degree that
such a yearning historically tended to move in quietistic or oppressively
manipulative directions, the conformative thrust of Scripture's figural
ordering poses an ethical choice, ever to be made again and again: shall
we hope in the *world's* Maker and God, and shall we live in such a hope?
The ordering calls for a reading; the reading is itself an articulation of
the Christian vocation, whose distance from our daily habits, in this
culture more than many, cries out for these habits' refashioning. If it is
difficult to read the Scriptures figurally in our day, it is a difficulty in
whose overcoming our own calling will emerge. And this is surely true
whether we teach or preach or pray.

In his astonishing homily 6 on Ezekiel, Gregory the Great compares
Scripture to a vast ocean (based on Ezek. 1:16 Vulgate) and the reading
of Scripture to baptism itself and its life of humiliated crucifixion in
Christ, whose power leads us through the waves of our temporal pilgrimage. He enumerates, in detailed and vibrant colors, the kinds of virtues
that derive from and are caught up in the practices of threading one's
way through the figural pathways of a biblical text, at once an exodus,
a journey of the magi, a pilgrimage to Jerusalem, a walk up Golgotha, a
promenade to Emmaus, a voyage through the wheels of heaven's throne
room. Who shall enter this realm of discipleship but the one who is ready
to follow? And in the labors of this grace, wherein faithfulness in walking with Christ the Master is figured in the exertions of scrutinizing the
Scriptures in their figural depth, one discovers, Gregory says (foreshad-
owing Duguet!), sweetness in proportion to the obstacles and a vision
of sublimity in proportion to the majesty of God's providence. What
occupation is this, but that of saying yes, in the mystery of our election,
to the voice who calls beside the sea?

# Part 3

# The Rich Indwelling
# of the Word

*Life Together*

*Let the word of Christ dwell in you richly, teach and*

*admonish one another in all wisdom.*

—Colossians 3:16

# 6

# The Figure
# of Truth
# and Unity

This is the history of the Church given by Solomon: Now, in this Song, hear told the mysterious story of the Incarnation: how the fallen human race is raised; how she is bound, but is freed; how she is corrupted, but receives again her virgin wholeness; how she is banished, yet brought back to paradise; from prisoner, she becomes free; from alien, she becomes citizen; from slave she becomes mistress; from lowliness, she becomes the queen and bride of the Word of God, worthy to receive his kisses. (Apponius, *Commentary on the Song of Songs* 1.4)

This is a traditional assertion for all ecclesiology: that the mysterious story of the incarnation is also the story of the Church, and that its story is one of a peculiar love in which the struggle of the partners represents a drama of engagement between a holy God and a hopelessly vile creature. This struggle of love is the whole Church's, wholly bound to the single redemptive grasp of God in Christ Jesus. And in assessing the nature of the Church—of its life, of its virtue, of its health, of its call—we stumble if we choose to pick at and tear apart the wholeness of this story, which is not simply a story, but the shape of God's life in time.

This basic narrative foundation for ecclesiology informs the following reflections in this and the subsequent chapters in part 3: how do we practice our faith—in preaching, in sexual expression, in dialogue and teaching, in discipline—in the midst of the present reality of tension now felt within our churches between aspects of doctrinal commitment and continued ecclesial and jurisdictional relations among differently committed bodies within their single denominational wholes? The question, briefly put, is this: in what sense is there or ought there to be communion between Christians whose beliefs seem to differ profoundly on a number of significant topics, from scriptural interpretation to creedal exposition to moral teaching to the church's political ordering? Does it make sense to speak of communion at all within such circumstances? Any right answer to this question cannot escape the historical reality that the Church's story must also embody the story of a divine union whose only possibility lay in the suffering of its divine inappropriateness. The hopelessness given in ecclesial contention and division is overcome only by the divine victory given in the body of Christ; it is a victory coincident with the life of the Church, however, and thus its historical form for the Church can be observed only within the scriptural realm of ecclesial conformity itself—truth and unity joined in the divine suffering of the body's fractured life itself.

This is now an almost forgotten observation, for many Christian thinkers persist in distinguishing unity and truth within the life of the Church as two distinct elements of practice that may or may not at a given time qualify Christian life in a given place. And when this distinction between unity and truth has been made, the fulfillment of these elements as characteristic of the Church has required, in the minds of such thinkers, their coordination in some fashion, usually according to some hierarchical scheme of appropriate dependence—no unity *until* truth, or no truth *unless* emergent from unity.

Certainly, unity and truth have struck many Christians as potentially incompatible characteristics at a given time, ranged against one another in a zero-sum game made necessary by the travails of the moment: sometimes unity but at the cost of truth, or sometimes truth at the cost of unity. This sense of potential temporary incompatibility appears regnant at present in the minds of many within our churches. It is, furthermore, a tension with a long history behind it that crosses all kinds of theological boundaries. Liberal Episcopal Bishop John Spong complains, in the preamble to a recent call for an overturning of traditional doctrine, that most church leaders are more interested in unity than in truth. But so can his conservative critics, like ex-Episcopalian Samuel Edwards, who attacks the same corporatist mentality as does Spong and who insists that right faith always be the priority to organic unity.

In the sixteenth century, the tension between unity and truth was expressed by both sides of the religious debate among Reformers and Catholics. John Jewel for instance, the great sixteenth-century Anglican apologist, could assert that unity was less important a mark of the Church than doctrinal truth, whose integrity was subverted by an evangelically false tie with Rome; while Tridentine apologists for Rome argued that truth was expressed only within the communion established with the pope, all else being substantive falsehood. At the start of the modern ecumenical movement, in the heady first days of Faith and Order, there was much open discussion about the need for truth to found any turn to reunion. It is a conviction that has since been reinterpreted in various directions, from the pluriformity of truth to the diversity of communions.

But while we can note this long history of attempts to play off unity and truth against each other or to relate them in some form of resolved tension, we ought first to ask ourselves whether unity and truth, as distinguishable elements, actually *do* fall within some specific category—or set of categories—of distinction and whether the method of their coordination within the Church may not rather be peculiar to the gospel itself. Do they, for instance, represent capacities whose realization depends on certain quantifiable resources (moral, intellectual, etc.)? Are they perhaps temporal aspects of the Church, whose historical embodiment may or may not be simultaneous, because one depends upon the other, sequentially, for its realization? Are they virtues of discipline, whose presence in the church follows the varied progress of certain maturing skills? Do they stand as parallel and hence potentially unequal qualities of moral commandment, to whose obedience differing degrees of fulfillment can be assigned?

It should be clear that when answers to these kinds of questions are assumed, they lead in significantly different practical directions. If, for instance, unity and truth were viewed in parallel with pneumatic fruit (Gal. 5:16–26), their coordination would be of a profoundly different kind than if they were viewed as variously attained aspects of obedience. We do not tend to see gentleness and patience as ever being in tension; we do not ever place kindness and self-control over and against each other as two elements whose individual consummation may require their subordination one to another in time. St. Paul does not do this, presumably, because the fruit of the Spirit belong to a singular existence that has been joined, as one, to the crucified life of Christ Jesus in its coherence, a life incapable of being parceled out in distinctive elements. Though in walking by the Spirit, a Christian may fail to exhibit one spiritual fruit or another, such failures pertain to that life as a whole, to the character and shape of its discrete pneumatic history, and not to separable histories of particular virtues, as if one could say, "Until now, I have worked on love; only when this is achieved can I turn to joy."

To observe in what way the aspects of truth and unity are embodied in Jesus' own life is to see the appropriateness of this parallel with our own existence in the Spirit. For it is just through the Spirit's self-expression in Jesus that he is said both to embody the truth of the Father and to live at one with the Father. No richer discussion of this occurs than in John 14–17, where the textured witness to this reality is explored from a number of angles: "I am the way, and the truth, and the life. . . . Believe in me that I am in the Father and the Father in me. . . . When the Spirit of truth comes, he will guide you into all the truth. . . . He will glorify me, for he will take what is mine and declare it to you. All that the Father has is mine" (14:6, 11; 16:13–15).

In Jesus' case, there is no coordination of these twin aspects of truth and unity, for they each express, in their fullness, the whole of his life. And if they are distinguished it is only through the particular articulations we apply to the narrative extension of his historical existence: we can speak of his teachings as truth or of his confession before Pontius Pilate (1 Tim. 6:13); we can also speak of his prayer in unity with the Father or of his authoritative healings and signs. Any discussion of truth and unity as they apply to Jesus, because they are identical to the pneumatic character of his incarnation, requires only our reiteration, through various narrative schemes, of his temporal form. As with any attempt to articulate discrete characteristics—for example, mercy and justice—as they apply to God, we are forced to acknowledge the formal illegitimacy of the material distinction, even as we fall back upon purely historical-scriptural discourse to enable their linguistic articulation: we can *describe* God's justice and mercy historically, but we cannot apply them to God logically other than in a unitary fashion. While God's attributes are not synonymous with respect to their historical expression and apprehension, as Aquinas argued, God's perfections are one through God's simplicity. And Jesus, as the God-man, stands as the embodiment of this fact.

Any discussion of truth and unity as divine attributes expressed pneumatically through Jesus, then, must be tied to the unitary figure of Jesus' own historical existence. To describe these aspects as distinct semantic entities can go no further than to articulate the life of Jesus as a whole. And to describe the aspects of truth and unity with respect to the Christian life of the Church, therefore, cannot go further than to articulate the history of the Church's representation of Jesus' existence in the Church's temporal form.

For instance, Jesus speaks of the unity of the Church as correlative to the unity of the Father and the Son: "[I pray] that they may all be one; even as thou, Father, art in me, and I in thee" (John 17:21). This similitude of unity is not given any metaphysical explanation by Jesus, to be sure; but it is nonetheless granted a fundamental status that moves from temporal coincidence to pneumatic participation in the living holiness of God's existence: "*The glory which thou hast given me I have given to them,* that they may be one even as we are one, I in them and thou in me" (17:22–23 [emphasis added]). Divine participation of this kind, however, is given in forms of historical existence, describable in terms of the world's temporal perception of God's worldly acts: I pray for the Church's unity "*so that the world may believe that thou hast sent me* . . . and hast loved them even as thou hast loved me" (17:21, 23 [emphasis added]).

On the matter of unity, then, we can conclude that if the church is one, its unity will involve a participation in the historical form of the Father's sending of the Son in time, an act synonymous with the incarnation's narrative.

Similarly, the truth of Jesus is expressed in terms of the Word's manifestation in the midst of Israel, the Word's own home and people (John 1:11). As the light whose testimony is true, Jesus ties his truthfulness to a history of encounter and manifestation within Israel, from Abraham on, in which divine promise and command in the form of law and prophecy experience a complex mixture of obedience and rejection (John 8:12–20; Luke 16:19–31; Matt. 23:29–39). This truthful aspect of Jesus is given consummation for the world, not in an extrication from this history of difficult witness within Israel, but in its final suffering in voluntary acceptance: "I, when I am lifted up from the earth, will draw all men to myself" (John 12:32). Not only does Jesus here refer to his manner of dying (12:33), but its historical fruits for all humanity are an expression of the very law of Israel (12:34–36).

On the matter of the Church's life in the truth, then, we can conclude that the sending of the disciples as witnesses to the truth must therefore involve a refiguring of this relationship of accepted encounter, both with Israel and the nations (Matt. 10:16–23; cf. John 16:29–33).

The passion narrative, in this light, becomes the temporal embodiment of Jesus' pneumatic character, including the aspects of truth and unity together. It demonstrates not the coordination of distinct elements, but rather their unitary expression through the suffering of their historical burden. Perhaps the most transparent episode in this respect is the relationship between Jesus and Judas, especially at the time of the Last Supper. Judas, whose complete and satanic rejection of Jesus is explicitly underlined in the Gospels, is nonetheless present as one of the Twelve; he shares in the covenantal meal by which Jesus establishes the participatory receipt of his body and blood; and he is even served by Jesus as the Lord washes their feet. In all this, Jesus holds Judas close to him within the group of his closest friends quite knowingly and despite being aware of Judas's deceit and ultimate role in his betrayal and death.

This event has long puzzled and exercised commentators, especially in the early Church, whose sense of demanded purity for the gathered body could not comprehend the capacity of truth and unity to embrace such patent treachery. Logical and exegetical contortions were made in order to distance Judas from the divine realities of the Last Supper and somehow to protect Jesus' own spiritual integrity and the integrity of his acts shared with the Church from their seeming contradiction exemplified in Judas. Yet the whole passion is nothing if not a repudiation of such protective motives. The truthful witness of Jesus to the Father is given precisely in the refusal to part with the perpetrators of deceit and the willingness to share communion, in the literal sense even of the Lord's Supper, with contradictors of that truth.

Not until Augustine—and even his insistences were widely ignored—did anyone acknowledge Jesus' sacramental embrace of Judas as a profound challenge to the Church's own accepted form of life within the context of its self-ordering in history. Such a self-ordering, Augustine asserted, would achieve pneumatic integrity only to the degree that it expressed the single cup imbibed and shared with the passional figure of Jesus (Mark 10:39)—a mixed cup (Ps. 75:8) for a Church who suffers the moral mixture borne patiently by its exemplary Lord.

To speak of the conjunction of mercy and truth—of communion and truthfulness—for the Church, then, is to describe the history wherein the experienced indignation of God forms the context out of which such pneumatic attributes emerge as an embattled form (Ps. 85:4, 10), reiterative of the figure of Jesus. There are various and alternative scriptural narratives through which the Church's life, in this fashion, can be explained, narratives by which Israel's agonal life as a people is directed toward the fulfilled servanthood of Jesus and whose temporal form is then shared, through the participation in his passion, with the Church. And the ecclesial task of adjudicating the claims of truth and unity in times of contestation and conflict ought properly to reduce itself to the scrutiny of and subjection to these narratives, insofar as they reveal the enacted and directive power of Christ's Spirit as it conforms the Church to the figure of its Lord.

In a brief chapter like this, we can touch upon only one example of such a scrutinizing vocation, but it is worth attempting even in such small compass, because it offers a perspective on Christian contestation that is clearly distinct from our usual reactive postures. Those who claim, for instance, that there are peculiar moments when the virtues of (doctrinal) truth claim precedence over the demands of (ecclesial) unity, or vice versa, are called to subject themselves to the shape of those scriptural narratives that describe, in their corporate application, the form of Jesus' singular embrace of these two aspects together. What could this mean?

A *locus classicus* for such a narrative, one that describes the ecclesial figure in its temporal conformance to Christ, is the Song of Songs, and we might ask ourselves how this narrative exerts its pneumatic pressures upon a conflicted social existence. The book's figural import is popularly associated with a now-discarded tradition of mystical application descriptive of the contemplative experience, whose well-known interpreters move from Origen to Bernard of Clairvaux. Even today, evangelical writers like Watchman Nee maintain the individualistic exegesis that explains the nuptial metaphor of the book in terms of the Christian soul's advance in personal relation to Christ.

From the first, however, Christian reading of the Song of Songs used the personal and individual aspects of the poem, even when interpreted literally, as a buttress for the ecclesial figure that St. Paul outlined in Ephesians 5:29–33: the embodied relation of carnal marriage figures the real relation of Christ and the Church. Origen himself advanced this approach to the Song of Songs, and after him great commentators like Apponius, Gregory the Great, and Nicolas of Lyra continued to explore this scripturally indicated application.

The characterization of Israel's existence in relation to God in terms of sexual allurement is a common Old Testament theme, although the visage of the partners is variously described. God's attraction is often given the face of a woman—Wisdom, the law itself—whose beauty is both ensnaring and often abused or repulsed (cf. Proverbs, Wisdom, Baruch). Sometimes, the relation is reversed, as Israel takes the form of a potential bride, debased at times, adorned at others (cf. Isaiah). And having recast people and Lord in these sexual terms, the abstractive characteristics of religious existence—including, for instance, the virtues of obedience, faithfulness, mercy, and so on—are given their concrete appearance as emerging elements of a historical relationship, whose identity is grasped only in the course of the enacted whole of the drama. The wholeness of the drama, then, turns back to challenge the dissection of virtue outside of its unitary narrative role.

What are we to make, for instance, of religious virtue within a history as described symbolically by Hosea, where people and God engage in an alternating relation of sexual profligacy, seduction, faithlessness, persistence, spurned desire, and incapacity? Consummated union in such a context of assaulted integrity is both a goal and a variously embodied posture, whose form surfaces continuously and fleetingly in the course of a similarly rendered story of struggle over obedience with which it is murkily entwined.

The Song of Songs represents an epitome of this scriptural approach, in which truth and unity, for instance, are presented as thickly textured aspects of a single story of passional attraction, the details of which continually confuse themselves, even while the whole moves with difficulty toward a resolution of embrace whose permanence lies beyond temporal description. Figural ecclesiology, in this context—and in a way that many early commentators hinted at in their historical exegesis of the book—demands that we place the church in the midst of the story as a single character, whose variegated experience in relation to its Lord and lover never undermines the singularity of that link, but only underlines its temporal difficulty. The repeated refrain (Song 2:7; 3:5; 8:4), "do not awaken love *until*" the pleasing season, points to the way in which the union of Church and Jesus, its complete conformance to the shape of his life, is something achieved only in the course of time; yet the story itself is an account of the integral character of that achievement. Ecclesial history is an ascetic history, one that moves, prepares, and shapes the Church for a final outcome; but just because of that, it is a history through which divergent expressions of virtue are consistently integrated and used for a single purpose.

The structuring form of the Song of Songs is, of course, much debated. But even early readers were aware that it constitutes a complex narrative, wherein any dramatic development of the characters, of the bride and groom's mutual approach, for instance, was fraught with feints and adventures, obstacles and attractions, which seem not so much to advance the drama of union, as to constitute it in itself; the final call of the maiden—"make haste" (8:14)—is but a single answer to its own initial yearning—"draw me after you, let us make haste" (1:4). If this response represents some kind of narrative progress, all that takes place in between—desire, delight, encounter, loss, searching, enemies and friends in help and in opposition, sorrow, renewal—must therefore form the historical matrix within which the larger movement of union and conformity takes flesh. And the confusing interplay of the partners in this movement—not only the bride and groom, but the "daughters of Jerusalem," the "watchmen," Solomon himself, and the onlookers—contributes to the single and mutual momentum of the gathering haste whose final expression refuses to deny or exclude any of the preceding relations.

As a figure of the Church in the course of its Lord-conforming history, then, the Song of Songs is a bracing challenge to any attempt at its evaluative dissection on the basis of identifiable virtues. There is simply no room, in such a narrative, for assessing degrees of integrity and then acting distinctly upon them. For the existence of such degrees—the church of the more or less truthful, or more or less loving, or in more or less communion within its parts, upon which distinctions we must make decisions—cannot be detached from the single movement of its history in relation to its Lord. Indeed, any perceived distinctions in character are simply a part of this history and contribute to its single outcome.

The traditional notion that the bride signifies Israel as much as the Church, or that the brutal encounter with the watchmen of the city (Song 5) represents the assault of heretics within the body, or that the "daughters of Jerusalem" might refer to the lapsed or to the Jews—this way of reading the text, however debatable in its particulars, at least forces us to recognize the manner in which divergent pressures and even conflicts within the narrative cannot be sifted out of the integrity of the historical process by which the Church is in fact the Church *of Christ*. The maiden's loss of her love, her fruitless searching, her uncertain relation to friends and foes—all are intractably part of *her* temporal existence as beloved and as the consistent object of another's love. When this book has been used liturgically as a divine word about marriage, in the same category as St. Paul's discussion in Ephesians 5, we see but the articulation of the way in which union in its fullest integrity is given passionally—"love is strong as death" (Song 8:6)—in the manner of Jesus' own temporal achievement with respect to his relation to Israel and the world. That the Church should conform to its Lord is something that he simply suffers and that it, in turn, experiences as its own gifted suffering in return: "I adjure you, O daughters of Jerusalem, / if you find my beloved, / that you tell him / I am sick with love" (5:8).

One way of looking at the present conflict within our own churches is to see it as an insistence, on the part of various players, to heal that sickness and to rewrite the plot of the drama of which they are parts so as to exclude the length and detail of its anguished elaboration. In contrast, the history of the Church, which is the history of the Lord writ small and long, proclaims: It is for the sake of charity that we suffer our disagreements; it is for the sake of truth that we love the liar; it is for the sake of the bride that it receive as her gift her beloved's body as her own. The irony of Christian patience is that it is an eternal hastening into the midst of this story, rather than one that hurries to break out of it. And we are perhaps called to judge our practical reactions to the array of our ecclesial anxieties—over incompetent and unfaithful bishops, over corrupted prayers and unjust stewards, over shallow understandings and venal missions, over uncaring guardians and unheeding tenants—judge them according to the standard of such a passion.

No clear directives emerge from such a judgment. Those who wish to know if they must follow this line, or resist along that, or compromise upon this other, are given no certainties in their choices simply because they subject themselves to the scriptural shape of Jesus' life. But they at least know that they cannot run away—and, because it is ultimately his life, that there is even redemption in such staying put! There are not many bodies, some true and some false, some loving and some uncharitable. These are distractions from the one story, and the embrace of this story cannot sustain the parsing of proprieties that today so grips our distorted sense of integrity. Readiness for love—truth bound in unity—is a single and extended temporal exertion. It is embodied in God's subjugation to time in Christ Jesus, and the Church finds its own readiness in his form. There is no escape from this particular fate and promise. And therein are the kisses of God's peace for his people enjoyed (Song 1:2; 8:1, 10).

# 7

# The
# Nuptial
# Figure

## *Human Life in the Shape of the Gospel*

A wide literature has grown up over the past two decades, some of it located at the very center of the Church's life, that is designed to call into question both the existence of a consistent Christian tradition about marriage and the reality of that tradition's theological breadth.[1] Despite its often laboriously informed historical method, one of the goals behind this literature's design serves a quite practical purpose, namely, to cut loose our own understanding of Christian marriage not simply from the past, but from the defining weight of the past, so that we can

1. Cf. the work of Adrian Thatcher, especially his recent *Marriage after Modernity: Christian Marriage in Postmodern Times* (Sheffield: Sheffield Academic Press, 2001). Much of the impetus for this rethinking of the character of the Christian marriage tradition was spurred by the research of the so-called Annales historians, whose delving into the records of quotidian existence in Western Europe uncovered a vast documentation of practices, the seeming diversity of which has been picked up by revisionist social and Christian theorists who question the authority and existence of a Christian tradition in the first place. Cf. the magisterial multivolume series *A History of Private Life* (Cambridge: Harvard University Press, 1987–), originally published in French in the mid-1980s. An accessible example of this approach can be found in *Western Sexuality: Practice and Precept in Past and Present Times* (ed. Philippe Ariès and André Béjin; Oxford: Blackwell, 1985).

construct our understandings afresh, according to new theological criteria freed from the accountability of what is purported to be only a confused history of Christian discernment and submission on the topic.

I believe that both the design and the end of this project are not only flawed, but contributory to the grand spiral of ecclesial unease and despair within the Church. I suppose that an orthodox approach to marriage in our day might therefore try to prove that there *has* been a consistent Christian tradition about the meaning, purpose, and general form of marriage and that all the talk about confusion of viewpoints, debated significations, and diversity of form is historically misleading. But such a response would have limited usefulness. For those who are committed to refashioning the Church's traditional teachings on any given topic, the historically consistent articulation of those teachings in the past rarely proves an obstacle or even a matter of concern. Witness the current debate over homosexuality. One of the *least* interesting elements in this debate has been the Church's consistent teaching on homosexuality. Either the teaching has simply been deemed wrong or, for conservatives, it seems to prove too little. So, analogously, what does it matter that Jesus, Paul, Augustine, Aquinas, and Cranmer—not to mention Catherine of Siena, Hildegaard of Bingen, and others—may have all had the same ideas about marriage? For most people today, the ideas are either crazy or correct, but for reasons other than their commonality! For all parties, the past has been sloughed off as a crust whose vital usefulness has slipped away.

In any case, most opponents of what is called the "modern Christian view of marriage" concede the point of at least a theological consistency in the Christian tradition on the matter. One of their most common tacks of argument is to draw a direct and singular line of misogynistic antisexualism from Jesus' limited affirmation of marriage, to Paul's valorization of celibacy, through patristic denigration of marriage in favor of virginity, on through medieval monastic ascetic demotions of marriage, up through Cranmer's or Calvin's avowed Augustinianism, which we have inherited in our Anglo-Protestant culture. It all sounds quite consistent. Surely, therefore, it is a rejection of this tradition, repugnant *in* its very *consistency,* that led people like Adrian Thatcher and others to call for "creating new theological understandings of holy matrimony." Why new ones, unless the traditional ones are no good any longer?

Certainly there is much disquietude, within our churches themselves, in the face of this tradition. For it is the tradition—that is, the evolved and evolving consensus of the faithful, as articulated in the councils of the Church and in the writing and examples of the saints—that conveys the currently debated ethical imperatives regarding the norm of heterosexual activity in marriage. It is the tradition that has imposed those stark limitations on fornication, adultery, and divorce that are so irritating today. I think it best, then, to leave the consistency of the tradition unquestioned—it is, after all, what everybody knows is at issue. What I think may be more useful to do than a tit-for-tat historical rebuttal of revisionists by conservatives is to defend the theological *integrity* of the Christian tradition's teaching on marriage, its wholeness and depth as a form of understanding the gospel. What the Church—and world!—needs to hear most at present is an understanding of the Christian tradition on marriage in a way that appreciates its central connection with the *most* essential aspects of the Christian gospel. Not only is this tradition interesting; not only did it make sense for a few passing cultural moments of primitive Europe; not only is it consistent; not only is it compelling on its own terms—but the tradition is bound up with what is *essential* to the gospel. Because, in brief, human marriage is a necessary tool by which God orders the destiny of humankind, worked out upon the redemptive axis of Jesus Christ. The tradition neither is expendable nor—because God actually shapes history to his will through it—is it escapable.

Let me outline how I will approach this topic. First, I need to explain why taking the tradition of the past as our guide on this disputed topic is compelling. I will do this by examining the nature of contested sacramental realities in general, using the example of the Eucharist as an aid. From this discussion, I will arrive at a basic statement about the very *nature* of sacramental reality, which must ground, I believe, any proper understanding of marriage in particular. That is, sacramental realities derive from and refer to the *person* of God in Christ Jesus; they are not defined by concepts or principles like sacrifice or love or mutuality, but by their representation of the historical existence of God's life in time. In this sense, they are intrinsically scriptural in their articulation. After this, I will give an outline of how this sacramental theology applies to marriage, through a summary of the gospel and the patristic vision of the practice that became normative for the Christian tradition. From this, finally, I will offer three central theological characteristics that qualify the Christian tradition on marriage. It will be clear in conclusion, I hope, why it is that traditionalists like me view this tradition as an essential aspect, not simply of moral behavior, but of the very enunciation of the gospel itself.

First, then, let us examine the authoritative role of tradition—of past accepted teaching—in sacramental disputes. It should be said, in opening, that many people no longer perceive the authoritative character of tradition in such contexts. If a topic is disputed within the Church, then, by definition, it is pointless to find some consistent truth concerning that topic articulated, however indirectly, within the tradition of the past; for surely, many seem to believe, the topic is disputed precisely because the tradition has been found wanting! Answers must then be constructed from the present. As if to say, "Well, people are arguing passionately—and acting out their diverse convictions—over questions of divorce, extramarital sexual relationships, conception, homosexual partnerships, and so on—all in ways that contravene any shared sense of an obligatory tradition from the past: therefore the past's tradition is either itself confused or misled or both at once. Certainly not an authoritative *focus* of attention."

A person's interpretation of what the tradition is, of course, may be debatable. But what I need to emphasize at the outset is that it is proper to *seek* after the accepted core of past teaching in the case of a disputed question, like sexuality and marriage today. It is even an *imperative* for the Christian to do so. Christians have discerned God's will and purposes in the past quite simply because the past is the most clearly defined location of God's life and action, the present still being unfixed and blurred. (This seems both so obvious a point and so completely dismissed today as to give cause for wonderment.) We seem to recognize this, however, in areas of dispute other than sexuality. When it comes to the Eucharist or baptism, we do not gather in small groups with newsprint to share our personal feelings, experiences, and reactions, hoping to discover the spirit's leading in contemporary society toward the new meaning of Holy Communion. And, as we know, the Eucharist has been in dispute among Christians for centuries. In fact, the example is instructive. There would be no growing ecumenical consensus about what the Eucharist is were not all the various parties in dispute agreed *at least* that there is such a thing as the Eucharist, that its character and meaning lie embedded in the past life of the Church and its churches, and that a common examination of that tradition, moored in the Scriptures, will give up from its store, however encrusted or smothered, the divine truth of a divine gift. And so Catholics and Methodists, Orthodox, and Lutherans gather to study Scripture together on the matter, to read Augustine and Cyril of Alexandria, Paschasius and Maximus the Confessor, Lanfranc and Luther—not just to compare notes and have articulate examples upon which to bounce off personal feelings, but out of the conviction that the Eucharist has done its work over centuries and that this work is not different, but consistent, and therefore consistently described by the ablest saints of the Church's life. Were we to hear them aright.

This conviction as to theological method, in the face of disputed questions, has been shared from the time of the early Church through the Middle Ages and the Reformation. And however inaccurate have been some of the fruits of this method, the conviction has been constant. Further, it is not an odd conviction for Christians to hold. For it rides on the faith that what God promises in his gifts to the Church God fulfills, in some fashion or another. What God promises in baptism, in the Eucharist, in marriage even, God enacts according to the fullness of that gift. What, for instance, Reformers like Calvin and Catholics like Bellarmine sought to apprehend in their polemics on, say, the sacraments was not the direction *now* given by the Holy Spirit for some new construal of a tired concept or practice. Rather, convinced that God's gift of the Eucharist was *not* empty, they sought to apprehend how the Holy Spirit worked to enact that gift in the course of centuries of ecclesial experience often marred by rebellion, apathy, and sin, such as to give rise to the current disputes in the first place. They disagreed about the Eucharist the way we disagree about sex. But for them—as for almost all Christians before them—pneumatic discernment on disputed sacraments referred to the revelation of God in the Church's past.

How did they discern the fullness of God's sacramental gift, when the sacrament itself was disputed? At the time of the Reformation, Protestants and Catholics sought to uncover the constant power of the eucharistic gift, for instance, by observing the way that, in the Scriptures, Jesus' body and blood at the Last Supper could have such wildly differing results for Judas and for the other disciples: for one it was a poison, and for the other the food of redemption. Yet always the same divine gift! Depending on one's polemical perspective, this divine gift wrought destruction through the blasphemies of the Catholic Mass or through the parodies of the Protestant Communion service. But to say that God was not consistently at work in deploying the power of his eucharistic gift was something neither side would admit. For to do so would be to deny not only the promises of Scripture, but the very way Scripture itself made prophetic sense of the past. For Scripture does nothing except embody the shape of Jesus' own cosmically decisive life. And is not the Eucharist (at least!) a coming-to-memory of the death of Jesus, the one who himself expired on the cross in both judgment and mercy in the reception of vinegar and gall? If so, then the history of the Eucharist is the history of that body of Christ redemptively broken, and we must find in it the letters and words of salvation. The Eucharist was a kind of prophecy for them, because it contained in it the life of Christ according to which the world was ordered.

Protestant and Catholic together shared this sense that the outworking of the scriptural figures—prophecies, forms, images, events—of Christ contain, in some way, the truth of his teaching. It did not matter that people did not always get the truth. The truth will out, in the sense that the history of the Church will, inevitably, share the same form as the life of Jesus. And the Eucharist, for example, will be most truly grasped when it is most accurately perceived as mapping out that history, in some way, tracing, in its practice, the conformity of experience to the scriptural figures or images of Christ.

Here we approach the nature of an ecclesial sacrament. A scriptural figure, in Christian theology, is not a literary metaphor that brings to the intellect some deeper meaning when attached to another image. A figure is a form that God actually makes historical experience fit, like some providential mold. Similarly, when ecclesial enactments like baptism, the Eucharist, and even marriage were gradually given the qualifier *sacramental*, it was because of this historical character as figures that all Christian disputants eventually agreed they had. They agreed that acts like baptism and Eucharist have their origin in the promises of God, given in Christ Jesus and then tied to the very shape of his own life. Thus, their enactment by the Church makes them to be providential orderers of historical experience, according to the forms of Scripture. In God's providence, sacraments shape history according to God's plan. Put another way, what is sacramental about baptizing, doing the Eucharist, ordaining, and marrying—and doing this rightly and wrongly—is that these acts conform the Church, whether it likes it or not, recognizes it or not, to the prophecies of Scripture fulfilled in Jesus Christ.

Before discussing marriage in particular, then, I can underline why it is that the theological significance of marriage cannot be understood apart from its disclosure within the context of the Christian tradition. If we speak of the Eucharist in terms of Jesus' body and blood; if we speak of baptism in terms of Jesus' death and resurrection or the gift of Pentecost; if we speak of ordination in terms of prophetic and apostolic commissioning; and so on—if we speak of these particular acts in terms of the figures or images of Jesus' own life and actions, it is because, ultimately, sacramental realities embody, historically, the *personal*—that is to say, scriptural—forms of God as they have been revealed in the conformed life of the Church. In this sense, sacramental realities, including marriage, are inescapable: they are not defined by the evolution of a human idea or concept or principle like love or intimacy.[2] These are principles that can be gleaned from or applied to any natural act or event. But sacraments do not embody principles or concepts, however theological. Rather, sacramental realities are subject to the irreducibility of a *person*, in that they represent the personal shape of Jesus into which God transforms the world. They stand over the world and call it to themselves. Referring to marriage in Ephesians 5:32, St. Paul says, "This mystery [or sacrament] is a profound one, and I am saying that it refers to Christ and the church."

Why have Christians always searched in the pneumatic past for the truth of their debated sacramental life? Because ultimately, sacramental realities embody, historically and experientially, the personal forms of God, *given* in the historical life of Jesus.

As for the particular sacramental character of marriage, it is true that marriage was not given the technical designation *sacrament* until the early Middle Ages. But this technical application of the term was only a secondary articulation of marriage's character that had been *already* been termed *sacramental* since the time of St. Paul, when, as in Ephesians 5, he called it a "mystery," a Greek word early translated in Latin as *sacramentum*. This phraseology very quickly received a rich and authoritative exposition in the early Church, such that *theologically* the discussion of

---

2. My discussion of the nuptial figure is, therefore, quite different from recent attempts to extract from the tradition of Christian marriage certain nuptial virtues or symbolics, elements of behavior and relationship that can be abstracted and reapplied to, say, gay partnerships. The figure, because tied historically to the irreducible person of Jesus, is itself *sui generis*, a singular and discrete gift of God for the formation of human historical existence. While it is true that human (heterosexual) marriage is positively fueled by and embodies specific virtues and symbolic images whose Christian meaning is certainly transferable to a range of contexts, marriage can never be exhaustively defined by these elements, just because it is primarily figural in significance, and the figure itself retains its exclusive meaning. Virtues are specifically figural when they enfigure Christ in a particular and exclusive context, independent of their power to project analogies. Cf. in contrast, Eugene F. Rogers, *Sexuality and the Body: Their Way into the Triune God* (Oxford: Blackwell, 1999), part 3 (esp. 269–74). Rogers's view of providence—which he addresses clearly—in this respect is quite different from the particularized figural understanding of its reality that I use here. The fullest discussion of the nuptial figure in the sense I am using can be found in John Paul II's monumental *The Theology of the Body: Human Love in the Divine Plan* (Boston: Panline Books and Media, 1997), esp. I:1 and II:4.

marriage's Christian significance really did not alter until the Reformation, and even then, only superficially.

The early Church fathers applied the terms *mystical* or *sacramental* to the divinely providential character of reality as a whole, as it is revealed in Scripture. These words were synonymous with what was also called the spiritual or pneumatic nature of reality that the Christian lived and discerned within the world. What was spiritual or sacramental was that which God had ordered and shaped in history, according to the promises and figures of the Scriptures. And since the Scriptures themselves were fulfilled in the person and life of Jesus, the spiritual and the sacramental character of reality referred to those elements of historical experience that displayed the scriptural life of Jesus as they were ordered to his revelation and rule. The cross of Jesus, for instance, was a sacramental reality because it pointed to the destiny of human history as fulfilled in Jesus' life and person as Christ. And there were many other sacramental realities, like resurrection, that one could find embedded in Scripture and played out in the world. So-called figural interpretation of the Bible, however simple or complex, arose from this sense of sacramental reality as the hinge upon which Scripture and experience are connected. And the early Church saw marriage, like the cross, as having a special sacramental—or christically figural—meaning. Marriage was essentially a lens by which inquirers could decipher the very shape of God's ordering of human history, because marriage was one of the means of that divine ordering itself.

We can see why marriage should have assumed this role, for it held a peculiar prominence in the Gospels themselves. One thing that intensive scholarship in the early nineteenth century demonstrated on the topic is that the rapidly evolved marriage symbolism of the early Church—including St. Paul's—is derived almost exclusively from meditation on Scripture, especially Jesus' words. (I point this out because, in the late nineteenth century, all kinds of wild theories were nurtured regarding the influence on Christian theology of pagan Hellenistic and gnostic nuptial imagery and practice. These theories, which the ignorant occasionally resurrect today, are almost certainly nonsense.) In any case, it is hard for readers of the Scriptures, especially of the New Testament, to ignore the peculiar prominence of marriage as a topic of concern. Jesus speaks of marriage as often, if not more, than he speaks of the cross or of the ministry of service.

For the early Christians, this concern on Jesus' part could be divided into three broad categories: (1) Jesus taught about the contemporary practice of marriage when he spoke directly to issues like divorce and adultery, referring both to particular laws of the Scriptures and to the "historical accounts" of Genesis; (2) Jesus spoke of the relation of married life to the life of the God's fulfilled rule when he spoke positively of the condition of "eunuchs for the sake of the kingdom of heaven" (Matt. 19:12) and the abolition of human marriage in the resurrected life (Mark 12:25–27); related to this are his warnings about married life in the end time (Luke 17; Mark 12); and (3) most important for theological purposes, Jesus used the imagery of betrothal, marriage, and marriage-feasting with a frequency and breadth that made the figure an unavoidably key interpretive tool. He uses the marriage feast as the figural occasion for teachings about preparation for the kingdom (Matt. 22; 25), about messianic service (Luke 12:35–40), and about humility and suffering (Luke 14). Within these parables and also apart from them, he crafts a set of images that directly speak of the Messiah in his personal character and rule as a bridegroom who comes to marry an awaiting virgin, identified either as the faithful themselves or as the mistress of the faithful. On two occasions, Jesus is specifically identified as the bridegroom of God himself (Matt. 9:15–16; John 3:29): "He who has the bride is the bridegroom," John the Baptist says outright of Jesus.

These last images, parabolically and prophetically applied by and to Jesus, are drawn from the Old Testament—from Isaiah 54, 61, 62, and the Song of Songs in particular. But their use is similar to that of the rather marginal Old Testament prophecies regarding messianic suffering: they are not central to the Old Testament. *Jesus makes* them central, a fact so peculiar that his followers could not ignore them as keys to understanding who he was. By analogy with the historical cross of Jesus, it seemed clear to the first Christians that the historical phenomenon of marriage itself held within its experience a providential sign, whose exposition helped to unveil the very purposes of God for the human race.

So, when St. Paul talks about the concrete practice of marriage in Ephesians, he places it squarely within the mystery—or sacrament—of Christ and his Church, which elsewhere he defines as the "plan for the fulness of time, to unite all things in [Christ], things in heaven and things on earth" (Eph. 1:10). St. Paul's own discussions about the practice of marriage are given as he attempts to be sensitive to all three dimensions of Jesus' own teaching: (1) its rootedness in the historical foundations of God's creative ordering of human life—this lies behind Paul's clear affirmation of marriage's historical integrity (1 Cor. 7; Eph. 5); (2) human marriage's temporal relativity in the face of the fulfilled purposes of God's kingdom, wherein human mutual service between male and female is taken up in a subsuming union with God—hence Paul's cautious encouragement to celibacy in the face of the end time; and (3) Paul's sense of the overarching bridge by which human marriage stands as gospel image for the life, character, and purposes of Christ in his own self-giving to and redemptive integration of creation's historical destiny as a whole—here we can note Paul's use of historical marriage as an experienced figure of the messianic marriage of the Church to Jesus, the divine bridegroom (2 Cor. 11:2). This is the reality he describes as the mystery or sacrament that marriage enacts in its revelation of Jesus.

The understanding of marriage developed by the postapostolic Church is surprisingly faithful to this scriptural vision. Elements of this vision were stressed to the detriment of others at various times in the Church's subsequent history. But their integrated relation one to the other was always recognized, precisely because each element was uncontestedly given in the Scriptures and each was seen as representative of the very life of Jesus in his messianic destiny. Did not the Bible begin, in Genesis, with an account of human creation that made the exclusive union of male and female the basis of salvation history? And did not that history, as given shape in Scripture, end at the Lamb's great marriage feast (Rev. 19:17) with the clarion voice of a pneumatically redeemed humanity fulfilling its divinely created form by crying out to God's approach as the bridegroom: "The Spirit and the Bride say, 'Come'" (22:17)? A proper Christian theology of marriage has *always* seen the parameters of its guidance by the Holy Spirit as defining the articulation of the historical reality that lies between these two nuptial boundaries provided by Genesis and Revelation. In other words, the Christian theology of marriage has always sought to answer this question: how is the bonded sexual life of women and men ordered so as to give rise to the readied cry of the ecclesial bride to her holy heavenly spouse?

The early Church outlined a theology of marriage, then, that was at root a kind of theology of *history*, because it sought to show the historical connections between created human existence, in sexual terms, and the messianic *fulfillment* of human destiny. And in doing so early Christians sought to do justice to the breadth of Jesus' own remarkable attention to marriage as a human practice and a divinely providential figure. For brevity's sake I will refer to only one representative example of this theology—but he *is* representative—and that is Methodius of

Olympus's fourth-century dialogue on virginity, known as the *Symposium* or *Banquet of the Ten Virgins*.

Methodius's *Symposium* presents an elaborate hymn of praise to the life of deliberate chastity, which may seem an odd context in which to find a normative theology of marriage. But let us remember—and here I address those who complain about the influence of the celibate upon our tradition—that virginity was always recognized as a *minority* vocation pursued in order to inform the *majority* vocation of married life. Methodius explicates this minority vocation through a complex figural and allegorical exegesis of various parts of Scripture. What is crucial to realize is that this figural discussion is rooted in a vision of salvation history that is itself explicated in terms of the experience of *marriage*. The very shape of our ultimate redemption is given in the experienced history of human marriage. Methodius argues that salvation itself is nuptial, is a form of marriage with Christ Jesus, embedded in God's life. The end of humankind's historical destiny is a life united with God's, given in the heavenly union of a betrothed Church with the divine bridegroom, according to the prophecies of Revelation. Western theologians call this end *societas divina* (divine society or fellowship). It happens in the future, but its primal shape is given with the creation of the first man and woman, whose life together was designed as a figure for an existence that would overcome creation's estrangement from its Maker.

In any case, it is this final condition of ecclesial betrothal that embodies the preparation in virtue that the ascetic discipline of celibacy engenders. The condition of being betrothed is a condition not of consummated love, but of love that is purified and readied for a marriage that has not yet taken place. Virginity for Methodius thus acts as the historical context in which individuals are formed in the virtuous life that the Church, in its entirety, will embrace as it is presented "holy and blameless" to Christ, as Paul predicts (Col. 1:22). Virgins are firstfruits of the Church's destiny, in that their particular form of disciplined life acts as a figure of that holiness that all Christians in the Church will eventually embrace at the moment of their perfect readiness for their union with Christ.

But celibacy is a figure, all the same. Sexual virginity is itself but a shadow of something fuller to come, a shadow, that is, of the purified life of redemptive reconciliation. Human marriage is also a figure of that future life—not of the purity of betrothal, but of the perfection of consummated union. Each figure is grounded in a particular dispensation of history. Marriage was established in creation by God, as a larger historical context in which the destiny of humankind might take form; virginity was established, later in history, as a particular though necessary aspect of preparation for that destiny's final fulfillment. Marriage's dispensation is more sweeping, temporally speaking; but virginity's dispensation is superior in that it is closer to the end and could not be unveiled until Jesus himself came on the scene.

This dispensational distinction carries with it a distinction in the virtues of each estate, for marriage provides the context for a set of figural virtues that differ from virginity's: namely, the virtues of creative propagation and of mutual care in the midst of death. And these societal virtues themselves stand as images of the Church's historical existence in raising up Christian offspring and in disciplining human life within the virtuous contours of Jesus' own forms of self-giving on the cross—that is, through mutual subjection and care to the point of death.

Taken as a whole, then, human marriage anticipates the final historical union of Christ and his Church's people at the end time. But it also foreshadows the way that God brings this union to pass in time. That is, marriage foreshadows God's own incarnation, a union of two natures, within the person of Christ Jesus. Hence, human marriage is a figure, not only of the *end* but of the *means* of salvation. And the Church frequently speaks, as does Methodius, of marriage as an image of the second Adam, joined to the Eve of created humanity, whose incarnation, passion, and resurrection makes of the fleshly figure of union a divine reality.

Methodius is careful to point out that these differing existential figures—of virginity and of marriage—run side by side historically. One does not supplant the other, and most Christians are called to marry until the final consummation of time in the great wedding of the Lamb. Marriage and celibacy *together* offer the exhaustive nuptial vocation of humankind as a whole. And they must be kept together as the social bounds of the Christian community, in the same way that the Scriptures provide the community's communicative bounds.

It is important to see this larger picture in trying to understand the patristic and later Christian tradition on marriage. Marriage is dispensationally distinct and prior to the vocation of celibacy, but it is not thereby dispensable. The marriage of woman and man in an indissoluble union, whose fundamental outcome is procreative abundance and communal righteousness, remains for the tradition an essential providential figure or divine instrument for the ordering of the human race toward its full redemption in Christ. And over and over again, the Church reiterated this historical indispensability of marriage. The most succinct affirmation of this kind is perhaps the first canon from the Council of Gangra, held somewhere around 360, and constantly reiterated as authoritative, in its content, by successive ecumenical councils: "If anyone shall condemn marriage, or abominate and condemn a woman who is a believer and sleeps with her own husband, as though she could not enter the kingdom [of heaven] let him be anathema."

Augustine, let us admit, says no more than Methodius and in fact writes a treatise—*On the Good of Marriage*—to uphold and explicate the affirmation that a council like Gangra legitimately sanctions. It remains, now, to delineate the ways in which this normative outlook defined the figural, or sacramental, indispensability of marriage's historical enactment. For purposes of concision, I summarize this definition under three headings, each of which, I believe, ought to stand as a limit upon contemporary discussion of marriage's significance. Each also reflects some form of Jesus' own life and is, in this sense, literally given by God.

In the first place, the character of human marriage is traditionally understood as being *consummative*, in the sense that it is ordered toward the consummation of human destiny in Christ Jesus. I deliberately use the term *consummative* in its double sense of pointing to a divine end through the sexual act. Only Jesus Christ truly consummates the purposes for which human marriage's physical consummation is a sign. Only Jesus Christ. *Historically*, then, human marriage is penultimate—it will disappear as a form of life—prior to the true marriage of the Church and Christian with God in Christ. (This is why, for instance, the Mormon teaching on the eternity of human marriage must be judged in error.)

But note well: if human marriage is temporally penultimate and consummative in its figural orientation toward the kingdom, then it is also the case that human marriage is *subject* to the providential ordering of history by God. That is, human marriage, as penultimate, is subject to the gracious revelation of God's will as its shape is represented in Scripture. This, after all, is what is meant by the spiritual or sacramental aspect of the practice: marriage is subject to the Holy Spirit's own shaping of its purpose according to the scriptural forms of Jesus. There is no way to *disengage* marriage, in other words, from its scriptural basis, as if it were a human institution that the Bible merely interpreted in its own way. The opposite is the case.

The criteria for just sexual relations, therefore, are precisely those forms of life toward which human marriage points figurally: the purified condition of indissoluble union between created human nature and the divine grace of the incarnate bridegroom. And this condition is alternately embodied in the virtues of sexual celibacy: marriage, because of its consummative character, must mirror celibacy in its relational practice. Hence, the Christian tradition of a chaste or continent marriage—which has little to do with an asexual relation—referred to married partners being called to live a life of unbreakable mutual devotion, in which adultery, divorce, and uncontained self-indulgence would have no place. Any other kind of marriage is a divergence from the figural end for which the practice is being used by God.

I emphasize "by God." For if consummative, then penultimate; and if penultimate, then subject; and if subject, then understood as an object of divine grace and not as a human function. In every respect, Christian marriage is seen, according to the tradition of the Church, as standing outside the realm of human manipulation, except to the degree that it is deformed by human rebellion.

Of course, human rebellion is a constant within human history. And the Christian tradition is nothing if not realistic about the vagaries of the human heart and body. If the liturgical and legal forms of married life have varied in the course of the Church's history, as some scholars stress, it is because the consummative character of the divine gift of marriage is embodied not only within a history under the pull of redemption. Marriage's history is also one whose pressures reflect the human origin of temporal existence—namely the estrangement of sin. Hence, a second aspect of marriage underlined by the Christian tradition is its *agonistic* character, its experience as struggle. As Augustine, among others, points out, marriage was given as a providential gift for the survival of the human race within a dispensation of mortality and physical affliction. Survival for the end of redemption—yet survival within the historical context of the assaults of fallenness. Not only was the redeemer of humankind given a future through the evolving temporal dispensation of human heterosexual practice, but that very dispensation imitatively embodies the redemptive struggle and victory of God over created antagonism.

Thus marriage is properly seen as a context impregnated with struggle—struggle against despair, betrayal, selfishness, hostility, loss and disease, anger, boredom, physical nihilism. Marriage is, in its own right, a school for virtue, an ascetic or disciplined environment in which both the yearning for redemption is revealed and the power to receive God's redemptive gifts is deployed. The mirror relation between the virtues of the married and virtues of the celibate is clarified in this agonistic context, for the discipline of virginity exposes, both figurally and practically, the tools by which married persons overcome the larger oppression of a world not yet fully reconciled to its Maker. If the strictures against fornication, adultery, and divorce are themselves part of the consummative character of marriage, their attractions and occurrence realistically inform the agonistic framework of mortality in which marriage is enacted. Realism about the assaults upon marriage, however, does not equate with a mitigation of marriage as an instrument of struggle *against* such assaults. This fallacious equation is characteristic of contemporary thinking on the subject.

Among the most pointed figures of this agonistic experience of mortality ordered to consummation are the burdens and sorrows of family existence, articulated in the curse of the fall. The struggle for survival, by which the husband expends himself in toil on behalf of wife and child and by which the painful and often deadly danger to which the wife exposes herself in the course of childbirth, represents the limits of agony reached in self-sacrifice on behalf of another: toil and childbirth each find their fulfillment in the creative ministry and passion of Jesus, both of which are given figures in the risks and promises of agricultural labor and maternal delivery. We should be aware that only very recently have these two realities—and mostly in the Western world—been mitigated by the advent of effective agricultural management and medical care. For very different reasons, we might wonder with Augustine whether the dispensation for family life is coming to an end.

With Augustine, however, it is a question we should reject. For, while embedded in the agonistic character of marriage, the final aspect I would underline, marriage's *procreative* nature, is tied to the concrete ethical imperative any form of sexual relation ought to follow within the dispensation of penultimacy that human marriage figures. For, at its root, the procreative outcome to marriage represents the human embrace of God's providential ordering of history as a whole: the actuality of offspring, as well as their withholding in a marriage through infertility or their destruction through premature death, sustains the embodied character of marital life, burdened as well as blessed, in the course of a figured existence. To affirm the procreative character of human life within marriage is to affirm the whole realm of God's providential ordering of human existence from its fall to its redemption in Christ: it is to affirm a divine plan, the sustenance and direction of the human race, the calling of a people, Israel, through the progeny of Abraham, the raising up of a ruler from the line of David, the birth of a divine Savior, the sharing of God's promises with the human race through the ordering of virtue and the suffering of discipleship joined to the body of that Savior, and the fulfillment of creation's purpose in its union through grace with God. To call marriage the "Nursery of the Gospel," as St. Francis de Sales did, is simply to reiterate its procreative center.

Consummative, agonistic, and procreative—these are only terms to refer to an integrated understanding of marriage that has remained constant from the early Church's first meditation upon the New Testament. We find it enunciated in medieval village preaching far outside the confines of the cloister; written down by the spiritual writers of the late Middle Ages whose work sparked the elaboration of a lay mystical movement among married couples in the early modern era, both Catholic and Reformed; we find it reiterated especially within an Anglican tradition whose devotion to married and family life was informed by a liturgically figural imagination that would finally give rise to that great exponent of revived patristic exegesis, John Keble. Keble's poetry produced one of the few hymns for marriage that has survived, "The Voice That Breathed o'er Eden," although precisely in its figural outlook it now seems crudely anachronistic. He anchors human marriage in a grand trinitarian, christological, and eschatological representation:

> Be present, awful Father,
>   to give away this bride,
> As Thou gav'st Eve to Adam,
>   a helpmeet at his side.
> Be present, Son of Mary,
>   to join their loving hands
> As Thou didst bind two natures
>   in Thine eternal bands.
> Be present, Holiest Spirit,
>   to bless them as they kneel,
> As Thou for Christ, the Bridegroom,
>   the heavenly Spouse dost seal.
> . . . . . . . . . . . . . . . . . . . . . . . . . . .
> To cast their crowns before Thee
>   in perfect sacrifice,
> Till to the home of gladness
>   with Christ's own Bride they rise.

Keble himself outlined, in a still-formidable essay on biblical exegesis (see chapter 4), the shift in modern sensibilities that must inevitably undermine the integrated vision that informed the Christian marriage tradition until this century. In particular, he notes our present disbelief in divine providence as a real force ordering historical experience; he points, as well, to our revulsion at disciplined moral living of all kinds, not just of a sexual character; and, finally, he wonders at our simple incomprehension in the face of a living communion of saints, whose lives and witness sustain the providential value of the past. Obviously, within a universe marked by such modern attitudes, the figural realm of Scripture's prophetic contours can have little informing value for our conceptions of marriage.

But Keble raises another, more fundamental theological question: is it possible to avoid, with the rejection of such a figurally informing sense of scriptural providence—is it possible to avoid a religion that has slipped into another, sub-Christian Arianizing gear? What if the shape of human historical existence is excluded from a providential ordering according to the scriptural forms of Jesus' life? This ordering, after all, stands behind the Christian tradition on marriage; and if we exclude it, then have we not insisted upon a universe in which the infinite demands of divinity have also been excluded from the incarnation itself? If we cannot accept that human history, constructed through the experience of normative practices like marriage, should itself reveal the shape of God's own self-giving in time, then have we not simply either human-ized or departicularized what we call the "tabernacling of God with humankind" (John 1:14)?

This, at any rate, is the fear that some of us hold. Informed by this tradition, it derives from our seeing the theology of marriage as an es-sentially christological, not a limited moral, concern. For myself, the scriptured universe and the gospel of our God made flesh are one and the same; and it is not prudery or sexual repression that urges us to hold on to the particular norms informing the Christian marriage tradition. It is rather that these norms are embedded in a rich soil of scriptural forms that sustain the history of Christ's salvation. To pull scriptural form and gospel life apart is to deny not only the history of the tradition, but a human history whose redemptive character is shaped around the providentially chosen realities of the life of Jesus. The gospel is not love or intimacy or mutuality. It is the person of Jesus, whose own nuptial form displays the very meaning of the all-too-human practice we call marriage. I do not think that this broken and ruthlessly competitive world we live in—now almost the social apotheosis of our own nation's culture of bourgeois self-regard—can afford to relativize the evangelical core that human marriage represents.

We need not end on a note of fear, however. Christological dilution may well be a modern trend that qualifies far more than our churches' evolving views of marriage. But perhaps, in the end, it is the very integrity of our marriage tradition that can encourage us as to the fate of the truth's apprehension. "The days will come, when the bridegroom is taken away from them, and then they will fast" (Matt. 9:15). Then again, the days will come when we shall call out, with the Spirit, for the bridegroom's coming (Rev. 21:9; 22:17). Wherever we are now in history, between these two terms—of fasting and of readied feasting—we may safely expect that God will order our fates according to the form of his nuptial promise. In sorrow or in hope, even in confusion, the shape of life around which the Christian marriage tradition takes form will most certainly do its work.

# 8

# Sex
# and
# Reticence

*Homosexuality and the Figure of the Church*

The evolving pluralism of Christian attitudes and teachings, bolstered by the all-embracing religious market of modernity, has rendered it almost impossible in America even to hope for the apprehended reality of such a thing as Christian teaching. Yet the hope is there, and the sense of there being a church whose visible community represents a definable character continues to motivate reflection around important matters of faith and life. Alas, under these circumstances, discussion and discernment have rapidly translated into contention. Indeed, contention has become a way of life to such an extent that its dynamics are easily clothed in an array of changing attire to meet the various principles of civic and intellectual existence in the modern world as they arise. Democracy, scientific debate, liberative struggle, and so on—all justify today the further rending of the body's seamless garb. Although the market itself has never loosened its grip on the underlying forces of Christian interaction, participants are able, within this grasp, to don varying intransigent and exclusivistic roles, through which the exercise of power becomes the tool for autonomous self-expression.

Among the many nodes of contention, our churches and denominations continue to flounder in disagreement over the matter of gay sex—its status within the Christian community and the proper Christian response we are to take in the face of its practice and defense. The topic has, in fact, so dominated the energies of denominations in America and of American Christianity's relationship with the rest of the world that one wonders if sexuality is not some grand projection upon the blank walls of worldly faith of some deeper struggle within the soul of the bridegroom's spouse, wandering through time (Song 5:6–8). But perhaps this is the nature of sexual character itself within our world; that is, it does not exist on its own, but only as the expressive tool of the interior spirit, chained to some cinematic duty of disinhibition. Much as our contemporary culture seeks to replicate its own tortures through the videos—the artificial visions—of its commercial and private self-expressive media, sexual expression has become the propaganda of spiritual writhing, projecting our religious dislocations into the theaters of social and political struggle.

Of course, to the degree that churches accept or promote this dynamic, they themselves become the projected images of the restless objects of their prayer and proclamation. Perhaps that is inevitable; but at least some measure of self-awareness ought to inform such an ecclesial descent into the experienced tunnels of imprisoned souls (1 Pet. 3:19). The cleansing of the temple, hoped for and long desired on the part of Christians for their own precincts, would seem even further to demand some distancing from the contended wrestling of the sexual figure bent and wrapped around the spirit.

On a purely political level, I have, with others, long advocated a moratorium on legislative debates and actions around sexuality.[1] The immediate motive for these kinds of appeals is a particular reading of

---

1. "As a response to the continuing crisis surrounding the church's teaching and practice regarding homosexuality," George Sumner (principal of Wycliffe College, Toronto) and I proposed the following resolution to the 1997 General Convention of the Episcopal Church meeting in Philadelphia. While it gained some public support, it never came before the convention and remains, in the minds of many, either a naïve irrelevance or a reactionary subterfuge: "Current resolutions of General Convention forbidding the ordination of noncelibate gays and upholding the normativity for sexual relations within marriage will be maintained without new resolutions or legislation aimed at their revision or abrogation. This will be understood to be the official and public teaching of the Episcopal Church on the subject. This moratorium will extend to revision or expansion of official liturgical forms that would contradict the above resolutions. Bishops will abide by these resolutions so as to avoid public scandal. The exercise of episcopal or priestly conscience counter to these resolutions, but in a way that does not cause public scandal, will

the condition of a given church at a given time in history and a concern about its members' continued communion. Such proposed moratoria, therefore, have more to do with assessed contingencies and their relation to fundamental theological principles regarding the church, for example, its unity, than with particular arguments about sexual ethics. But there is obviously a profound connection between the two—the threats to the church's already fractured unity at a given point in time and God's direction of our sexual lives—that it is worth considering. Especially since, if our sexual lives end up in fact being the images of our spirits' shape even as this shape is given over to the molding hands of Christ's own form, then sexual ethics on some basic level is an aspect of ecclesiology (because bound to the providential order of Christ) and vice versa. The present chapter, then, is an attempt simply to show that, were one to accept the contingent judgment about the danger of our church's contentious disintegration over the issue of sexual practice and were one to accept the overriding imperative of maintained communion, then the strategy of, say, a legislative moratorium is at least coherently grounded in a theological vision concerning the relation of public and private sexual practice that is rooted in the Church's scriptural hope.

In fact, I will not claim that this theological vision ought to be normative for sexual ethics as a whole (though it might be), since one of the contingent judgments that would motivate a plea for reining in contentious legislations over sexual ethics is that such normative visions are not now capable of accepted articulation, the church currently lacking sufficient structures for consensus. All I wish to argue here is that the theological vision is plausible and hence that the decision to desist from the sexuality fight does not sink into theological perversion when it relies on the overriding principles of unity. Unity is *not* a subterfuge for power; it is the vessel for truth.

Of course, asking people to stop proposing legislation about sexual behavior will seem particularly uncomfortable to those who cannot stand to ride the vessel to its destination, but insist that truth is something on this side of Scripture's oceanic Golgotha. This will be so especially for

---

not be subject to public censure within the church. Public scandal on the part of bishops counter to the resolutions will be met with prompt episcopal censure but without disciplinary measures. Public scandal counter to the resolution on the part of priests will be met with the discretionary discipline of the local diocesan bishop. This moratorium will be understood to be in effect for a 'Sabbath of conventions,' for seven triennia, which is roughly the period of leadership of most of the current House of Bishops." Obviously, the 2003 General Convention of the Episcopal Church has now roundly rejected even the motives of such a "moratorium." The idea, however, still has some purchase in the wider Anglican Communion.

both traditionalists and revisionists on the matter of homosexuality: it counsels consistency of a public teaching that prohibits the official affirmation of noncelibate homosexuality while also urging freedom of conscience and discretion in the tolerance of such a way of life. The best that might be said about such a position, perhaps, is that it is muddled; the worst, that it is destructively hypocritical. Therefore, although there are many aspects of the theology of sexuality that deserve attention as it relates to ecclesial order, I shall limit my argument to what I assume will be this more generalized sense of dissatisfaction with compromise between public prohibition and private tolerance. After all, compromise is itself something that may well reveal the form of Christ if adopted from a particular posture that derives from him and not simply from the strategies of political survival. In any case, our discussion here will take us back over material regarding the sacramentality of marriage, already touched upon in our previous chapter, but now looked at in the specific terms of ecclesial discipline.

## Unveiling the Veiled

It would be historically naïve, I need to stress, to think that the Christian Church has ever actually avoided living with the disjunction between public pronouncement and private practice. To take but one example: the Church's promotion of the indissolubility of monogamous marriage in Western Europe was a centuries-long process, with and without tensions, of continually changing the balance between a religious vision and deep-seated cultural behaviors that favored concubinage or bigamy or serial partnerships or privatized contracts.

Not until the sixteenth century did the Church actually "Christianize" marriage definitively in its social estates, moving it ritually into the sanctuary and imposing (even then unevenly) its meanings upon popular practice as a whole. Whatever the Church's actual teachings on the subject may have been,[2] parish priests and bishops had, for hundreds of years, been living with alternate conjugal arrangements among their flock (and sometimes among themselves!). And this kind of evolving balancing act between public discourse and private practice pertained and pertains to other areas of sexual behavior as well.

2. These teachings were strong and clear enough, however; and I am hardly arguing here for a culturally constructed evolution of attitudes; merely of discipline. Cf. chapter 7 above. But the evolution of discipline is not without its theological ramifications.

Of course, historical practice in and of itself cannot count as a theological argument. What it can do is indicate the possibility that theological authorities in the Church—the traditionally interpreted Scriptures—can still maintain (and sometimes enhance) their primacy, even within a realm of their uneven application to public and private spheres. To be sure, the contemporary culture of the West has shed most of the inhibiting elements that kept the overt expression of many aspects of sexual practice from assuming public stature and that hence helped to stabilize the reality of public-private dissonance. But even our current trend toward "pansexualizing" existence has had the value of reaffirming the uneasy reality of universal sexual irrationality that lay behind the earliest Christian (and scriptural) judgments about sexual practice; after all, if everything is sexualized, but sex is fraught with ambiguity and anxiety, then there is an evident social dynamic put in play to set public parameters around sexual expression. Thus even today's highly sexualized culture can point us toward refounding the original possibility of a balance between public discourse and private behavior that the later Church was able to enact.

In a sense, we are perhaps in a better position today than at any time since the early Church to distinguish the religious reasons why we can maintain this balance. Only in recent years, with the development of psychological science (rudimentary though it still is), has anyone seriously considered the possibility that homosexual behavior might be understood within the same psychological context as heterosexual behavior. And, if this can be done, then we can more aptly locate the Church's attitude toward homosexual life within a Christian theological perspective that embraces sexual life in general.

In large part, modern psychology demonstrates the way that virtually all sexual desire and behavior (especially among heterosexuals, this being the most widespread) is governed by a range of irrational impulses that might seem perverse if publicly known by others. (Actually, the early church understood this as well, which is why it never got too exercised by homosexual behavior as a specific vice.) Few of us are open with others about our sexual desires and fantasies precisely because we realize that there are some people who will find them odd or distasteful and because we ourselves assess them ambivalently. Psychologists in the late nineteenth and twentieth centuries, for the first time, began to expose many of these common desires that we harbor with a sense of embarrassment. Before this era, the peculiarities of interior desire and its concrete expression were publicly veiled and emerged into open view only indirectly, if at all.

Certainly the Bible, for instance, has nothing to say about sadomasochistic sexual acts (among many other kinds) between husband and wife; and it is not at all clear how Scripture, in this case, conforming as it does to the long-standing cultural pattern of veiling interior desire, can offer us any direction on such particular, though for many consuming, elements of sexual passion. Further, although many of us instinctively consider such sadomasochistic behavior perverse, it appears from modern psychological research that many otherwise normal—and no doubt Christian—people pursue it.

Psychology having brought to light the universal character of sexual shame and relative perversion, it was logical that the limited types of sexual perversion from the past would appear less odd (though not necessarily less ambivalently considered). And this is the case with homosexuality. The numbers of homosexuals within many historically accessible societies are shown to be greater than people in the past were willing to admit (although just how much greater is still contested), and the oddness of their behavior seems less distressing in comparison with the oddness of much of our sexual behavior in general.

As contemporary people turn to the Scripture's teaching about sexual relations, we do so with a knowledge of what men and women normally do with each other or with themselves that no other group of people in the history of the world has possessed in the past. We understand our own sexual desires in a far more conscious way than people in the past. And we now think we know what many of the Israelite wives and husbands likely did with each other in the privacy of their homes, things the Bible does not mention.

What results from such embracing knowledge of what once were private secrets? It might seem, at first glance, that the contemporary unveiling of desire has in some sense relativized overt scriptural prohibitions by indicating their almost arbitrary enunciation within a presumed collection of unspoken, though licit, perversions. For instance, we have now noticed—though it was there all along, if obscured by the unquestioned cultural assumption of a certain set of sexual practices—how many of the Bible's teachings on sexual relations fall within a set of teachings about cleanness and uncleanness that we have long since rejected as no longer theologically compelling as a category, because unsystematically applied and seemingly unprincipled. Has homosexuality, which falls within this now relativized category of Old Testament purity legislation, been thereby liberated from its scriptural prohibitions?[3]

## Universal Disorder Judged

Only one place in the entire Old Testament really gives a clear teaching on homosexual acts: Leviticus 18:22 (repeated in 20:13). (The story of Sodom and Gomorrah, in Gen. 19, is only indirectly pertinent, since, on the face of it, it concerns not only homosexual practice in and of itself, but also the forcible rape of strangers.) In Leviticus, homosexual acts are called "abominations," which simply means something that God hates. This may seem clear enough, and it is, within the context of the Old Testament. The problem is that the term *abomination* (Hebrew *toebah*) is used for a wide variety of practices, many of which either the Christian Church from the beginning no longer considered abominations or which later Christians, like ourselves, ceased to think of as crimes against God.

Some things called abominations in the Old Testament are still considered by most Christians as sins: incest, bestiality, child sacrifice, worshiping idols, sorcery, cheating. About other practices, however, also called abominations in the Old Testament (in Leviticus and Deuteronomy especially, in the same context as the prohibition of homosexual acts) attitudes have changed: having sex with a menstruating woman; eating pork; eating shellfish; eating squid; touching dead animals of various kinds; touching anything unclean, such as a leper, menstrual blood, semen, a pagan, and so on; men wearing women's clothes (e.g., a skirt?) or women wearing men's clothes (e.g., slacks, ties?). Christians no longer consider these things abominations as the Old Testament taught that they were.

How shall we determine whether homosexual acts are to be seen as equivalent to sorcery or as equivalent to having sex during a woman's period or eating clams? If equivalent to the former, such acts are to be condemned on scriptural grounds; if equivalent to the latter it may be possible for us to reevaluate their moral status. While it is easy enough to

---

3. This argument has been forcefully made by, among others, William Countryman in his *Dirt, Greed, and Sex: Sexual Ethics in the New Testament and Their Implications for Today* (Philadelphia: Fortress, 1990). While I will not address this currently influential argument specifically, I will simply register my sense that the argument itself is a scripturally baseless attempt to disengage the reality of divine holiness from moral (and sexual) behavior. For a discussion of the place of law in New Testament ethics that completely undercuts Countryman's approach, see Markus Bockmuehl, *Jewish Law in Gentile Churches: Halakah and the Beginning of Christian Public Ethics* (Grand Rapids: Baker, 2003).

point out that Jesus "declared all foods clean" (Mark 7:19), and therefore eating oysters no longer need be considered an abomination, he had nothing at all to say about menstruation's new purity. The latter is a decision that the Christian Church itself made, not only on the basis of Scripture but on the basis of what might be considered implications of its understanding of what Christ demands. (Although this process was itself slow, limitations on menstruating women still applied, for instance, in the so-called Apostolic Canons accepted as binding by the Eastern Church at the end of the seventh century.)

In addition, however, to making the levitical prohibition of homosexual sex a limited cultural phenomenon, the unveiling of desire in our day has also had a very different, even opposite, effect, which places its reality within the framework of a more universal problem. The modern realization that sex of all kinds and for all people is fraught with irrationality, confusion, and a sense of shame makes us more open to another facet of biblical teaching, a facet that also makes it harder for us to single out homosexuality as a form of behavior that requires some kind of special concern, because it is only derivative and ancillary to a more fundamental pattern of human failure. Indeed, whatever we may make of levitical injunctions—and their continuing significance in light of the coming of Christ is not obviously one of simple abrogation, though we cannot discuss this here—the Old Testament canon itself worked to expand the reach of the logic of abomination in a universalizing direction.

It is not the case that only books of the law, like Leviticus and Deuteronomy, speak about abominations in the context of ritual purity. The Book of Proverbs, for instance, also says a good deal about things that are abominations in God's eyes: pride, deceit, self-promotion, arrogance, and so on. And while Christians are (usually) willing to call these characteristics sins, most agree that they are universal: they are acts in which all of us engage, Christians included. The question arises: if we are to deal with, say, homosexuality the way that we deal with pride, what would we do? Or, conversely, if we were to adopt toward people who are arrogant (including ourselves) the same attitude adopted toward homosexuals, how would we treat ourselves?

This is an important question because asking it helps us better to understand what to do with the only New Testament text that speaks theologically of homosexual behavior: Romans 1:26–27. It is probably fair to say that, even if the Leviticus text taken on its own cannot be used by Christians in a clear way to prohibit homosexual behavior, this text in

Romans shows that, from a Christian standpoint, such behavior is not viewed positively (and therefore that the Leviticus text needs somehow to be incorporated meaningfully into Christian reflection). But exactly how is it viewed? To give a comprehensive answer, one has to read the whole passage, beginning with 1:18 and ending with 2:11. In viewing the question in this context, we can see that St. Paul evaluates homosexual behavior as part of a universal fall from God's truth, a fall, however, that touches each and every one of us, heterosexual and homosexual alike.

In this passage, Paul describes how the human race turned away from God, a movement that resulted in an inescapable pattern of futile thinking. Mired in a kind of blindness about who God really is, human beings turned to the created order to find their gods. This condition of blindness and self-worship, which Paul describes as being founded on a basic misdirected desire (the "lusts" of 1:24), has two main results.

The first result (1:26–27) is "dishonorable passions," among which Paul includes homosexual behavior. In speaking about passions, he is pointing to the realm of our sexual lives being disordered by the fall. This is what he means by calling homosexual acts "unnatural": they are part of the human existence from which, in general, the truth about God is obscured. Paul also writes (1:27) that the penalty for these passions is contained in the acts themselves. (This is a mysterious phrase: what does Paul mean? Perhaps he is referring to the fact that homosexual sex precludes having children and hence contains its own unnatural punishment and outcome in sterility.) In this he seems to be saying that the wrath of God against these passions takes place in their own practice, not in some further punishment: they are dead ends, as it were, in and of themselves.

A second result of our blindness to God is what Paul calls a "base mind and . . . improper conduct." Here, in distinction from sexual passion, Paul is referring to our more public human relations. These too have been disordered, and he gives a long list of how, including greed, malice, gossip, insolence, lack of love, violence, pride, arrogance, and so on (1:28–31). The list contains many of the sins spoken of in Proverbs as abominations. They are also—as well we know—rather common. Yet for these common failings, "those who do such things deserve to die."

In Romans 2, St. Paul then brings his description of fallen humanity to a conclusion: "Therefore you have no excuse, O man, whoever you are, when you judge another; for in passing judgment upon him you condemn yourself, because you, the judge, are doing the very same things"

(2:1). Paul, then, has painted a picture of humanity in which all people, all women and men, no matter who they are, stand before God as blasphemers, as committers of abominations. Indeed, he lays much greater stress on the condemnation of the sins of "base mind and . . . improper conduct" (the heart and the deed) than he does on the sins of disordered passion (sex). It appears that our sexual lives are images, projected *simulacra* of our moral lives, and their disorder is but part of a larger disorder of the spirit. Further, that disorder is universal: it touches every single person. And because universal, it is all part of the reality that God alone can redeem, in Christ Jesus.

As noted, St. Paul here clearly casts homosexual behavior in a negative light. But he makes it a part—and a very distinct and limited part—of a condition we all share. And it must be emphasized that the relational sins he lists—pride, lack of love, gossip, greed, and so on—are sins that still beset all people, even Christians. We have only to read the end of his letter to the Romans, not to mention most of Paul's other letters to Christians, to realize that these sins are our sins, despite our new life in Christ Jesus. And so, his question, "How do you judge another?" gains special weight: If heterosexual Christians condemn gay people for their homosexual acts, they inevitably condemn themselves even more so (for their own pride, arrogance, lack of love, etc.). The point here is not that what is right in God's eyes is unknown, but that what is wrong in human eyes is obscured by self-righteousness.

## Marriage as Redemptive Sacrament

In a sense, then, St. Paul himself also offers a kind of theological unveiling of human sexual desire, in such a way as to disclose a universal implication in alienated disorder and liability before God. From one aspect, this unveiling effects a delimitation on the practical discipline upon such behavior. If we interpret Romans 1:18–2:11 as saying that homosexual behavior is a historical sign within the human race that exhibits, in a peculiar way, the same sin we all share, then such behavior falls within the category of disordered passions, which we must consider as physical signs of our common fall. But obesity, to the degree that it manifests a disordered passion for consumption, is also such a sign (as is any sort of lust of the flesh, which includes much that passes for the needs we fulfill secretly or often publicly in our lives).

We must be careful, therefore, not to assume that homosexual behavior can be segregated from the host of patterns that inevitably define us (in the way that our imperfections are inevitable in this world and our bodies are still not fully redeemed). We must treat it, rather, as part of the ordinary features of our fallen existence, which include each of our own inordinate sexual and nonsexual appetites and desires, as distinguished from the more root sin of our self-love, which Paul says is prior to any of this (Rom. 1:22–25) and thus, in a real sense, the worst and controlling sin.

Further, the way the Christian Church must deal with homosexual behavior is therefore going to be very different from the way it deals with the more extraordinary figures of our fall, figures in which we normally call upon social sanction in the public sphere (e.g., murder, robbery, abuse). We must deal with it the way that we ask the church to deal with us in our own personal failures and weaknesses—through the discretionary and edifying influence of the Christian community's disciplinary tolerance.[4]

At the same time, however, St. Paul's universal unveiling of desire, while it may delimit public discipline, also places homosexual behavior, along with all other disordered elements of our appetitive existence, within a sphere that is subject to redemption. This is the positive side of his anthropology, which reasserts the applicability of the broader claims of scriptural proclamation. If subject to redemption, then homosexual behavior is subject—in the sense of being conceptually dependent in the realm of its public description—to the figure of Jesus Christ. To speak properly in Christian terms about homosexuality, one must then speak of it within the logic of Christ Jesus.

This logic, as it turns out, is itself described in those terms given in Scripture that, on its own coherent basis, propose heterosexual marriage as an essential grammar for reordered humanity (see below). The linguistic metaphor—description, logic, grammar—is appropriate here (and the iconic metaphor of image and figure even more so) because Scripture itself presents the relationship between the concrete existence of Christians in this world and their full redemption in the image of God

---

4. Having said this, however, we must consider that, at various contingent moments of time, certain sins assemble in a cultural mass that has the result of potentially overturning whole orders of virtue and that the exigencies of these moments may require particular attention and focus on some aspects of disordered behavior more than on others. Is sexual behavior in our time one of these demanded foci? Of course, who demands? The present ecclesial and public contention over sexual expression may well be a providential clue.

as one of increased and progressive correspondence, in which image and meaning become more and more adequately manifested and communicated as a unity.

This presses us to go beyond Scripture's discursive details about sexual behavior to its configurated meaning within Scripture's "master image" (to borrow a concept from Austin Farrer),[5] supernaturally given in the form of the incarnate God to which all other images (including public sexual expression) are destined to conform. For, clearly, there is much in Scripture bearing on the issue of homosexual conduct that does not explicitly treat it. Primarily, we have scriptural teaching on marriage as the primordial (that is, the first in God's purpose) union of male and female from the beginning of creation (Gen. 2:24), which is made the supreme enacted symbol of God's love (cf. Hosea), upheld by Jesus (Mark 10:6–9), and then proclaimed as the divinely effective image of Christ's own self-giving for the world through the Church (Eph. 5:29–33).

This last text, given its placement in the larger scriptural tradition concerning marriage, is hardly peripheral. Indeed, it forms the summit of a consistent scriptural teaching on the shape of divine redemption that explicitly describes it as bound to the logic incarnated within human heterosexual marriage. That Paul calls it a mystery—the background to the Latin term *sacrament*—and that it thus pertains to the very act of salvific purpose given in Jesus thereby founds marriage itself as a key figure or image of redemption, a practice communicative of the gospel, to which, therefore, homosexual behavior must somehow give way.

As a mystery—and this is ultimately the sense of a sacrament—marriage is denoted by St. Paul as being representational of Christ. The representational character of the sacrament must be distinguished from any expressive quality it might have (as if what were sacramental was anything that somehow articulated some deeper abstract meaning about Christ). It is not love in general, for instance, that marriage expresses: homosexual unions could do that too, in many cases just as well. Rather, it is a precise description of Jesus Christ in particular, through which the historical agency of his life is given for participation, that is presented in the condition of Christian marriage; and this is what makes of it something sacramental.

---

5. See Austin Farrer, *The Glass of Vision* (London: Dacre, 1948), chaps. 3, 6. Farrer's is a great book, a modernist's attempt, not always convincing, to ground the patristic metaphysics of scriptural figure (i.e., scriptural providence) in something coherent with contemporary literary sensibilities; it deserves a place at the top of any list of creative and faithful hermeneutics.

Further, the representational force of marriage lies not in some features intrinsic to its biological or natural contours—Paul does not mention these—but simply in its historical assumption by God, in Christ, as the communicative image of his own life. Such a voluntary assumption of a communicative sign, by God or anyone else, is at the basis of any language or iconography. God speaks through human marriage; we are to listen.

These two outcomes of St. Paul's unveiling of desire—the presentation of marriage as a redemptive mystery and the delimitation of discipline against desire's disorder—correspond, in practice, to the balance between private discretion and public prohibition of homosexual behavior that we have been examining. Therefore, although judgment passed by one Christian on another regarding the character of their sexual desire and practice is generally self-condemnatory, this fact cannot undermine the public witness that the church must offer to its redemptive foundation. The normativity of marriage is something that the church proclaims, makes public, in that it is, in its practice, an enunciation of the gospel of Christ Jesus. And homosexual behavior, like all sexual life, stands toward Christian marriage as something subject to its redemptive enunciation, not as something equivalent or supplemental or even irrelevant to it.

Yet the public proclamation of the gospel is not the same thing as its historical fulfillment, the latter of which involves a complex and confused process of individual and mutual self-denials, advances, retractions, attempts, and redresses, wherein the Holy Spirit works with each of us differently and at different levels and moments for a larger goal of transformation into the fullness of our human stature in Christ that is not immediately apprehended by any one of us. In this historical realm, under cover of its public proclamation, the Church as a body acts with comparable flexibility and variety with individuals and groups, balancing the needs (or confusions) of the times with the clarity of the ultimate mission confided to it.

From a purely scriptural perspective, then, there need not be dissonance between public prohibition and discretionary private tolerance. And this conclusion derives, at base, from the perception that the sacramentality of marriage, as it emerges in the New Testament, includes this balance between public and private within its very meaning. This perception now bears further examination, because it is upheld, I believe, by the actual interpretation of the early Catholic tradition that began to formulate the basic understanding of sacrament eventually given technical precision many centuries later. It is, in addition, an understanding that is not coincidentally tied to a vision of the unity of the Church joined from a welter of diverse moral practices, a vision to which I believe the churches must, for the moment anyway, commit themselves.

The sacramentality of marriage is something that bears careful consideration with regard to the issue of public sexuality and sexual practice in the church. Indeed, I believe it is absolutely crucial to distinguish heterosexual marriage as sacramental from marriage as an ideal. When seen merely as an ideal, heterosexual marriage is an imagined form of life that simply does not fit the real world and thus cannot by definition be a norm. But as sacramental, heterosexual marriage is instead something through which God acts to form the Christian people, drawing them through their common history into a specific future. Through the temporal enactment of the sacrament, God fits reality in time to marriage, not the reverse. And this movement has important implications for the relationship between private and public expressions of sexuality.

## Social Figuration in Augustine

It is worth noting, before going further, the general absence from the Church's discussion of sexuality of any serious examination of the historical logic governing the concept of sacramentality already implied in the scriptural correspondence drawn between marriage and Christ's redemptive relation with the Church. Failure to take seriously the sacramentality of marriage has led to a misreading of history, to an inability to see that variety of sexual practice outside and within the church is irrelevant to the issue of what the Church actually says about marriage (and sexuality).

Indeed, the theological conception of marriage's sacramentality was forged by the Church during the first four centuries of its existence precisely in the midst of diverse sexual practice. And far from mimicking any socially normative behavior of the surrounding culture, the sacrament of marriage was the deliberate theological construction of an independent norm, extrapolated from Scripture and ongoing Christian practice, that, as we know, was only loosely adopted by the larger populace for centuries. The cultural independence of this sacramental construction of marriage, in fact, is what allowed it to function as a formative element of the Church's evangelical ministry, rather than simply as an instrument for the hypocrisies of successive sexual eras.

To see this clearly, we must return to the historical moment when the concept of marriage's sacramentality was being teased out of the social experience of the Church's prophetic existence in the midst of a sexually confused culture. In this regard, it is appropriate to turn to Augustine, not only because he stands as the crucial expositor of the tradition on the matter, but because, for clear thinking's sake, the myth of his role as the West's originator of sexual repression needs to be dispelled. Far from elucidating a coercive sexual ethic based on St. Paul, Augustine was the articulator of a kind of inclusive theology of sexual practice—inclusive in the sense of a realistic acknowledgement of diversity—that was capable of nourishing Catholic faith and existence. He did this, historically, by staking out a path between thoroughgoing sexual asceticism and worldly libertinism, as well as between moral sectarianism and the uncolored contours of non-Christian culture.

In one sense, it was fortuitous that Augustine carried on a pastoral role within an African church torn by the Donatist schism. For among other things, the experience impelled him to work out a notion of efficacious sacramentality with respect to baptism (and, derivatively, ordination). Like the Eucharist, these two acts of the Church were sacraments (to reiterate, a Latin translation for the Greek word meaning "mystery") insofar as they were socially embodied deeds through which God acted concretely within the Church (whether it actually bore positive fruit within an individual life). A sacrament, for Augustine, was any historical reality by which God openly pointed to and publicly enacted some aspect of his plan for the Church. The term was not, initially, tied to a closed set of ritual practices.

Against the Donatists, who saw the practices of the Christian church as corrupted and corrupting because of the sinful character of particular priests and lay people who might participate in them, Augustine insisted that Christ's sanctifying work in baptism and ordination, in particular, was effective over and beyond whatever sullying secrets were harbored by Church members who might participate in these rites. Since God alone effected his plan for the Church through these rites, the disposition of human participants was not determinative of their value for the Church (or world) as a whole.

## Marriage as Saving Institution

Augustine extended this aspect of sacramentality to marriage, drawing on the Greek "mystery" language that St. Paul uses for marriage in Ephesians 5. In doing so, as in his *On the Good of Marriage,* Augustine elaborated on what a sacrament is and opened up an understanding of marriage that proved remarkably strengthening of the Christian community: marriage was not an institution contributing to individual hypocrisy (a public cover for deviance from the norm), but rather one that saves the Church from the corrupting effects of corporate hypocrisy.

How does this happen? First of all, Augustine emphasized that the human fellowship of male and female precedes and founds the shape of sexuality and that marriage presupposes this primary good of human companionship. While mutual joy is the foundational purpose of sexual relationship—a point worth remembering in Augustine's much-maligned theology—it is true that the "goods" of marriage, understood in institutional terms, lie not immediately in such fellowship, but in the procreation of children, the mutual faithfulness of wife and husband, and finally in the sacrament that marriage embodies.

This list of goods is obviously contestable. That mutual pleasure in sexual activity is not listed (and is, in fact, called a venial sin within marriage) is repugnant to most modern sensibilities. We need not follow Augustine along this path of condemnation, however, while still remaining challenged by the suggestion that pleasure can never be autonomous from the social good that marriage (or anything else) promotes. The notion that autonomous pleasure can legitimately be pursued is a modern moral invention whose narcissistic origins bear some scrutiny.

Further, those who criticize the procreative bias of Augustine's framework must grapple with a remarkable twist in his argument. For in surveying these goods, Augustine is nothing if not realistic: children are not, he acknowledges, always given nor are they always sought; in addition, the pact of faith between husband and wife is constantly violated, by adultery and other extramarital sexual practices. What then is left of marriage's good in the real world? Only the sacrament.

And for Augustine, as for the tradition he merely exemplifies, the sacramentality of marriage was signified by its indissolubility—the unbreakable union of male and female within the Church. Calling marriage a sacrament means primarily that whatever the partners do, however they act, no matter what they practice, even if they leave each other, the marriage somehow sticks, it holds and welds. In this sense, it is normative.

But what can this mean? What is the point of insisting that marriage is indissoluble within the Church, that it is a holy mystery, when it is constantly violated and repudiated in practice? The answer that Augustine gives is a short summary of what he means by sacrament in general. With respect to marriage in particular, he says that, in a basic sense, marriage is not defined by its practice, but is rather a gracious sign, one that God grants and works through in the Church exactly because of the variety, caprice, and perversion of actual sexual practice. That God is actually doing something in marriage is something that contemporary critics of the institution's normative status fail to grasp. If marriage were only a human phenomenon, its elasticity and even relative contingency could be more easily acknowledged. Seen in terms of sacrament, however, marriage was instituted as divine gift and divine action, independent of its human recipients.

What God does is to grant marriage the power to shape Christian society. It is here that Augustine provides theological nuance and force to the reality of sacrament. The effective sign that marriage is can be looked at in three ways. First, the sacramentality of marriage as communicated by the church is *informative*. That is, marriage tells Christians something about who they are, people different from the world in their destiny to fellowship in Christ with one another. Second, the sign is *formative:* by being consistently enunciated in the public life of the church, marriage shapes the common lives of Christian members into the form of their membership in Christ's body. Finally, and in a way that summarizes the two previous aspects, the marriage sign is *figurative,* that is, as entered into, marriage is a participatory indication of something still being realized in the Church by God's power. In Augustine's interpretation of Paul, this figure is the oneness of the nations joined in Christ, in other words the Church as the redeemed flesh of humanity joined to the flesh of Jesus. Taken together, the sacramentality of marriage means that marriage embodies a present and public mission into a divine future. Nothing less.

From a cultural standpoint, we must not fail to note that in the tradition that Augustine encapsulates it is the sacramentality of marriage that distinguishes marriage from all other relationships. This bears emphasizing: the distinctive feature of Christian marriage is not the worth of childbearing nor even the faithfulness of the partners to each other (in contemporary terms: committedness), but sacrament. Why? Because this figurative and figurating character of sacrament sets out for the Christian the parameters of our hope and the borders of our social mission in Christ, in the face of every alternative practice within and outside the church. (An important question here is whether, going beyond Augustine, we might apply this point to marriage in general, and not only Christian marriage: is Christ given to the nations evangelically in the very act of natural marriage? This would be a truly mysterious and astonishing grace! And therefore all the more a spur to the Church's promotion of marriage in any culture.)

As in the performance of the Eucharist or in ordination, so in marriage: when the Church "says" it, as it were, God acts even in overcoming the resisting secrets of our participation. Thus, the notion of hypocrisy is irrelevant to Christian marriage in any fundamental way. It is only when the Church stops speaking the sacrament consistently—offering it, stressing it, defending it—that corrupting hypocrisy creeps in: claiming God's power at work in its common life, the Church excludes one of the primary vehicles for God's formative presence.

Because of this, the aspect of indissolubility is only on a secondary level referred to in an individual couple's concrete marriage relationship, that is, on the question of divorce. On a primary level, indissolubility refers to the Church's unyielding commitment to express the norm of marriage in the face of whatever particular deviations from the norm its members pursue, within premarital, extramarital, or homosexual contexts. (This is why the continuously varied concrete attitude of the Church to particular cases of marital instability never undercuts the significance of the marriage sacrament itself.) The exclusivity of the marriage norm is contained in this commitment to the figurating agency of sacramentality.

While Augustine, for instance, recognized the historically developmental character of certain sexual institutions—for example, from polygamy to monogamy—a character that, in theory, might not rule out the possibility of homosexual unions becoming permissible in time, he grounded any such change in the common assent of "nature, custom, and [scriptural] command" (a coincidence that no one today could claim exists in the Church for any sexual relationship other than for marriage).

The point in asserting this three-pronged common grounding to any change was simply to express, in terms of human deliberation over a matter, how a sacrament in fact functions: the shape of the world (nature) is molded through the social agency of the Church (custom) according to the form of God's self-offering (scriptural command). Outside this cohesive congruence between history and scriptural form, there can be no discernment of some new sacrament, for example, homosexual union. And the sacramentality of marriage, thus, appears to demand its own permanent, persistent, and precluding enunciation.

## The Redemptive Veil of the Sacrament

All this, however, is to stress only one side of the sacramental issue involved with the Church's attitudes toward homosexual activity. The other side points to the hidden plurality of sexual practice, a reality in which the Church actually has a quite flexible interest insofar as it remains private. It is, of course, crucial to appreciate that, in any era of Church history, a common and commonly formed understanding of the Church's enunciatory mission within the public realm is the very substance of the sacrament. But it is equally critical to realize that beneath such consensual and traditionally legitimated sacramental constructions lie a host of secrets—secret lives, secret habits—practiced yet unknown to the Church's public. This holds true even in our own pansexualized culture and is particularly pertinent in an era of confusion where private conscience has properly been given a special role.

I do not know the kind of sex in which my neighbor engages. Nor does the sacrament of marriage drive me to seek to know. While relevant to individual consciences (and perhaps their confessional partners), these secrets are relevant to the Church's conscience in only the most variable, and usually muted, ways. Clearly, the Church has an interest in anything that might affect the spiritual condition of an individual soul—a sister or brother in Christ, a "little one"—before God. The question is how the Church chooses to approach the host of individual characteristics that pertain to such a condition, for example, envy, pride, anger, parsimony, and even sexual behavior.

The fact is, even at the Western penitential system's most florid moments, the Church, through its official public ministers, addressed particularities of individual holiness or unholiness in a wholly discretionary manner, balancing the realities of personal formation, social context, and public persona and vocation with a discernment of times and wills. In the process, private life was often left untouched in favor of the transformative power of the Church's corporate witness. Is this gap between corporate inflexibility and private discretion a problem? Hardly, precisely because the divine goal of the Church's sacramental mission is achieved through its public enunciation and cannot be measured through its individual appropriation at any given point in time.

The conviction governing an appeal for legislative moratoria on matters of sexual behavior outside of marriage, then—and it is probably a popular if unarticulated conviction within the Church at large—that sexual practice ought to be a private affair and diversity tolerated as long as it forbears publicly scandalizing marriage norms within the community, turns out to be a fairly accurate intuition of marriage's own sacramental character. The Church, of course, is deeply concerned with aspects of private life that tend to the abuse and destruction not only of mutual relations but of personal health. But within such constraints, the appeal's theological payoff is easily, if baldly, summarized: sexual activity is a relentlessly private affair, and heterosexual marriage an expansively public affair within the Church. Further, while God may well be graciously at work in the private realm of sexual practice, such grace is demonstrable publicly only in marriage.

The upholding of a public norm of marriage that acts as a potential cover for private deviation has little to do, in the end, with any impulse toward hypocrisy on the sexual front. Rather, it presses toward a communal understanding of Church membership that can both protect individual practice and conscience while maintaining a divinely directed corporate vision. This is particularly relevant precisely during a period of public (and divisive) contention among individuals and leaders within the church. To say that the very character of the marriage sacrament, which figures the image of Christ Jesus, can even help us to live with a tension between public speech and private behavior peculiar to this era, is only to say that God has graciously given us a means to live through times that try the faith, while avoiding the compromises of hypocrisy. The marriage sacrament, expansively embraced and discreetly explored, is an instrument of profound hope, because it represents the form of Christ.

There *is* a theological coherence to the discipline of forbearance at this time, then, and it lies in a recovered understanding of the marriage sacrament's character. Its usefulness as a moderating platform for a divided church can be stated in the following three summary implications, whose acceptance, I believe, can form the contingent basis for the kind of discussion on the topic of sexuality that must take place over the next few decades if the Church is to be readied to formulate consensually—and faithfully—deliberated doctrine on the matter.

First, the sacramentality of Christian marriage, defined here in an exclusively public and social aspect, implies that human personhood cannot be construed primarily in terms of sexual desire (as distinct from relational behavior). Basically, it does not matter to the Church what one feels or how one senses erotic energies. A human person is embodied as a female or a male simply and quite apart from expressive sexuality; and the Church's catholic society is signified (figurated) by the fellowship of male and female, irrespective of desire. Clearly, sexual desire is important to individuals and their mutual sexual relationships; such desires are, further, matters of concern, even moral concern, to individuals in their relationships with God. But they are matters of concern in a nonsystematic fashion that is linked variously to their location within individual ascetic vocations. We are not persons on the basis of either our heterosexual or our homosexual urges, and the Church's public teaching is under no theological obligation to acknowledge the public expression of erotic desire as a divine right. The sacrament of male-female marriage—defined by an indissolubility that is efficacious for the Church over and beyond individual desire—sees to it that sexuality, in the limited sense of object-oriented desire, is irrelevant to Christian personhood.

Second, the realm of actual sexual practice, within the cover of the Church's sacrament, is understood as decidedly private and open to Church exploration only in a limited and discretionary fashion. Even historically, while cultures like that of ancient Rome and early medieval Europe subjected the first intercourse of a newly married couple to public scrutiny, the whole life of sexual practice has, nonetheless, been deliberately shrouded from the popular eye. The modern affirmation of homosexuality as a condition of personhood is really a subtheme of a larger narrative that brought all sexual practice into the public square. If the Church chooses to follow this lead, we will ourselves threaten the structures of secrecy demanded by the sacramentality of marriage, whose public figure is designed to shelter individual idiosyncrasies (of virtue and sin) under its molding and proclamative force. When all sexual desire and practice take on the relief of public display, the formative Christian culture to which the effective sacrament contributed is consequently weakened. With no behavior left private, conduct in general ceases to bear surprising, let alone scandalizing, potential—which is merely another way of saying that the community has lost a compelling identity of a kind.

Third, the sacramentality of Christian marriage, and the private and secret realm into which it assigns actual sexual practice, insists thereby that the Christian Church be characterized and enlivened in its public mutual relations by values of an order other than sexual conduct altogether. This should be a warning to both conservative sex-brigades within the Church and revisionist ideologues who think the marriage norm irrelevant to social justice. The surprising equanimity with which the early Church (Augustine included) greeted the reality of sexual practice and deviance among its members—that is, when contained by a privacy that did not burst into public scandal—is explained by the much higher premium placed by early Christians upon nonsexual virtues like friendship, mutual care, and service. We are all well aware that virtues like these have been formatively eclipsed of late within our church, and it is important that revisionists and traditionalists alike rediscover their centrality in a way that is not erotically dependent.

The indicative figure that the sacrament of marriage represented for early Christians—the catholic Church of many nations unified as one body in Christ Jesus—called on forms of human interrelationship that consciously transcended the sexual sphere altogether. In our age, the Church wearies itself futilely in trying to figure such attitudes for any sexual orientation. The defining penumbra of desire looms as too dark a shadow for such habits to be seen clearly, and the Christian collective fragments itself along libidinous lines. From this regard, celibacy, un-encumbered by such pulls, stands not so much as an option for sexual expression, but as the only truly divine sexual vocation alternative to heterosexual marriage, designed to serve the Church in its search for clarity within the thickets of its desires. Celibacy for the kingdom is in service of the same reality the sacrament of marriage figures, a pointer perhaps to what ought to be our Church's future constructive consensus on matters of sexuality.

# 9

# Apologetics
# and
# Unity

*Confessing the One Lord*

I have been arguing that common discipline, in ecclesial order or sexual expression, is hardly a peripheral matter to the Church's integrity. Such commonality in order is tied to the heart of the gospel's own articulation in the world. Creed and canon are intertwined, in and through the very body of our Lord. But where is the body itself? How shall we describe it? It would be an odd claim to assert, in arguing for such interconnection in our era, that the right response to unity lay simply in buckling down to uniformity. Unity itself masks the terms of the discussion. Creedal claims, even joined to some canonical focus, splinter and slither away in the ears of bystanders. Why does our confession of "One Lord, Jesus Christ," given in the Apostles' Creed itself, the first baptismal proclamation, seem to so many today, both outside and even in the Church, so incoherent? Incoherent not because this person or that person, this group or that group, this church or that church, does not know what they mean by the confession, but incoherent because they all mean so many different things. It is an irony, felt by many with acute pain, that when we say with the creed, "We believe in one Lord"—in the sense of Ephesians 4's "one body, one Lord, one faith"—we necessarily contradict ourselves right from the start. Christians of all kinds are eager enough to evangelize, and do so with admirable enthusiasms; new churches proliferate around the globe. But where is the body?

It is picked apart. Picked apart by the ecclesial incisors of group identity; picked apart by scholars whose scriptural reflections themselves are fashioned with the scalpels of clarifying dissection. In this chapter I will take a side glance at the historical-critical study of Jesus, which stands as one of the great, almost unconscious, and ultimately voracious alternatives to perceiving the providential scope of the Church's scriptural unveiling we have been looking at. It also constitutes a minor obbligato to the melody of missionary chaos in the contemporary world. I will argue here that historical-critical study of the Bible has been fueled, since its inception in the seventeenth century, in large part by a desire to resolve the incoherence of disunity that is rooted at the center of modern Western Christianity. The contemporary marshalling of historical facts about Jesus—whether by the orthodox or by the unorthodox—represents, I believe, a consistent form of response to an ecclesially untenable diversity of Christian commitments and practices. But because it is a response, the search after the historical grounds for the Christian confession of Jesus as Lord is neither an original cause nor a viable solution to the incoherence itself, which is far more profound than a simple variety of opinions held by otherwise amicably related Christian believers.

The practical issue here is enormously important, because it encompasses the possibility of evangelization and conversion itself. The market has worked hard to keep the word at bay from living within our midst and from spurring our speech into realms of persuasive vigor. Disintegration of witness in word and deed represents the effective dampening of the world's belief, even while it has instigated the myriad practices of ecclesial denotation that so mark today's calculating Christian communities, trussed up in methods of church growth, cultural manipulation, and consumer ethics. As an alternative, as the only alternative in fact, the struggle for Christian unity represents the vehicle for light and the vessel by which Christ "draw[s] all men to [him]self" (John 12:32). It is a struggle that itself ought to shape the form and content of apologetic discourse and the postures of moral witness. It is, furthermore, the way that God has given us time to be turned into history. It was on the basis of this providential truth about mission, grounded in Scripture, that Charles Henry Brent inaugurated the modern ecumenical project with his opening address to the 1927 Lausanne World Faith and Order Conference, citing John 17:20–23: "The call to unity is primarily from God to man. It is for our good that the appeal is made. Through unity alone can the Kingdom of God be set up among men. Through unity alone can the world believe and know that the Father has sent Jesus Christ to reveal Him to the whole human race. It stands as the unalterable condition on which He can fulfil His mission to mankind. This no one doubts who accepts Jesus Christ as Lord and Savior."[1]

Unity of witness in God's time, rather than the rational evidence of critically analyzed history, is what Brent proposes for the evangelization of the world. Yet the proposal stands in sharp contrast to the wearied labors of the last few centuries that seem to have assumed that, if we could at least prove Jesus' concrete existence, for lack of ecclesial integrity, then some kind of personal recognition and allegiance might be forthcoming. The assumption has proved vain indeed.

In what follows, then, I shall give a broad explanation of why the attempt to ground belief in Jesus as Lord on the basis of Jesus' historical factuality arose only in seventeenth century and not before; and in particular I shall try to contrast positively some of the theological and ecclesial realities that made possible the early Church's noncritical commendation of the faith in Jesus, Messiah, and Lord with our own critical, but intrinsically inadequate, attempts to do so today. As a conclusion, I will suggest that our confession in Jesus Christ as our one Lord, however we consider it in orthodox or traditional terms, must be tied to some demanding and probably painful ecclesial practices that will overstep the narrowly theological and certainly the narrowly political avenues of vocation to which we have consigned confessional belief in our day.

Let me start with an observation about a well-known contemporary and historical-critically literate commentator on Jesus, Bishop John Spong of Newark, whose interests actually coincide with many other revisionist scriptural scholars like Marcus Borg. The observation is this: Spong's revisionist efforts at reading the Bible and at describing the reality and meaning of Jesus spring from a deep desire to *commend* Scripture and belief in Jesus as Christ to contemporary people. All his talk of the Gospels as midrash and his theories about the disciples' projections of their weaknesses and insecurities upon the scriptural record and so on—which many find offensive or compelling or simply silly—are attempts by Spong,

---

1. *Faith and Order: Proceedings of the World Conference, Lausanne, August 3–21, 1927* (ed. H. N. Bate; New York: Doran, 1927), 3–4.

as he himself claims, to commend Christianity to a critical, scientifically ordered, pluralistic audience. It is crucially important to note, then, that Spong is an *apologist* of sorts for the Christian faith. Indeed, most practitioners of the historical-critical study of the Scriptures, since the seventeenth century, have used their studies apologetically as a primary means of commending a vision of Christian truth—they have been believing Christians, however idiosyncratic, or if not quite Christian, they have been apologists for a kind of religiosity that might at least embrace Christianity. And this is crucial to bear in mind, if we are to take accurate stock of the means at our disposal to gain clarity about our confession of Jesus as Lord. Historical-critical examination of the person of Jesus has almost always been offered as an effective tool to come to know this Lord and to persuade others of his reality and significance.

The fact is, however, that it really did not occur to Christians to ground their faith on the critical study of history for almost 1,600 years. This is not to say that Jesus' historical reality was not significant until the post-Reformation. Only that for 1,600 years the establishment of that historical reality was not deemed a significant ground for believing in this man as Lord. This fact, furthermore, should strike us as odd, for it goes so against our instinctive grain. Today we have philosophers arguing over whether our beliefs need to be founded on a certain epistemology; we have arguments over the Jesus of faith and the Jesus of history; we have debates over the place of factuality in the proper interpretation of the Gospels as literary genres; and so on. Is it not odd that we should wait so long for these discussions? Is it simply the case that prior to around 1600 all Christians were credulous or superstitious or, more fashionably, precritical (which sounds suspiciously like *un*critical)?

Let us briefly examine, therefore, the early apologies for Christianity offered in the first centuries of the Church. It is not the case that *non*-Christians simply did not care about the issue of historical fact and did not need to be answered on that basis. One has only to read Origen's reply to the pagan philosopher Celsus, his so-called *Contra Celsum* (Against Celsus)—to realize that Celsus's now-lost work, written toward the end of the second century, was filled with exactly the kinds of critical questions that continue to pop up in books similar to Spong's: the gospel accounts are not credible as historical evidence, but represent projections and fabrications by the first Christian community; we can read back through their patina of retrospective justification to discover the real Jesus, who was the bastard son of a country slut, with a politically unsettling itinerant movement of socially marginal followers, moored to a sectarian Judaism. It appears, from Origen's discussion, that Celsus raised just these points, and thus that people *did* ask these sorts of questions and give these sorts of answers long before Galileo and Newton. No, the historical questions of modernity are not themselves novel to the period.

Furthermore Origen, fifty years after Celsus, attempted to mount a kind of scattershot response to these kinds of questions. But while he does offer a few critical answers to Celsus's interpretations, what is striking is the way that these rarely coalesce into an integral historical defense for the Church's picture of Jesus. Instead, they keep pointing away, through a certain general skepticism about historical research altogether, to other apologetic concerns. Near the beginning of his long work *Contra Celsum,* Origen states outright that "the endeavour to show, with regard to almost any history, however true, that it actually occurred, and to produce an intelligent conception regarding it, is one of the most difficult undertakings that can be attempted, and is in some instances an impossibility."[2] Origen, we should stress as well, was one of the very few Christians who even bothered to acknowledge queries like Celsus's on their own ground.

For on the whole, early Christians—Origen included—were amazingly insouciant to the historical doubts or concerns about Jesus that critical study might resolve. This is what is surprising. And this insouciance, it appears, was due in large part to their seeing another approach as far more persuasive and, in the end, coherent with the truth they were attempting to commend to an unbelieving world. A survey of the extant apologetic works of the early Church supports the following gross generalization: Christian thinkers defended their faith in Jesus as their Lord on two grounds: the consistent moral conversion and moral superiority of Christians compared with non-Christians, and the compelling witness of the Old Testament prophecies to the general history of which these Christians saw themselves as part. Particularly odd is that, in many early apologies like those of Athenagoras, Aristides, or Theophilus, Jesus as a historical person is actually not mentioned *at all.*

First let us look at the issue of Christian morals. It is perhaps logical that the apologists should have stressed Christian moral integrity since, in many cases, their defenses of Christianity were written in response to

2. Origen, *Contra Celsum* 1.42 (trans. F. Crombie; Ante-Nicene Fathers 4; repr. Peabody, Mass.: Hendrickson, 1994), 414.

persecution and to the specific charges of social corruption made against Christian manners. But this turns out to be only an occasional cause for the emphasis on morals. More crucial to the moral emphasis was the common sense of early Christian apologists that a certain realm of life was involved in the Christian gospel that needed both to be acknowledged and entered into as a condition for apprehending truths that pertain to God—and by extension to God's Son, the word himself. This was the realm, in scriptural terms, of *holiness*, and it embraced the goal of the Christian life as well as provided the terms by which the origins and explicators of that life could be grasped. To know God one must be, in some measure, like God; to live with God, one must reflect God's own nature, as the apologist Theophilus (among others) stressed so clearly at the start of his work *To Autolycus*.

We are familiar with much of the early church's doctrine of salvation being distinctly oriented to the issue of moral conversion. And most moderns know that the more elaborate theologies of the incarnation that are given early (e.g., by Clement of Alexandria) and later (e.g., by Athanasius) stress the way in which the coming of the Word in the flesh of Jesus took place precisely in order to transform human beings into vessels of righteousness and holiness, whose image conforms to that of God himself. In their apologetic mode, Christians simply took this central understanding of salvation and turned it to the purposes of persuasive argument. "The pious Christian alone is rich and wise, and of noble birth, and thus we call and believe him to be God's image, and also His likeness, having become righteous and holy and wise by Jesus Christ, and so far already like God," writes Clement in his *Exhortation to the Heathen*.[3] The critical test for the argument lay in the manner in which Christians actually exhibited the holiness that they claimed was gained for them by God's Word come in Jesus.

Here is where the apologists aimed their heaviest artillery: Christians, they asserted, are demonstrably better, holier, more righteous, and more loving people than non-Christians. It is an argument that few historically informed twentieth-century persons would today wish to make with much conviction, perhaps. (Although it is still negatively affirmed by those, for instance, who view the decline of American economics and moral culture as a result of its slide into dechristianization.) The argument from Christian holiness, in any case, is certainly pressed with an

---

3. Clement of Alexandria, *Exhortation to the Heathen* 12 (trans. William Wilson; Ante-Nicene Fathers 2; repr. Peabody, Mass.: Hendrickson, 1994), 206.

astonishing consistency, vigor, and prominence by the early expositors of the faith, from Justin to Tertullian and beyond. Look at us, they insist: to understand our religion, observe our sexual abstinence or marital fidelity, note our generosity to strangers, mark our treatment of those who persecute us, attend to our use of money or the way we treat women and slaves or deal with issues of violence and injustice, poverty, and want.

To our post-Reformation sensibilities, this might all seem inappropriately moralistic. But even Augustine, the anti-Pelagian virtuoso, adopted the same line as his predecessors when speaking of the window through which the world can see the illumining clarity of Christ Jesus. Indeed, it is the historical connection they draw between enacted holiness and Christ that is fundamental to distinguishing the early Christian apologists from insistent moralizers. I underline the word *historical* because history and the Jesus of history were crucial to their persuasive presentation of the Christian faith, but in a way that, for very particular reasons, was not available to the enterprise of historically *critical* reflection. This brings us to the second common feature of early Christian arguments for the lordship of Jesus Christ, that is, the fulfillment of scriptural prophecy.

When Justin or Tertullian or Origen called upon pagans to look at the witness of Christian holiness, they took pains to derive that witness from the actual teachings of Jesus, culled from the Gospels. If Christians welcomed the stranger, it was because their master had taught that one is "to give to whoever asks"; if they were obedient and peaceful, it was because the teacher whom they followed had spoken of turning the other cheek, of loving enemies, of being servants and not masters; if they accepted death rather than deny their master, it was because he had showed them the life of the spirit, of the resurrection, and of the heavenly treasure that the cross could attain.

These teachings of Jesus were often mentioned *without* reference to the details of Jesus' own life. But they were described as much more than philosophical principles for virtue, for their force was commended in terms of the *coherence* between actual teachings by an actual person and the actual lives of his followers. The issue was historical consistency. This was further underlined by the apologists when they attempted to link these teachings of Christ and their fulfillment in the lives of his followers with the lives and teachings of the scriptural prophets who lived long before Jesus and his Church.

The way that these early defenders of the Christian faith relied upon rehearsals of the Old Testament prophets as they addressed *non*-Jews must mystify us. Why would anyone who did not read, let alone believe, the Jewish Scriptures care about what Moses or Isaiah said? And why would anyone be convinced by Christian claims that certain elements of these prophecies were historically fulfilled in Jesus? This kind of modern question is pertinent, because when, in the seventeenth century, the orthodox defense of the lordship and divinity of Christ Jesus took up with a vengeance the argument from the fulfillment of prophecy, the argument increasingly crumbled in the face of historical criticism, to the point that it is rarely heard today even in quite conservative circles and is openly dismissed by most revisionist critics like Bishop Spong.

For the early Christians, however, the compelling character of fulfilled prophecies lay not in the way that discrete predictions came to pass. Rather, prophecies were taken as a whole, often without order, to demonstrate the way a whole range of historical realities hung together: the prophets claimed that God's holiness had a certain form, that their own lives reflected this form, that Jesus' teachings were consistent with this, and that the Christian Church, in contrast with pagans and Jews, was in historical conformance with all of this. The early Christian stress upon the fulfillment of prophecy lay in its demonstration of what we can call the historical coherence of the practiced faith of the Christian religion. This demonstration, finally, found full flowering in the great works of historical synthesis by Eusebius, Augustine, and Orosius, who attempted to discern in the events of time, especially in the Roman world, a broad *amelioration* of corporate sanctity, even in the midst of social disorder (and despite the sorry spectacle of fourth-century Christian divisions). The world and historical experience itself *fits*, they insisted, with what Christians believe and with the writings they engage at the center of their common life.

Two things are to be noted here. The first is the shape of the argument itself: if Isaiah's prediction of a messiah or king whose rule is given in overwhelming justice is indeed fulfilled, this is so because its confirmation is given in the contemporaneously demonstrable life of the Christian community. The second thing to be noted is that this demonstration is the ground for apprehending the content or the significance of the asserted religious truths themselves: who God is, and how the prophets actually relate to God's power and Spirit, and who the man Jesus is and why he is called Christ and is our Lord—all this is exposed, not in the confirmation given by the Church's life, but in taking on that life, in entering it—that is, in Theophilus's or Clement's terms, in entering the realm wherein the purification of the heart through the instruction of Scriptures, the guiding form of Jesus, and the grace of God's governing Spirit opens one's eyes to the glory of his nature and presence.

The early Church's approach to historical reality, then, can be described in this way: the *fact* of the Church's sanctity, explicated by the Scriptures that point to or describe Christ Jesus, demonstrates the ordering providence of God. And it was a faith in that ordering providence that founded the compelling reliability of the scriptural history. Church, Scripture, history—they were at one with each other; they existed in a *unity*. So if the details of the historical Jesus' life were rarely examined by the apologists, it is because their very existence could not be noted apart from this assumption of the providential ordering of the world by God. They belonged to that ordering. The critical testing of historical detail was simply *unnecessary* once such details were understood as forming a part of *God's* providential ordering of history and Scripture as a unit; God, after all, took care of and had already taken care of the details.

What *could* be noted was the way the Church itself, in its historical coherence with the affirmations of prophecy, made such an ordering plausible, even compelling. As Origen wrote, "It is because Christ was the power of God and the wisdom of the Father that He accomplished, and still accomplishes, such results," converting "not only the wise" but "the most irrational of men, and those devoted to their passions," such that none have "withstood the progress of his doctrine—kings and rulers, and the Roman senate, and governors in all places, and the common people."[4]

It is possible, in contrast, to move directly to the modern era. It is a big jump, but one can skip the intervening millennium in large measure because the apologetic outlook of the early Church remained stable during this time, though much constricted. We can note, however, that in moments of revival, evangelistic preaching—among, for instance, the Canons Regular of the twelfth century and the Franciscans and Dominicans of the thirteenth century, even the Wycliffites of the fourteenth century—remained tied to the primordial theme of historical coherence, wherein Christ Jesus was to be discovered in the assumption of an existence (in his entry into the world) of a corporate body temporally conformed to the holiness of God described in the Scriptures. Scoffers there no doubt were. But the history of Jesus was never called into question, never became a matter of concern, because the premise of a unitary

4. Origen, *Contra Celsum* 2.79 (trans. Crombie), 464.

coherence between Church, history, and Scripture—within which Jesus' life and form assumed a providential force—was still plausible.

A radical change of perspective, however, did indeed take place somewhere in the sixteenth century. And by the early seventeenth century, already, the significance of the Christian faith began to be explicated in a new fashion. The difference between the seventeenth century and this long stretch of time before it lay in the novel realization that the historical coherence between Scripture and Church, which formed the access to an apprehension of Jesus Christ, had become fractured. Whatever the troubles of the Church in the past, the sixteenth-century division of the Western Church, with its resultant religious hostilities and outright warfare—lasting well into the seventeenth century—proved an absolutely devastating contradiction to the prevailing apologetic reliance on the fact of communal holiness wrought within the sphere of God's historical providence. The permanent disintegration of the Christian community into antagonistic and competing groups wholly subverted the mutual relation of both sides of the affirmation—scriptural providence and ecclesial virtue together.

This is a well-worn observation, and it is reasserted in our own day by prominent intellectual historians like Richard Popkin and Stephen Toulmin. But the practical theological consequences of the sixteenth-century Church's loss of scriptural and historical credibility, with which we continue to live, have, I think, been underestimated. Protestant apologists adjusted to the new situation by cutting loose scriptural authority from ecclesial virtue altogether, while Catholics tidied up the integrity of providence by simply excising Protestants from the realm of church itself. The ripples of these adjustments magnified over the centuries and determined much of our present ways of tackling theological matters. Most importantly for the present topic, what was lost in the process was the conviction that the historical experience of the Christian community, because of its conformity to the scriptural narrative and claims, provided the window of access to a clear knowledge of Christ Jesus. The devotional legacy of this evolution still haunts us, with its radical individualism and loss of communal humility.

The apologetic legacy was even more disruptive. For with the deep skepticism set loose about the historical coherence of Scripture and Church, other avenues were sought after that might demonstrate the attainability of virtue and the kind of sanctified amelioration of existence that the early Church had used as its demonstrable access to the person of Jesus. Indeed, by the seventeenth century, history itself—with its newly recognized embedded divisions and conflicts, intractable even to the Christian Church—history itself needed to be bypassed altogether, if salvation could be properly described and thereby sought after. The rise of historical criticism, in the realm of scriptural study anyway, represents, ironically perhaps, just such an attempt to bypass the historical experience of the Church in its relation to scriptural prophecy, in an effort to get back at the origins—the origins of Jesus, the origins of his teaching, the origins of his intentions. If Jesus could be described in a way that was independent of the ecclesial contradictions that had asserted themselves in the sixteenth and seventeenth centuries, independent of what Catholics or Calvinists or Anglicans or Quakers or Baptists said, then perhaps the still vaguely apprehended salvation he promised might yet be salvaged.

That this salvation now came to be almost exclusively defined in moral terms by the self-consciously modern apologists is not surprising, for it was this moral aspect that ecclesial experience contradicted, and it was this aspect that seemed so patently demanded by the times, in the face of religious quarrels that had subordinated its importance. Already in the mid-sixteenth century, Christian proponents of religious tolerance like Sebastian Castellio were finding themselves drawn to a rationalistic approach for the reading of Scripture that tried to strip it of any historically providential power it might once have been thought to have had, in favor of its distilled moral teachings. By the mid-seventeenth century, lapsed Jewish philosopher Baruch Spinoza detailed what can stand as a kind of primitive manifesto for the historical-critical study of the Bible in his *Tractatus theologico-politicus* (Theological-political treatise). Here he called for the writing of a "history of the Scripture," in the same way one might study nature, that would identify all the historically contingent and conditioned elements of the biblical texts—their time and place and context of origin, their authorial idiosyncrasies and projections, their ethnic and socially specific perversions, and so on—and then relegate all these elements from positions of normative religious authority. Having done this, Spinoza contended, one would be able to affirm the basic and consistent moral principles that ran through the Bible as a whole, Jesus included, principles that all people could reasonably accept and follow. This historical approach to the Bible, Spinoza insisted, was absolutely necessary if people were to be freed from the violence brought on by those who, under the "mask of godly zeal" in using the Scriptures to advance their own interests, pressed for "discord and implacable hatred" in attempting to "compel all others to be of their own opinion."[5]

Only a few decades later, English philosopher John Locke, from a more explicitly Christian vantage point, attempted to do the same thing, searching for a universal access to moral life in the Scriptures that might somehow bypass the real antagonisms and particularities of the now-warring factions of disintegrated Christianity, particularly obvious in seventeenth-century England. While Locke was not a historian, he felt that an apprehension of the real Jesus of the Scriptures, discerned on his own independent terms, would yield a doctrine wholly conformable to universal human reason and hence immune to the sectarian strife to which so much of his own writings are responses. Many of Locke's followers soon realized that this real Jesus of a universal morality of reason was not quite the same as the Jesus of traditional Christianity, and with sharpening critical tools, they went about the job of constructing a nonsectarian religion of virtue that could be culled from the Bible, even while the religious particularities of Scripture were rendered obsolete or time-limited—and therefore discardable—by their efforts at historical analysis.

With an oddly constricted perspicacity, eighteenth-century critical historians like Edward Gibbon were able to grasp the apologetic force of early Christian holiness,[6] but they were also incapable of seeing how such holiness was tied, at least in the Christian outlook, to firm providential and scriptural moorings. (Gibbon, for instance, roundly denigrated early Christian apologists precisely for their reliance on scriptural prophecy, a method he deemed useless.) It was this truncated eighteenth-century vision of Christian origins that led directly to Nietzsche's contempt for Christianity's supposed "moralizing weakness"; indeed, it still informs, if in a less hostile fashion, much contemporary sociological analysis of Christian origins.

One way to characterize the whole historical-critical enterprise as it relates to the Bible in the modern era and continues in our own day is to see it as the embodiment of the motive behind a popular bumper sticker that reads, "Jesus, save us from your followers." And who cannot fail to have at least some sympathy with such a hope? Alas, the hope itself is illogical, and its pursuit destructive of its own religious object. For without

---

5. Baruch Spinoza, *A Theological-Political Treatise* (trans. R. H. M. Elwes; New York: Dover, 1951), chap. 7.

6. See especially Gibbon's discussion in *The History of the Decline and Fall of the Roman Empire*, chap. 15.

his followers, it makes no sense to speak of a Jesus who saves. Christ Jesus may remain faithful while we are faithless, as Scripture claims (2 Tim. 2:13); but in that case Christ Jesus also remains unknown. Stripped of a Church whose life in history conforms to the object of its worship, this Jesus becomes wrapped in obscurities and hidden by arbitrary claims of the moment.

It took some decades of struggle within the divided Church before religious tolerance and denominational pluralism became recognized by Locke and others as the logical outcome to nascent historical criticism's universal morality. And who is not, again, at least a little grateful for the social benefits of that recognition? But even before this process became apparent, John Donne was able to note, if ruefully, the apologetic harvest necessarily reaped by entrenched, accepted, and socially protected Christian division. Himself the product of a family and personal life torn by the Catholic-Protestant rift, Donne wrote in his *Essays in Divinity* that once the Church is "reduced to such Unity and agreement," then "discharged of disputations, and misapprehensions, and this defensive warr, [she] might contemplate Christ clearly and uniformely. For now he appears to her, as in *Cant.* 2.9, *He standeth behind a wall, looking forth of the window, shewing himself through the grate.* But then, when all had one appetite, and one food, one nostrill and one purfume, the Church had obtained that which she then asked . . . [to be] a *savour of life unto life* [that] might allure and draw those to us, whom our dissentions, more than their own stubborness with-hold from us."[7]

This Christ Jesus, whom we confess to believe in as Lord, yet now quarrel over, recriminate over, divide communion over, is but glimpsed in part, says Donne, as through a distant window grating. It is interesting that Donne makes this remark in the midst of a discussion on the diversity of the scriptural witness, its variations, seeming contradictions, messiness of reference—all elements of what would later become the grist for historical criticism and its orthodox opponents (like the indefatigable Nathaniel Lardner, who in the eighteenth century produced fourteen volumes attempting to iron out the supposed historical discrepancies within the Gospels). But such labors proved fruitless. We cannot see this Jesus clearly within this text, and the Scriptures strain to give us access to his form, Donne implies, because the Church itself does not embody the Scripture's providential unity coherently in its own life.

7. John Donne, *Essays in Divinity* (ed. Evelyn M. Simpson; Oxford: Clarendon, 1952), 52.

The problem facing the divided Christian churches of our modern era, a problem that both orthodox and less orthodox critical historians cannot hope to resolve, seems to be this: as long as Jesus cannot be affirmed coherently to be the Lord of our history as a Church, he inevitably, no matter what we claim doctrinally or devotionally on our respective ecclesial turfs, is reduced to being an object, a mere object, contained by the unordered history of the past, glimpsed at through the literary fragments of a collection of documents we call the Bible. Historical criticism is a gross reflection of this impasse.

Can we simply go back, as John Keble hoped, to recover a patristic view of providence, of typology and Scripture, or of asceticism and thereby say of Jesus Christ "*Ecce homo*, behold the man"? Our emphasis upon early Christian apologetics is not designed to necessarily suggest this, nor is our calling to construct or reconstruct some picture of who Jesus is that will compel and convert or prove our own faithfulness in the face of the apostate. There are plenty of pictures from the last two thousand years that are more than adequate to the demands of God's truth. Still, we must face the sorry fact that we have built a wall around them, through the defenses we have erected around our own Christian communities, one from another, from which we have sallied forth only in hostile pride. The coherence that our history as a Christian community ought to provide such pictures—the witness to the lordship of Christ that holds together Scripture, time, and Christian faith—has been lost; and the commodified culture of the Christian market in America is perhaps the nadir of such privation.

By contrast, we can certainly assert the following: our confession that "we believe in one Lord, Jesus Christ," will be explicated and the Scriptures that fulfill that explication will be opened when we are willing to submit our churches to their historical and temporal reshaping into a unified posture of reception from God's ordering hand. That is the note on which this chapter might justly stand aside in favor of more constructive critical efforts: theological articulation must be yoked to the mission of ecclesial reconciliation if it is to have *any* apologetic force at all. Our confession of faith in the one Lord Jesus Christ is not simply a declaration of conviction; it is today a profound challenge to any single denomination and to the larger fractured Church of which we are a part. Our continued confession ought properly to be heard today, less as a proclamation than as a plea that cries out: let us stop the hemorrhaging that our quarrels, our moral dissipation, our self-righteousness, our greed and pride have continued to foster and that we threaten to display to the world anew with each succeeding step we take. Instead, let us do the work of rebuilding, from the ground up once again, a temple indwelt by the Holy Spirit.

This is not a challenge simply to ratchet up ecumenical dialogues or to "just get along" as some church leaders impatiently urge. It is a challenge to recognize and respond to the enforced incapacity of ecclesial witness in our day. The goal, however, and as we all sense, is elusive. As institutional churches, as formal Christian communities, we now stand in the same condition as that of the first Christians after the resurrection. We have no articulated theology, we have no proven structures of authority, no experienced framework for the reading of Scripture that is common to us as a church. Is this an opportunity, in the optimists' parlance? Certainly it is. But we have been *reduced* to this opportunity, through the judgment of God's history, not raised to it. And we will not receive from this condition the grace and power of God in Christ Jesus given for life, if we do not first let go of the political and material structures of our institutions, which we continue to use for our self-justification, and then rather hold all things in common, as in that young Jerusalem of Christ, and pray together and search the Scriptures anew, in the humble posture of the chastised many, not of the holy few.

Each week in every congregation, each month in some church meeting of one kind or another, in one diocese or denomination or another, there will be a point when all the gathered will proclaim, "We believe in one Lord, Jesus Christ." At which point the Lord himself, master of mercy and forgiver of sins, as in the past, will offer us yet another chance.

# 10

## Bad Bishops

The demise of denominational integrity has focused our attention on many things. One of them is on Christian leadership and, in the ecumenical sphere, on bishops themselves (or the unspecified "overseers" [episcopoi] that the Lima Agreement proposed as being universally necessary for the ministry of all churches and denominations). We have seen, for all kinds of reasons, their images reproduced in magazines, their words quoted in newspapers, and their arguments, statements, resolutions, and objections ingested into the ongoing debate of the larger Church's public life. In the process of this revived public exposure, theologically heightened by ecumenical discussions among mainline denominations over the forms of unifying oversight, the character of bishops, broadly understood, has come in for renewed examination and, given various forms of public scandal, more often renewed disdain. Why allow our church's public life to be led by the nose at the hands of incompetent and often wayward leaders invested with impossibly fulfilled potencies? Organized religion comes in for plenty of criticism, and the turpitude—doctrinal, moral, and intellectual—of so many prelates, episcopal or otherwise, seems to be a crowning source of denigration.

In particular, the struggle within the American Episcopal Church over the doctrine and discipline touching upon sexuality has focused special attention on the integrity and meaning of episcopal oversight and authority, which, in a certain respect, has contributed to the already fallen status of bishops in the public's eye. Clergy conferences among Episcopalians in this country, for instance, find it necessary at times to openly express their desire to refrain from malicious speech, particularly as it refers to local bishops. This commitment, of course, flies in the face of a long tradition of contemptuous speech aimed at bishops, who make up a large section of any index on folkloric ridicule. Clergy especially are familiar with gently complaining stories like the apocryphal story of an Anglican and a Presbyterian arguing over whether the episcopacy is established in the Bible. The Anglican finally says, "I can prove from the very words of Scripture that Saint Paul himself was under the authority of a bishop." "How so?" wonders the astonished Presbyterian. "Observe 2 Corinthians 12:7," the Anglican replies, "where Saint Paul writes, 'To keep me from being too elated . . . , a thorn was given me in the flesh.' If that's not a proof that Paul had a bishop, I don't know what is!"

It is worth noting, however, that even superficial tales like this show a positive character in the bishop's burdensome person, one that is informed by its link with a scriptural insight about grace and about God's providentially gracious use of bishops in their painful mode. And this positive character, vestigial to the weary scorn felt toward the episcopacy, is perhaps a clue to something more profound governing episcopal-type ecclesiologies, like Anglicanism. In what follows, in any case, I will attempt to use the figure of the "bad bishop" as a key to understanding—at least partially—the essence of the episcopacy within the church. The purpose of this attempt is not to give credence to the assumption that there are not plenty of good bishops around. Without a doubt, there are. Furthermore, the character of the good bishop is *also* critical—and primarily so—to the essence of the episcopacy. And we should labor for good bishops, without ever becoming comfortable with the bad. But bad bishops can, nonetheless, help us get clearer about all this.

That we should talk about essence at all, with respect to bishops in the Episcopal Church, is, of course, inevitable. The Chicago-Lambeth Quadrilateral, for instance, lists the "historic episcopate, locally adapted" as one of the "inherent parts of this sacred deposit" of the "Christian Faith and Order committed by Christ and His Apostles to the Church unto the end of the world" and "essential" to the restored unity of the Church. This is part of Anglicanism's basic claim concerning bishops and one shared, in theory, with other ecclesial exemplars of traditionally ordered Catholicism. The late nineteenth-century Quadrilateral's affirmation of this essence has, in fact, given rise to what is—however little appreciated—a revolution in ecumenical discussion. The 1982 so-called Lima Statement of the Faith and Order Commission of the World Council of Churches entitled "Baptism, Eucharist, and Ministry" was extraordinarily significant in this regard, although its affirmations have had little practical impact on common Christian self-understanding. Among the agreed-upon assertions was this one: "Among these gifts [of the Spirit for the Church] a ministry of *episcopē* [i.e., oversight] is *necessary* to express and safeguard the unity of the body. Every church needs this ministry of unity in some form in order to be the Church of God, the one body of Christ, a sign of the unity of all in the Kingdom" (§23 [emphasis added]). While the Lima Statement does not make the historic episcopate an explicit element of the essence of the Church, it does recommend its explicit adoption and, indeed, could be interpreted as implicitly defining some local adaptation as part of that essence.

This revolution in ecumenical theory ought to alert us to something that, on first glance at the Quadrilateral, has always surprised people, namely, that episcopacy ought to be central to who we are as Christians. It surprises people, because its character seems so formal and institutional (bad things in the present culture) and therefore so antithetical to the spiritual bequest of Christ. In addition, as noted above, we do not really grant to bishops much public deference. But although we play down this institutional essence, probably simply in reaction to our present relativization of almost every evangelical essence apart from numerically quantifiable growth attached to the contentless name *Jesus*, our episcopally ordered churches are being driven, nonetheless, by their ecclesially centered focus on bishops in particular. If we had no bishops who taught or prayed or acted in ways that caused many Christians sorrow and anger, the issue of our churches' health and institutional future simply would not arise with the energy, anger, fear, and passion that so grips us today.

This chapter will address the question of the essence of the episcopacy, by offering conclusions to the following three areas of concern.

First, the question of the episcopacy's essence is in itself crucially at stake in current tensions within our own American Christian context: it is framed, usually unconsciously or only by implication, in often angry discussions about the episcopal ideal and its lack of embodiment among many working bishops in the church. Episcopal essence is usually identified in terms of this ideal, and the ideal itself takes the various forms of doctrinal integrity, and personal moral integrity: the wholesome example for the flock, courageous opposition to spiritual error and ethical disease, and so on. By focusing on the question of the bad bishop, I want us to ask if the essence of episcopacy—which we claim is itself essential to the Church—is to be measured by the fulfillment of such ideals. The conclusion I would give here is this: probably not.

Second, the question of how Episcopalians in particular, as a denomination, choose to understand and respond to bad bishops has, quite frankly, a larger ecumenical implication. Explicit Episcopalians are not the only episcopally ordered denominations around, nor the only such denomination to have bad bishops. But Anglicans—now joined by scandal-ridden Roman Catholics—are the only ones facing, with such force, the problematic challenge of bishops. (Of course, every denomination carries enormous burdens when it comes to the public image of its leaders.) And because Anglicans have staked their claim on the episcopacy as a denomination itself, this problem renders their witness to the larger Church crucial on this issue: either Episcopalians shall demonstrate the ancillary, as opposed to the essential, character of the episcopacy through their demolition of its constructive status, or they will lead the way for other Christians to better perceive their ecumenical opportunities within the larger purpose of God for the Church as they are tied to the episcopacy. In any case, the future and vocation of Anglicanism in the larger Church—and thus of the ecumenical promises made on the basis of *episcopē*—hangs, in part, on what we understand to be the evangelical location of bad bishops. Traditional Catholic ecclesial entities like episcopal synods and councils, let alone diocesan structures, have little to offer anyone, apart from a hopeful answer to this question.

Finally, either there is or there is not an evangelical basis to the essentiality of the episcopacy. In allowing the problem of bad bishops to address our churches in a central and basic way, we will perhaps be helped in getting to the core of the Christian gospel itself, that is, we shall perhaps learn something of Jesus himself as the Christ of God and as the center and animator of the Church as his body.

Let me begin with a historical observation: far more is written, within the ordering documents of the church, about bad bishops than about good bishops (although this tendency began to shift in the twentieth century).

There are of course notable works on the positive character of the episcopacy: we can recall, for instance, Gregory the Great's *Pastoral Rule*, which is tied to a number of earlier works on basic elements of Christian leadership associated with the priesthood by Ambrose, Gregory of Nazianzus, or Chrysostom. These works have even achieved some classic status. Much hagiographic literature, furthermore, has been written about Christians who *happen* to be bishops—these tend to stress miracles and asceticism, and their stories are often interchangeable with those of other saints. None of these stories, however, have achieved any normative status for the Church—an interesting fact about holiness as a (non)determining element in Western ecclesiology that merits further exploration. But beyond Gregory the Great, in any case, little *ordering* literature about bishops exists, that is, ordering in terms of defining the nature, character, meaning, duties, and calling of bishops. Rather, what have from the beginning driven the definition of the episcopacy in our tradition are the canonical documents—the church laws—and these, significantly, speak at great length to the *problems* challenging the church as it faces the reality of bad bishops.

The canons of the early church—ecumenical, conciliar, so-called apostolic, and so on—say, to put it bluntly, far more about what to do with bishops who are drunkards, sexually fallen, financially corrupt, doctrinally incompetent, ethically unjust, jurisdictionally wicked, and so on, than about how to call, discern, and train good bishops or about how good bishops should conduct their ministries.

As I noted above, this has changed in the twentieth century. The change is evident not only in the plethora of writings about the ministry for ministers—part of the self-help outlines in career management that have Dale Carnegie as much as the Holy Spirit behind them—but it is a shift also apparent in the purely canonical documents of the contemporary church. The constitutions and canons of the contemporary Episcopal Church, for instance, stand in stark contrast to the early Church's in the relatively abbreviated weight now given over to bad bishops. We might think this a gain, a redressing of the balance of concern. But is it? In any case, it is a significant shift. Why, for so long, did bad bishops loom so large?

On a basic level, the issue is one of power: bishops had it back then, they do not now. Nowadays, in fact, we can afford to ignore bishops in many ways, because of broad changes in social relations within modern, democratic nations. The question before us, however, is not the status of bishops in general, but of bad bishops in particular. Why care so much about the bad ones that the good ones seem to be allowed to take care of

themselves, canonically anyway? We can explore two reasons: first, the figural importance of the episcopal institution itself, in terms of its perceived
embodiment of Jesus' form within the temporal life of the church, was
significant in the past in ways it no longer is; second, in the past this figure
implicitly lifted up institutional *unity* in particular as the mechanism by
which the christic form is maintained. It is no novelty to say that, in the
Catholic view of episcopacy, certain institutional aspects have evangelical significance. This is well known; but it is also shied away from in our
voluntaristically oriented modern view of religion, where institutions are
suspect as purely human and unspiritual (and hence usually oppressive)
entities. What is important to stress is how the early Church located the
evangelical significance of its institutions precisely in the realistic assessment of the humanly fallible as the necessary context for the Spirit's
deployment. The struggle for the *unity* of the institution in particular
within conflict and fallibility, a struggle that was focused upon the office
of the bishop explicitly—both as its cause and its instrumentality—was
seen in the past to be a central vehicle of ecclesial grace.

First, we can note how the episcopacy was understood as a figure of
Jesus. The seeming hierarchical character of the episcopacy in its origins
is well known, if regretted these days. It goes back to St. Paul's own image
of apostolicity, of course. For St. Paul, his ministry as an official apostle
of Jesus' gospel made him the father to those he had converted, much
in the image of Jesus' paternity. And Paul passes this paternal role on to
Timothy, providing a reminding ministry of imitation (1 Cor. 4:14–21;
cf. Philem. 10; 2 Tim. 1:11–14). Although Jesus instructed his disciples
to "call no man your father" (Matt. 23:9), Paul seems to have no trouble
staking apostolicity on that very term and relationship, precisely because
apostolicity is about Jesus, not about Paul at all.

But the most famous defining exposition of the episcopacy as a figure
of Jesus is found in the writings of St. Ignatius of Antioch. It is sufficient
only to outline the general form of Ignatius's vision, which places in
the center of the church the bishop, as one who represents *God himself*
(the male pronoun is not without significance for Ignatius's trinitarian
symbology) in the midst of his people and obedience to whom mirrors
subjection to *God* himself (*Letter to the Ephesians* 5.3). Ignatius is more
supple in his characterization of hierarchy than this, however. He will
locate the bishop as an imagistic part of a larger scheme of figural inter-
relation: the bishop indicates God, presbyters indicate the apostles, the
deacons indicate Christ; or, in another image, bishops are the Son, the

presbyters represent the Father, the deacons point to the Holy Spirit—and all of them, as located among and working in mutual relations with the people of God—form a unity of love that is, at once, the body of Christ perfected: "Make a real effort, then, to stand firmly by the orders of the Lord and the apostles . . . in body and soul, in faith and love, in Son, Father, and Spirit, from first to last, along with your most distinguished bishop, your presbytery . . . , and your godly deacons. Defer to the bishop and to one another as Jesus Christ did to the Father in the days of his flesh, and as the apostles did to Christ, to the Father, and to the Spirit. *In that way we shall achieve complete unity.* I realize you are full of God."[1]

Hierarchy for Ignatius is clearly important here, but not in the way we assume today—taking orders, groveling, and so on. Hierarchy was a totalizing image for the church in its entirety, as it conformed to the image of Jesus—the "form of a servant" or, in Ignatius's words, "Defer to the bishop and to one another, as Jesus Christ did to the Father." This is the figural relation he stresses: servant-deferral. To be in this form was to be a community in service of holiness, in subjection to its demands of obedience and love. The *institutional* structure of the church, according to Ignatius, is designed to figure this service through a range of mutual subjections: "We are fellow slaves," as he puts it (*Letter to the Philadelphians* 4), linking this service to the single Eucharist under the one bishop. The bishop's role, as Ignatius makes clear, is simply to be a central example of this—hence Ignatius's joy in the clarity that his arrest and impending death offer to the church at large. Hierarchy, in its individually concrete and corporately diverse yet practical modes, is the means of conformance to Christ—which is another way of translating Ignatius's notion of the unity of the church with God: when you are conformed to Jesus, you are in unity. And because it is mutual subjection, its unity is also always demonstrated in its own visible life within itself. The church at unity under and with its bishop is the church in conformance with Jesus.

Although he says much about the evils of schism, of acting apart from the bishop, Ignatius nonetheless says little about problematic bishops, bad bishops. But the subsequent elaboration of canonical literature about the unity of the church to which Ignatius is committed centers around just this problematic element: the question was not so much, "How maintain unity in the face of bad bishops?"—our own era's question—but rather, "How does our unity as a church express itself within a body in which bad bishops

---

1. Ignatius, *Letter to the Magnesians* 13–14 in *Early Christian Fathers* (ed. and trans. Cyril C. Richardson; Library of Christian Classics 1; Philadelphia: Westminster, 1973), 97 (emphasis added).

figure?" The answer is obvious when posed this way, given the premises: bad bishops do not, in themselves, represent a subversion of the life of mutual subjection in the figure of Jesus; rather, they represent the possibility of that life in a particularly acute form.

Let us take but one example. The Apostolic Canons—and there are parallel forms in other canonical literature (e.g., Council of Carthage)— which may be based on fourth-century originals, spend an inordinate amount of time dealing with two issues: what to do with bad bishops, and how to protect the integrity of diocesan boundaries from the predatory authority of external bishops. These two issues, coincidentally, dominate current Anglican episcopal concerns in the communion. Both issues are addressed with excruciating detail: what procedures are to be followed, who is to accuse whom, who is to decide, what provincial council, what trial, what decision, on what basis. On the one hand, the canons are concerned to deal with the reality of bad bishops; but, as we know, the procedure for thus dealing with bad bishops is so complicated and long that it is hardly clear that responses will ever be decisive enough to re-solve the situation in anything but an illegitimately aggressive fashion. (We might consider, as a parallel frustration, contemporary processes of presentment within modern Anglican churches.) Further, and because of this, we may see these two concerns as potentially in conflict: if bad bishops are a problem, as they appear to be for many dioceses, and if it is so complicated and hard to get rid of them, then surely the integrity of diocesan boundaries ought not to be upheld idealistically; one ought to allow a good bishop from outside to intervene in the diocese led by a bad bishop. All this has a modern ring about it.

But this is not, in fact, the reasoning of the early Church. The enor-mous integrity of diocesan boundaries that early Christians insisted upon and the grave error of blurring their lines is critically linked to the enormous gravity of episcopal conduct, doctrinally and morally. It is *because* the unity of the church is so critical to its conformity with Jesus that individual conduct is brought into line with the image of Christ only through an ordered, if often ineffective, process of mutual subjection that does not allow for shortcuts. Or, put another way, the integrity of the episcopacy as an apostolic image embodied in time is maintained only through the mechanism of institutional unity. The bishops of the early church will sometimes speak of the "blessed unity" of the episcopacy, and do so in the context of dealing with bad bishops (cf. the Letter and Canons of Constantinople) and of healing the injury that they do. Follow the process, they say, because of this blessed unity we have. Unity is a blessing, which means a saving balm in itself, by which evil is allowed to be expunged from the church. It is so because its maintenance *in itself* represents the mutually self-subjugating character of the conformed life of Jesus by which unity with the Father is achieved. Extraordinary patience is required in dealing with bad bishops, as seen in canon 6 of the Council of Constantinople, which in its tedious and contorted demands for due process would make any normal person despair of ever punishing a once-accepted heretic. But this convoluted process is explained in terms of giving honor to the "order of the church" embodied in its laws, whose bequest of temporal breadth upon the body (i.e., patience) allows for the flourishing of virtue over time.

Practically speaking, the ecclesiological consequences of this theologically informed canonical attitude are this: bishops are not primarily *individual* representations of Jesus; they are so only to the degree that they are part of a *larger ecclesial figure of mutual subjection* in the image of Jesus. This larger figure allows for individual discrepancies—bad Christians, bad priests, bad bishops—and it allows for these precisely because their presence in the Church, however unfortunate and disruptive, can never subvert the possibility of service and can, in cases of extraordinary challenge, even heighten them. Augustine, as we know, has much to say about the blessings that come from living in a mixed church (cf. his exegesis in his homilies on the Gospel of John about the presence of Judas among the apostles). It is not the case that bad bishops are really good; they are always bad, and there are mechanisms by which the faithful church is asked to reform or remove them. But these mechanisms are slow, hard, and often weak. And in this context, bad bishops can indeed always be a tool for the larger apostolic figure of "strength in weakness," as in all those canons that touch upon putting up with episcopal oversight; in the case of bad bishops, the tool is specifically one that can reveal the character of corporate grace as it molds the Church's ongoing life.

For instance, we talk of Jesus' subjection in death, his obedience: is there a practical way to distinguish the object of his submission? Is it to the Father that he submits, or to his own Jewish leaders, Pilate, and the people's wrath? The latter can be grasped only as an extension of the former. He submits to both, surely. It does not matter the level on which we parse this. The creed contains the central fact of "crucifixion under Pontius Pilate," not simply to emphasize the historical concreteness of the Lord's death—this is what we hear said in explanation today—but,

more profoundly, to remind us of the inescapably self-subjecting character of his life in time, whose bowing under the burden of human
folly orders the whole subsequent character of human salvation, in the
Church above all.

One of the richest images used to describe the relationship between
mutual subjection, instanced in the continued existence of bad bishops,
and the figure of Jesus is given by Gregory the Great in a letter to one
of his fellow bishops (Epistle 17, to Felix of Messana).[2] The question
that Gregory was asked to answer was how to deal with those who vex
a bishop—by complaining, accusing, blaming a bishop's conduct and
character, even his teaching. Gregory has no real advice to offer, except
to say that such accusations, however justified in themselves, are inappropriately expressed in public with respect to a bishop. He uses the hierarchical model to explain this by emphasizing how we should willingly
be subject to the throne of a bishop, whatever his conduct: "Subordinates,
whether clerical or lay, . . . are to be admonished that, when they observe
the deeds of their masters, they return to their own heart, and presume
not in upbraidings of them."

The primary scriptural figure that Gregory indicates in this, however, is
not simply one that describes the natural relation of subject and authority, in terms of some divine *social* hierarchy. Rather, Gregory chooses an
image from among the most lofty possible, that is, the example of David
and Saul: "For, if David who was the most righteous of kings presumed
not to lay his hand on Saul who was evidently already rejected of God."
That is, the Messiah himself, who was divinely legitimated in his kingship, refused even to undermine the oppressive and illegitimate king
whom God himself had overthrown! Such is Christian subjection rightly
embodied. The use of the messianic figure by Gregory is deliberate, of
course, for he ends his discussion by subsuming this posture in the very
life of Jesus, quoting from Matthew 10:24, "A servant [is not] above his
master," the master, that is, of the universe itself, whose self-subjection
to the world's evils and the evils of his own people embraces the very
calling of God's people as a whole.

It is not surprising, then, to find Gregory frame the discussion in terms
of two familiar themes that, as we have seen, characterize the early church's
traditional attitude toward the episcopacy in general: first, that any relation to the bishop is a relation to Christ Jesus: "Vexation or detraction

2. Gregory the Great, Epistle 17 to Bishop Felix of Messana (trans. James Barmby; Nicene and Post-
Nicene Fathers, Second Series 13; repr. Peabody, Mass.: Hendrickson, 1994), 109–11.

of [the bishop] touches Christ," he writes; and second, that this relation, which exists in subjection, is therefore given its significance in terms of the burdens of unity: "Our Head, which is Christ, to this end has willed us to be His members, that through His large charity and faithfulness He might make us one body in Himself.... From the citadel of the Head let nothing divide us, lest, if we refuse to be His members, we be deserted of Him, and wither as branches cast off from the vine." The case of the bad bishop, figured in Saul and then fulfilled in the life of Jesus' relation of passion to the authorities of Israel and Rome, unveils the very character of the Church's divine vocation and destiny.

We must be clear about the basis upon which this entire outlook of the early Church is founded. For it goes back quite literally to the character of apostolicity itself—which the episcopacy embodies—as lifted up by St. Paul. Paul, as we know, legitimated his apostleship precisely in terms of his experience of submission to the travails engendered for him by his own people: "Are they [other so-called apostles] Hebrews? So am I.... Are they servants of Christ? I am a better one—I am talking like a madman—with far greater labors, for more imprisonments, with countless beatings, and often near death" (2 Cor. 11:22–23). And so the catalogue of Paul's woes of submission follows, which he sums up with the flourish: "If I must boast, I will boast of the things that show my weakness" (11:30). This is what it means to be an apostle, Paul asserts; and this is the relation that the ongoing character of the Christian leader assumes with the larger Church and world. Thus, Paul writes to Timothy, "For this gospel I was appointed a preacher and apostle and teacher, and *therefore I suffer as I do*.... Follow this *pattern* ... you have learned from me" (2 Tim. 1:11–13 [emphasis added]).

If we were to transpose this to the explicit discussion of the episcopacy, we could say that Paul is talking about the self-subjecting character of the *good* bishop—that is, himself! But this character, as we know, assumes the central orchestrating role for the entire Christian ethical life of the Church, as elaborated by Paul himself and Peter too in that genre of Christian moral summary given in the so-called household code so common in the Epistles and so maligned today. "Be subject to one another out of reverence for Christ," Paul writes (Eph. 5:21), placing the form of the Christian life under this one subsuming and submitting banner of mutual relation—slaves and masters, husbands and wives, and so on. Peter, for his part, outlines the shape of Christian duty in just these terms of mutual subjection in his first epistle, but now stated explicitly as offering the means of our conformance to Christ. And Peter stresses, more than elsewhere in these lists of relations, how this conformance is given especially when we suffer the burdens of these relations *unjustly*. It is worth laying out the order of relation as Peter explicates it in this letter:

> Jesus suffers patiently, giving us an example to follow in his footsteps; he does not lash back, he does not resist, he trusts only in God's judgment (1 Pet. 2:21–25).
>
> As Christians, we are called to be subject to every human institution ordained through the Lord—whether emperors or governors—acting as slaves of God (2:13–17).
>
> Slaves are to be subject to masters, even when unjustly treated (2:18–20).
>
> Wives are to be subject to husbands (3:1–6).
>
> Husbands are to be similarly ordered (the mutual relation is properly understood as implicitly pressed through the rhetorical shape of the argument), and they are to understand that women are coheirs with men of God's promises (3:7).
>
> Elders (i.e., presbyters) or shepherds—the church's leaders—are to be willing examples of Christ's sufferings for their flock (5:1–4).
>
> Finally, all others in the church are to be subject to the elders themselves (5:5).

The governing rubric in all of this is the joyful sharing of Christ's suffering (4:13), which is explained as being given within the church's life of mutual humility and love (3:8).

In this scriptural light, obviously, the focusing importance of bad bishops is not a plea for their benign toleration. What we have here is rather a general description of the character of an episcopal church as it understands the essential quality of its self-ordering. Transferred to our own era and institution, we could say that apostolicity is a reminder of mutual subjection, and it is institutionalized—ordained, stuck into the middle of our lives—like a lightning rod. We enter this "episcopal" church in order to be buffeted, ensnared, shaped, and molded through our formal encounters—with Scripture, the liturgy, but also with the order of the church—into the shape of Jesus' self-giving.

The classical shape of this outlook should be familiar to those conversant with church history, in the form of the monastic virtue of obedience, related especially to that of the abbot. One way of looking at Anglicanism in particular—and this is a topic worth investigating—is as a laicization of the ideals of religious communities, with all the *theological* alterations such a democratizing must make necessary. (Even the defining Protestant issue of justification by faith within Anglicanism can be interpreted in this way, along with a number of other classic reforming doctrines.) In any case, simply translate obedience by mutual subjection and define the bishop as the popular bond, in his or her official role, of this mutual subjection, and much of the Benedictine teaching on the virtue of obedience makes transferable sense in the terms I have been using. This is true especially in relation to bad bishops. We can use, as a test case here, a classic text of Dom Columba Marmion: *Christ the Ideal of the Monk* (1922), especially the magnificent chapter entitled *"Bonum obedientiae"* (The good of obedience).[3]

Marmion describes the virtue of mutual subjection in terms of Christ-likeness: the monk is to follow the footsteps of Christ, much like the mistreated slave and all Christians are to do in 1 Peter's exhortation. Marmion himself uses the image of Philippians 2 and Hebrews 10:7 ("Lo, I have come to do thy will, O God"): in the incarnation Jesus "darts through the infinite space that separates the created from the divine," and the humanity of Jesus is "drawn into an impetuous current of uncreated love" toward God that surpasses any other human being's, that is founded in the gaze of a human child straight into the face of the loving Father. "His whole existence is summed up in love for the Father," Marmion writes; "but what form will this love take? The form of subjection [obedience]: *Lo, I have come to do your will.* And why this? Because nothing better translates filial love than absolute submission. Christ Jesus has manifested this perfect love and this full obedience from the moment of the Incarnation 'even to the death of the Cross' (Phil. 2:8)."[4]

According to Marmion, within the monastic community the disciple is joined in this Jesus-figure through the exercise of mutual subjection as it is embodied in a relationship to the abbot, the superior, who stands, as St. Benedict says, in the "place of Christ" for the monk, just as Ignatius describes the bishop. The monk is to obey the abbot "as if the order came from God himself."[5] We are familiar with this aspect of the Benedictine rule. But it is not for the sake of servile self-abnegation that such subjec-

---

3. Columba Marmion, *Christ the Ideal of the Monk* (London: Sands, 1926), 250–290.

4. Ibid., 276.

5. Cf. ibid., 265

tion is enjoined; it is for the sake of the virtues of Jesus himself, virtues that can ground, as well as spring from, the act of mutual subjection: faith, hope, and love.[6]

For instance, we subject ourselves to the abbot in *faith,* faith that God will use my love for his ends, that my will offered up is usable, that my pride and insistence is expendable in the face of God's omnipotent and gracious act. Self-subjection is *hopeful* in a related way, in that obedience casts out fear and God is allowed to take our hand and lead us, as he led Moses through his mission to the promised end; and self-subjection is driven by and leads to *love,* the love of union with Jesus' own submission, the love for others, that their lives are held by God's, lives to which we can join our own wills without doubt or fear.

This is well-worn ascetical wisdom. But Marmion spends a good deal of space on the most vital context in which the virtues of subjection find their effective spirit: not in some ideal community of faith, filled with nice, faithful people; no, rather the virtues of faith, hope, and love in subjection are most fully exercised in the face of bad or incompetent or fallible authorities. Obedience to weakness is the key, Marmion explains. Self-subjection to another is like receiving the sacrament of the Eucharist:

> Our senses cry out, "that is not Christ! Only bread is there!" But Christ has said, "this is my body." . . . In the same way, Christ veils Himself in our superiors. The abbot, despite his imperfections, represents Christ for us. St. Benedict is formal on this point. Christ is hidden under the imperfections and weaknesses of the human being. . . . By reason of our habitual contact with him, we naturally see his deficiencies and limitations, and then we are tempted to cry, "this man is not Christ!" His judgment is limited, is fallible, he can be mistaken, he *is* mistaken, he allows himself to be biased. . . . Yet faith discovers Christ beneath the imperfections. . . . To obey the abbot because we have the same ideas as he, because we admire his talents, because we find him reasonable, is unworthy of us. . . . Why so?[7]

Marmion answers this question by stating that "as soon as we place ourselves on the natural plane" every person is the same, and we should submit to no creature—even a dazzling genius. "But if God says, 'This person represents me,' be he a man without talents, having the most bla-

6. Ibid., 267–79.
7. Ibid., 267–68.

tant defects, belonging to an altogether inferior set, I would yield."[8] For I would be serving God with my faith, with my hope, with my love.

All this is firmly part of the tradition. It stands in continuity with the most splendid spirits of the Christian church, like St. Francis, who in his *Testament* begins by urging his brothers willingly to cease preaching where they are forbidden:

> And if I were as wise as Solomon and met the poorest priests of the world, I would still refuse to preach against their will in the parishes in which they live. I am determined to reverence, love and honor priests and all others as my superiors. I refuse to consider their sins, because I can see the Son of God in them and they are better than I. I do this because in this world I cannot see the most high Son of God with my own eyes, except in his most holy Body and Blood which they—the leaders of the church—receive and administer to others.[9]

In the midst of our contemporary concerns over the urgent need for prophetic cleansing of the Church, we can ask ourselves: was St. Francis effective in renewing the Church of Christ? Or are we dealing here with a monstrous anachronism? Yet the cultural distance from our own that this perspective represents does not lie simply in our developed social structures that have done away with hierarchicalisms and self-denials in the face of the abuse of power. Marmion, as noted in the quotation above, is well aware that subjecting oneself to another creature is unworthy of who we are. Further, he is well aware that abbots can also err in matters of essential faith, in which case they are to be confronted in a legitimately sanctioned way—but not disdained and repulsed.

No doubt there *are* standards for the episcopacy to which it is necessary to hold bishops accountable and according to which bishops should be nurtured and upheld. No doubt there *are* doctrinal truths or moral conditions that the Church and its people are led to struggle for and guard. And the object of such struggle is worth defining and promoting. Further, the character and process of that struggle and guardianship are not simply up for grabs—we have canons and processes, which can even be changed and improved, through legitimate bodies of decision-making.

Be that as it may, what this present reflection suggests is a fundamental set of informing parameters for our relationships with *bad* bishops that

8. Ibid., 272–73.

9. As translated in Marion Habig (ed.), *St. Francis of Assisi: Writings and Early Biographies* (Chicago: Franciscan Herald, 1983), 67.

underscores our relationship with *all* bishops, because it derives from the very core of the Church's vocation to follow Jesus. Whoever may be the bad bishop to whom we are subjected—and there are many candidates whose names each of us could enumerate!—there is a legitimate process to follow in opposition, a process, however, that may be likely to result in juridical standoffs. In the meantime and subsequently, questions of relation are pressed, like: should the bishop be allowed to preach in the churches of the diocese, in my church? Do I pray for the bishop as my father—or mother—in Christ? Do I take Communion from his or her hands? Do I attend his or her diocesan address? Do I pay his or her salary?

These kinds of questions are pressed because proper subjection has bite in terms of *these* elements of relationship. The president of the United States, for example, is impeachable, but until legitimately removed from office remains "Mr. President," with all the authority to sign bills, conduct foreign policy, address the Congress and people, and be paid, whether he is good or bad. What we call moral authority—as opposed to sanctioned authority—is, in canon law, something that is recognized only retrospectively. And self-subjection, according to the gospel, is not something that is granted only to the moral authority. It is itself the basis of Christian moral authority. And thus, while the early Church canons can call bad bishops "no bishops at all," this moral judgment is attached to individuals only later and never translates into legitimate rebellion, but instead sharpens the moral character of the mutually subjected church.

It is not our heightened sense of autonomy that separates us from this consistent past in our tradition and so renders pointless any exploration of the gospel in such subjection. Rather, it is our sheer lack of faith that God has any good purposes to fulfill in the mutual submission that orders his church. We do not trust, not simply other people in the church; we do not trust God with the church's life itself. Yet that trust is crucial to the entire possibility of the Church's ongoing continuity in time. A letter falsely attributed to the early Pope Zephyrinus states: "Bishops are to be borne by laity and clergy, and masters by servants, in order that, under the exercise of endurance, things temporal may be maintained, and things eternal hoped for."[10] Hope for eternity, then, is here given as a ground for subjection, one perhaps lost today.

10. *First Epistle of Zephyrinus* (trans. S. D. F. Salmond; Ante-Nicene Fathers 8; repr. Peabody, Mass.: Hendrickson, 1994), 610.

Just so, the convictions of the early Church on the question of bad bishops and their indicating gift of hope through subjection are not ones that have been easily passed on to the modern era. Our own worries over independence, self-protection, and systemic integrity have inflexibly pushed us away from any recognition of virtue in mutual subjection. But it is notable how, even in Zephyrinus—and the letter was perhaps edited in the ninth century to defend the rights of individual dioceses against the power abuses of archbishops—a commitment to more democratic and local forms of church government turns out to be tied to programs of self-subjection in unity. This fact has some bearing on our own modern situation, where the rejection of episcopal authority for the sake of an assaulted truth is a constant temptation in, for example, Anglican affairs of the present: for among the most fervent Catholic defenders of episcopacy in a nonpapal perspective were those who stressed the value of suffering in love the depredations of unjust leaders. A glance at the early modern experience of the Jansenists makes this clear.

The Jansenists, a seventeenth- and eighteenth-century Roman Catholic reform movement, centered in France—Pascal, Racine, Boileau, among famous literary figures, were Jansenists—were deeply committed to an Augustinian reading of divine grace and providence and committed also to a generally Catholic ecclesiology. Rather than leave the church because of its corruptions and false teachings, which they felt acutely, the Jansenist understanding of unity was informed by a call to suffer mistreatment, a call that was itself connected with the most rigorist of moral and doctrinal commitments. Pierre Nicole, one of the great Jansenist apologists for Catholicism, is notorious for his argument against the Calvinists: despite the evils of the institutional church, Nicole insisted, you should have gone *without* pastors altogether, rather than alleviate your suffering through subverting the unity of the church by ordaining your own. For that unity will always be your vehicle of conformance, and you have now cast it aside.[11]

The one great moment in which Jansenists took independent power, ecclesially, can be seen as the repudiation, not only of the governing theological principles of Nicole's call, but of the evangelical effects that Jansenists claimed were associated with it. This occurred in the Catholic Church of Holland, which had, since the sixteenth century, been without a local archbishop, due to conflicts associated with the Protestant

11. I examine this outlook at length in my *Spirit and Nature: The Saint-Médard Miracles in 18th-Century Jansenism* (New York: Herder & Herder/Crossroad, 2002).

government.[12] Desirous of having their own bishop, but ignored in their pleas to the Vatican, the Utrecht cathedral chapter, which was rife with Jansenist sympathizers, took matters into their own hands. In 1724, they consecrated an archbishop of their own, Dominique Marie Varlet, at the hands of a suspended Jansenist bishop then living in Amsterdam. The subsequent history of this event follows in kind: Varlet's refusal to step down as a working bishop and his continued consecrations, the fear of abandonment on the part of many Dutch Catholics, the drift of the church into schism when Varlet's consecrations were not recognized (this is the origin of the so-called Old Catholic Movement), and the final virtual disappearance of the church into parochialism and eventual preciosity—all this came with a whimper. Curiously, the growth of the Catholic Church in Holland in the wake of the Reformation came in the *earlier* period of absent bishops—in the late sixteenth and seventeenth centuries, before the split with Rome took place.

One of the interesting aspects of this modern episode is that all French Jansenist bishops, despite their doctrinal and even institutional sympathies with Varlet and the beleaguered Dutch Catholics, refused initially to lead and later to participate in his consecrations, although invited to. And here the consistency of their position was demonstrated: Jansenists themselves were passionately committed to the promotion of good bishops; they wrote treatises on the subject, instituted reforms, opposed corrupt and lax episcopacies. But the ascetic competence, if you will, of the Jansenists also allowed them to see the providential capacities that bad bishops had for the welfare of the church, including paradoxically in the case of Utrecht the gracious consequences of *in*competent institutions that actually rendered flocks bishop*less*. That is, they saw that the Dutch Church could in fact flourish without a bishop, if that lack was accepted in a mode of self-subjection. In Marmion's terms, of course, this was a vision derived solely from faith—faith in the purposes of unity through mutual subjection that the *episcopē,* in both good and bad forms, was established to embody. The parallel of this episode to certain pressures now felt in our own churches' current conflicts ought to be obvious.

We could multiply examples from the history of the Church and its theology, examples of both accepting and rejecting, with sad consequences, the premises I have just asserted. But with the main point already made, let us turn back to our opening questions and attempt

---

12. An accessible historical review of this episode can be found in C. B. Moss, *The Old Catholic Movement* (New York: Morehouse-Barlow, 1964), 1–123.

some brief conclusions. These questions, to summarize, were these: (1) Is the evangelical character, or essence, of the episcopacy defined by an ideal? (2) What is the role of the episcopacy in our vocation as episcopally ordered denominations for the larger Church? (3) How, at root, is the episcopacy tied to and expressive of the nature of the gospel of Jesus itself?

With regard to the first question—the ideal of the episcopacy—I think we can conclude that the essence of the episcopacy lies *not* in the embodied ideal of the bishop, whether functionally or morally defined. The essence lies, instead, in the dynamic of relationship that the real, concrete bishop establishes at the center of a mutually subjected body of Christian believers. To put it with provocative bluntness: whether a bishop is a wholesome example to the flock or an effective or even truthful guardian of the faith is irrelevant to the essence of the episcopacy *in its individual exemplars*.

Obviously, the ideal of doctrinal and moral integrity is highly relevant to the overall, ongoing purposes of the episcopacy in God's ultimate designs. God did not order the Church episcopally with the final *purpose* of subjecting it to incompetent leaders. But *unless*, in individual instances, the continued subjection to bad bishops were not also essential to the salvific character of the Church, the Church itself would be a dead vessel in those ultimate divine designs. Since, however, those ultimate designs include the unity of the Church in the form of the servant Christ, the relations of mutual subjection, even centered in evil leaders, must work essentially for the Church's positive destiny. And what could be a better tool for this than the lightning rod of bad bishops?

I stress again that the process of confronting, correcting, and perhaps even removing bad bishops is also a part of the episcopal essence for the Church. But this process is governed by the order of the Church that itself is subject to the character of mutual subjection in unity that bad bishops actually serve to unveil. If the process were not itself slow, painful, and often ineffective, it would not be reconcilable to the very character of the Church's figural reality as an image of its Lord. In other words, the imperative of the process of opposing bad bishops cannot be seen as undermining the essential quality of mutually subjecting relations that the episcopacy in *every case* must embody and promote. In this light—the light of the relation and not of the ideal—I believe a number of our current tensions in the Church must be rethought.

To the second question, regarding the vocation of the Anglican Church within the wider Church universal, I believe we can draw a potentially encouraging, even exciting conclusion. Episcopally ordered churches are, at this point in history, the Christian denominations best placed to exhibit the full character of the episcopate for other traditions; and in so doing, they are the most ready to render a glorious service to Jesus' divine plea for unity among divided Christians and so to his call to evangelize an unbelieving world (John 17). As Anglicans, for example, we have bishops; we have bad bishops (and good ones too!); we are democratically and culturally dispersed, in ways that demand some deliberate form of relation; and, finally, we are in a situation of doctrinal, liturgical, and moral fragmentation that would render any ministry of painful self-subjection in unity a blazing light to the world.

When it comes to Anglicans, in any case, our vocation at this point in time is *not*, I feel certain, to be a bridge between Protestants and Catholics or to be an example of theological comprehension or tolerance or to be a model of diversity. Every major denominational church in America today is already running, with tongues hanging, after this set of supposed callings. A truly episcopal vocation, rather, is to suffer in unity, around our bishops, for the sake of embodying the shape of Jesus Christ in flesh and blood. The fruit of this suffering, as Dom Marmion might put it, will be the fruit of all faith, hope, and love—that is, the unveiling of Christ's Spirit at work in the world to convert the hearts of men and women to God's eternal purposes and life.

Finally, to the question about how the gospel of Jesus Christ is clarified by the reality of bad bishops. I will simply summarize much of what has already been said in my array of citations: Since we are talking about the *person* of Jesus, the body of Jesus Christ in the figure of his church, self-subjection in unity around a bishop of any kind is a profoundly *evangelical* act, a gospel act, a signal of corporate humility before God set in front of the nations (Isa. 66:19) that will bring Jew and Gentile together. This is the key to all faithful ecclesiology, as I will argue in this book's final chapter. *Servire est regnare* (to be subject is to reign), in St. Benedict's phrase. And this maxim is not to be taken in a weak or rhetorical sense. It is rather the very proclamation of the Lord Jesus Christ, stating clearly *who* he is: to be subject is to reign in the fullness of God's truth and glory, through which, in the action of Christ Jesus himself, he will "draw all men to [him]self" (John 12:32). There is no question about it: the gospel itself is at stake in how we relate to bad bishops.

# Part 4

# The Better Form of Providence

*Where We Are Headed*

*Since God had foreseen something better for us, that*

*apart from us they should not be made perfect.*

—Hebrews 11:40

# 11

# Enduring
# the
# Church

*How to Be a Fool*

To speak of the Church in our day is certainly, for many, to voice exhaustion. And there may well be a kind of idealism at work, however nobly attired, in speaking of a denomination's upward pull by God, its hoped-for redemption even through its internal struggles and battles. Could it possibly be true in the real world that arguments, bitter and divisive, over sex and bishops and the Bible and spiritual consumerism and the like represent the conforming pressures of the Holy Spirit? Yet if reading the Scriptures as the enfigurating denotations of the Lord's connoting power within time is itself a kind of mortifying gift, this is only because it prepares for and leads us into the divine discipline that is the Church of Christ. And if it cannot also help us stay within this realm of shaping, we read in vain. There is vanity in the joinings and leavings that mark our ecclesial lives. There is hope in staying put.

Here I would simply like to state, in relatively concrete and sometimes personal terms, why staying put is not and cannot be apostasy even in the face of ecclesial failure and self-deception. It cannot be apostasy;

only gift. It is a simple statement by one who knows well that truth is assaulted first and foremost by the Christian witness—by teachers and leaders, by bishops and priests, by wise men, scribes, and debaters (1 Cor. 1:20). And no one dares to call the family of fools his or her own. But let me be a fool in this one argument: God makes us his in such assaults, as we stand still long enough to be touched.

My main desire is to explain why theological conservatives like myself not only wish to remain working within the bounds and communion, in this case, of as confused a denomination as the Episcopal Church of the U.S.A., but also why I believe it is an evangelical imperative that we do so. On this score, what I write is pertinent to other denominations riven and confounded by debates that appear based on forgetfulness and willfulness. I write to all churches and all the weary within them. For it has been my role as an active ordained priest to embrace even the awkward, perhaps foolish, position of furthering the order of my particular institution in the face of theological questionings with which I often sympathize. And although this has brought pain, I could not be such a fool were I not convinced that, at root, such foolishness bears a necessary witness to a divinely inevitable vocation.

## The Crisis Is Real

Let me begin with some candor: I do not for a moment minimize the seriousness of the challenge, now mounted in many quarters within our various denominations, to the gospel as it has been handed down to us. I have heard the query raised by exasperated revisionists: "Why is the sexuality issue, for instance, one that seems to have broken the camel's back? Did we not survive civil rights, women's ordination, prayer book revision? Why are you conservatives so adamant on this topic?" It is a good question, but also one that is straightforwardly answered. I would start with three responses. First, the extreme novelty of recent revisionary teachings on sexual behavior is unique in our church's development and more than anything else offers up a seemingly culturally driven rejection of scriptural authority that has no precedents. One does not have to engage in the sometimes complicated theological and historical reflections pursued in previous chapters of this book to realize this. The revisionary program over sexual behavior strikes at the core of our biblical faith. Second, the kinds of reasonings that seem to lie behind the revisionary trend in our denomination—reasonings based on controlling definitions of justice, love, inclusion, and so on—are so distant from the particularistic and defined words and actions of Jesus and the Christian tradition's acknowledgment of his person that the revealed Christ appears to have become the servant of a greater principle that stands beyond him. This contemporary and perhaps only implicit form of the ancient Arian heresy—that Christ is to be identified with a reality not personally equivalent with God—strikes at the core of our catholic confession of Christ. Third, so many other Christians around the world perceive this threat clearly, and yet a significant and powerful part of our denomination seems oblivious to and even unconcerned at their pleas and warnings. This evidences a chilling lack of charity that strikes at the core of Christian communion.

And therefore the question that some people ask conservatives, "Why would you get so upset at all this as even to think of leaving the church?" can be equally forthrightly answered: many of the habits of the Episcopal Church, and not a few of the articulate teachings and examples now being promoted in our denomination, are so obviously contrary to the Christian principles that this church has consistently upheld until only recently that, simply put, the church to which many of us made ordination vows no longer—in many important respects—informs the church we serve. It is not only plausible, it is absolutely necessary under the circumstances that we now reconsider what the nature of those vows might be. If we are to stay put as I exhort, it will be with eyes wide open and in the unflinching face of a sorrowful reality.

Despite my conclusions about the call to resist the market, I remain puzzled by those who accuse conservative struggles with denominational allegiance as somehow mindlessly succumbing to a new congregationalism. If anything smacks of congregationalism, it is the ecclesial style of so much flouting of traditional Christian teaching and behavior over the past few years on the part of parishes disinterested in the commitments of the larger church. It has always been my argument that there is an essential connection between faithlessness and fissiparousness. If temptations must necessarily come, nonetheless "woe to the man by whom the temptation comes!" (Matt. 18:7). No, the issue at stake has nothing to do with how we think of the connectional church, with its institutional responsibilities and strategies. It has to do with whether the church exists as a divine body at all, and if so, where it might be and how it might survive with the integrity of witness to Christ's gospel that is its reason for being. These are not light matters, and they are matters very much up for grabs in most of our denomination at this time. Anyone who dismisses the necessity and profundity of this struggle that conservatives now experience within their churches is merely skating on the surface of the gospel.

## But It Goes beyond Theological Correctness

Having noted how theologically critical this struggle is, I nevertheless fear that the theological passion of the orthodox has misled us, as it has many conservatives (myself included) into a debilitating misreading of our vocation, one that seems to think that if we could just find the right idea, the right notion, system, criterion, confession, template on heresy, declaration—if we could just get this right and build for it the proper corral—faithfulness would be preserved. I'm not sure what to call this mistake: a Pelagian ratcheting up of the theological task? A kind of orthodox gnosticism?

In any case, it is a misleading task for several reasons. First, it obscures history. We already possess confessions, criteria, lines in the sand, and declarations galore, from Ignatius to Bonhoeffer. While it may be useful to own our personal versions taken from this storehouse, we must not confuse this with the major theological task of finding our way—God's way for us—in an errant church. More pertinent than yet another Barmen pronouncement is a deep sense of why the storehouse fails to have value for so many anymore. What is going on in this long line of enunciations that they appear so garbled to so many? This is the historical question of God's providence and human sin, to which I shall return in a moment.

The immediate point to which this leads, however, is that of the personal demands of God upon one's own self, in judgment and redemption. I fear that in reducing theology to the fuming bibliography of confessions, which this must inevitably do however much this or that item grants us light, we shall find ourselves gathering to ourselves the gold of orthodoxy so willingly that we shall be surprised when the voice comes, saying, "Fool! This night your soul is required of you." And what will we do with our confessions then? There are different kinds of fools; it is a matter of joining the right band on this score! Conservatives have increasingly lost sight of their mission within the church—even the errant church—and have retreated to their barns, institutional as much as convivial, exhaustedly taking what pleasure they can in their correctness. We are not an inspiring spectacle.

I have no doubt that all of us could provide an interesting—and accurate—list of essentials to the faith, which we could then apply to our denominations and thereby find each one wanting. We have already done it ad nauseam. Then we could decide with whom we want to be in communion and argue among ourselves about this or that point and this or that person, and then maybe find a set of folk with whom the arguments are less drastic and call them our fold. But we are missing the point for our own souls: the point that asks not, "How can I prove myself theologically correct?" but, "What is God doing to this church of which I am a part and how shall I serve it?"

That is the proper theological question—which is why I wish conservatives would stay a little while and not skip to Athanasius and Luther and Cranmer and the rest so quickly before attending to the fruit of what conservatives, as much as liberals, produce, not only here and now but in this place and that place, then and before. We have been going off half-cocked for centuries, and a great darkness and gloom has descended upon the land in which we—*we*—grope. There is a good deal, I am sure, to discover of God's hand in all of this, that awaits our scrutiny. And it goes beyond fixing the ideas. Although the fifth-century writer Salvian is no longer considered a great theologian in the realm of the history of ideas, he and others like him have much to teach us on this score: the providence of God rules the Church, and its travails are given to us as justice and mission to be received in humility and repentance. Curiously, Salvian's influence at the time of his writing was far greater than has been that of the critics of liberalism in the last century. (Yes, and *why?*)

My own sense is this: God is punishing this church, and many other churches. (O sinner, where will you flee?) Within the redemptive context of the gospel, of course, I would consider such punishment to be a chastening, and there is such a hope within it. (Again, can we discern it, describe it, give ourselves over to it?) And, as much as I resist the notion, I must at least try to believe that I am meant to be a part of this chastening, that I too deserve what has come upon my people (despite having the right ideas about everything). Scripture offers us much guidance on how to suffer this reality—kings and saints, prophets and commoners. We have a Lord, as well, who has lifted up the standard. And in the Christian Church, followers like Catherine of Siena live and speak to our own age most pointedly. (I suppose she would say that our vocation is to die for the liberal heretic in our midst! *There* is a thought worth sinking our theological teeth into.)

There is, to be sure, plenty of normal theological work to be done in the service of such a life—including the articulation, over and over again, of the truth! But what to *do* with it, how to let it render our own lives beneath the humbling hand of God, how to walk with Jesus in the midst of the wilderness of his—and our—people, this is a harder theological task, requiring far more immersion in Scripture and far more sensitivity to the travails of the body than we have hitherto been apt to embrace.

## Do Conservatives Have a Valid Ecclesiology?

This basic warning aside, I must now note that conservatives are often lazy theologians too. We are accused of being reactionaries precisely because too often we allow our convictions to do the work of thinking things through, and we often let our evangelical passion take the place of an informed Christian conscience that ought more acutely to frame our decisions. The emboldened fool might well believe, in contrast, that such thinking through of the current crises of our churches ought to lead into a renewed decision to stay within them, to witness here to the gospel as we have been entrusted with it, and to grow in greater likeness to our Lord in the midst of this commitment. It is the very depth of any crisis that has the power to unveil the evangelical profundity of our basic call to remain.

Part of our reactive temptation to do otherwise springs from the models of the church with which most contemporary ministers work, especially our models of the church in crisis. Our instincts since the sixteenth century have been well trained to sense that ecclesial error is simply something that brooks no compromise and association. Perhaps we think of Athanasius "against the world." In fact, though, careful examination of a defender of the truth like Athanasius displays many details that are hardly exemplary and more importantly pertain in any case to someone who lived in an era before the East-West schism and the sixteenth-century religious breakup of Christendom. One cannot think of Anglicanism or Presbyterianism or Methodism or any other denomination as a simple microcosm for the Catholic Church of the fourth century, despite our frequently annexing "Church" and its gifts to the autonomous groups we represent. The Episcopal Church (along with every other denomination) is, quite simply, a denomination among many. And the real models of the church with which we work have been bequeathed us by the Reformation division of the Church that led to denominational existence in the first place. We must take this reality seriously and try to evaluate scripturally the habits we have thereby inherited.

In general, three possible answers to the church in crisis were given in the sixteenth century: perhaps the church you were in was the true church (in which case stay); perhaps it was a/the false church (in which case leave); or, finally, church itself was an insignificant social entity (in which case stay or leave according to what caused the least pain—this was the [understandable] position of the disgusted humanist, which now has gradually come to rule the evolution of Christendom to marketplace). To this day, people unthinkingly relate to their struggles with their churches according to these options, even while the outcome to their choices has produced a very different kind of Christian reality whose integrity may demand new attitudes.

The past few centuries of denominational experience have undercut these sixteenth-century options for us. The inescapable development of a denominationally pluralistic society, as well as the vagaries of denominational development and ecumenical insight, have shown us that the Anglican church or any other denomination cannot simply be the true church; increased knowledge about and experiential exposure to other denominations have shown us that the criterion of falsity must logically be applied to all denominations in certain respects (though the historical data contradicting the claims of Protestant or Catholic Puritanism are often conveniently ignored in times of crisis); and finally, the Christian practices associated with devaluing church structures altogether—the developed culture of indifference to organized religion in our day—have demonstrated themselves as being hopelessly incompetent to embody the full gospel. And this goes for both liberal and evangelical versions of this outlook.

Beyond these options, however, what answers do conservatives have about the reasons for ever being members of this or that church in the first place and, therefore, for their concern with its devolution in teaching and witness? It is not enough to speak about affections for the church "I grew up in" or about the glories of, in my case, the Anglican tradition or about the admiration one has for Anglican balance between doctrine, liturgy, and other Episcopalian accoutrements. If the church is a divine body at all, how ought we to locate that identity within this church in particular—if only in the past—in such a way that a threat to this church's integrity is a cause for profound Christian concern? An answer must be attempted, or any debate within our church and any action we might take can be attributed only to the venal motives of human psychological drives.

If the twentieth-century development of both pluralism and ecumenism—not to mention increased acquaintance with the wide failures in Christian witness around the world—has had any religious payoff, it has been to begin lifting up a growing consciousness about the providential value of suffering Christian division as a means of growing in Christ. Both mainline and evangelical ecumenical struggles since the end of the nineteenth century have increasingly unveiled the destructive character of Christian disunity. But a realization has been emerging that we cannot move on toward the healing of such disunity within the will of our Lord, unless we, as it were, enter more deeply into the lived consequences of our divided loyalties as they have been bequeathed us.

We cannot, for instance, continue playing out the inherited habits of disgruntled Christians from the past. And God clearly wants us to face those habits from the past, with their outcomes, as part of our own vocation to move forward in his will. What shall we do? What was missing then that we can now take up in the face of our own crises? What has God allowed us to learn? Almost five hundred years after the sixteenth-century debates and divisions, we can no longer ask ourselves the same questions that John Donne asked (where is the true church and does it matter?). By contrast, I believe that the Scripture teaches us today the following: God has allowed us to come to faith and to practice our faith within divided Christian communities so that, forced to follow Jesus where we have been placed, we might learn repentance. And repentance marks the embrace of Jesus Christ's own form—he, as C. S. Lewis said (drawing, knowingly or not, upon a breadth of rich Catholic spirituality in his *Mere Christianity*), who is the perfect penitent.

We tend to think of repentance in terms of discrete acts—repentance for this or that misdeed or for this or that failure or betrayal. And so we should. But there is a larger kind of repentance as well. When Jesus exhorts the Pharisees to "go and learn what this means, 'I desire mercy, and not sacrifice'" (Matt. 9:13), he points to the character of a life that must be grasped as whole through a larger process of learning, of discipline. The providential character of denominational commitment, carried out in the midst of the divided community's sins and failures and now done in the service of the larger church's healing, provides the only real vocation of such learning, discipline, and repentance in our day, at least within the kind of robust embrace of the visible church that Anglicans and other mainline Protestant and even Roman Catholics have always upheld. That God has placed us in this church at this time must mean that he would have us grow in the form of life that bespeaks the Church's repentant readiness to be healed.

## Thinking Scripturally about the Church in Error

Of course, there is nothing conservative about this understanding of our ecclesial vocation—except that it is thoroughly scriptural and therefore thoroughly committed to a witness to the revealed Christ. The providential value of suffering division as a means of repentance is, in fact, the only theological model of ecclesial division that the Bible offers us. I refer explicitly to the history of divided Israel, a reality that is both the consequence of sin and the means of that sin's experiential redemption. No Jew, within scriptural testimony, is ever asked by God to choose between Israel and Judah, despite the fluctuating fortunes of their respective faithfulness; no Jew is asked by God to discern the future of that faithfulness in this or that community. Rather, God asks each Israelite to suffer these fluctuations themselves in faith and to allow that faithful patience to be molded into the shape of a repentant people by God's own acts upon them. This is the overall burden of prophetic discourse within the Old Testament, and it is carried through, albeit in a transformed shape, within the New Testament as well.

It is crucial for any Christian, conservative or revisionist, to identify this scriptural history as the interpretive center for their discernment regarding faithful responses to apparent falsehood within the body of Christ. For too long Christians have allowed their actions to be governed by a superficial hermeneutic that has simply gravitated to fragmented verses regarding repudiation of error. There is, however, no explicit discussion in the New Testament of Christian division, only ad hoc references to individual responses to false teaching that together offer no unified outlook. We see disagreements dealt with in various ways in Acts, in Paul's letters (and Paul himself adopts varying attitudes toward teachers with whom he disagrees), and in the Johannine literature. (If anything, the greatest common thread tying together many of these strands regarding repudiation of error in the New Testament is the rejection of greed, a concern rarely voiced, let alone heeded in the present day.) It is Israel, and Israel alone, that embodies the divine shape according to which the Christian Church's experience is to be evaluated historically.

And this is so for a very singular reason: Israel's life is fulfilled in, it typifies, Jesus' physical existence; and church is the body of Christ—that is, it in turn mirrors Israel in its own typifying shape, as we have discussed at length in the chapters above. In the matter of division and error, the Christian Church must look to Israel, so that it might see Christ; and in seeing Christ, we must move back, as it were, through the shape of his life, in order that we might faithfully adopt the form of God's chosen people.

It is therefore facile and ultimately misleading for orthodox Christians to identify, face, and respond to their churches' errors simply by saying "repudiate and separate"; it is ultimately misleading even if such a response is made only after long agonies of discernment. It is misleading for the single reason that this is not the shape of Israel's history—which must ultimately be our own—because it is not the shape of Jesus' own life. There is no other standard.

## Scriptural Figures of Christ at the Center of the Divided Church

Such scriptural reasoning here is richly textured. When it is pursued, of course, different Christians come to differing conclusions. But we must make that effort if we are not to succumb to a reactionary faith. Here, at least, are some traditional discoveries of this pursuit.

We can, for instance, identify a number of shaping forms within Jesus' own life that fulfill a broader scriptural history with regard to division and error. For instance, there is the whole image of Jesus' relation to the temple. How would we characterize its shape? Challenge and correction, certainly. But also unswerving commitment and participation. The governing image or type of this combined attitude, as we all know, is the cross. Correction and commitment to the temple are given divine flesh in Jesus' crucifixion. (Hence, Jesus fulfills the sacrificial purpose of the temple itself.) And the crucifixion, after all, is expressed historically in Israel by Israel's fate in destruction, exile, and repentance (cf. Lamentations). In ecclesial terms, in terms of the body of Christ, that can mean only that the divinely willed response of faith before error within the Church is the integrity of truthful patience that is willing to die in place, as Jesus died.

Or take another governing scriptural image that displays the relationship of Christ to the Church in particular. Particularly pertinent to our present dissension, this figure is worked out in Ephesians 5: "Husbands, love your wives, as Christ loved the church and gave himself up for her, that he might sanctify her" (5:25–26). This "profound" "mystery," which "refers to Christ and the church" (5:32), is of course the image of marriage, and it also refers to the shape of the cross. In this case, this shape is given experientially in the suffering indissolubility of fleshly union (5:31), the temporal outcome of which is the sanctification of the Church itself.

The marriage type as an expression of Christ's self-giving for the Church turns out to be a governing—not a transient—interpretive key for Scripture as a whole; and it also turns out that its applicability to the question of faithfulness and error within the people of God is crucial. How else ought one to read and fundamentally apply the embodied symbol of Hosea 1–3, except as a prophetic figure of how the body of Christ takes form within a realm of intrinsic sinfulness? "Go, take to yourself a wife of harlotry and have children of harlotry" (1:2) becomes a promised command for the history by which God pities his chosen and creates his people (2:23). It is a command to Hosea, to be enacted prophetically, because the marriage of harlotry will become the means of salvation by which Christ subsumes the sin of humanity and establishes the very character of the Christian Church. This master image or type is reiterated elsewhere in the Old Testament and lies behind the very meaning of Ephesians 5.

It is not so much ironic as it is theologically inevitable that one of the central issues currently in dispute within our denominations—the character of marriage—provides also the very shape by which faithful Christians are called to enter into this dispute: the cruciform union of love that suffers its rejection indissolubly. What is ironic is that some of those who would protect the human embodiment of marriage within the church should be tempted to contradict its ecclesial expression. We must not give in to this temptation. For if the web of Scripture is properly intact, then it must be the case that the greatest service to human marriage that we can offer will be given in the ecclesial acts of "not hat[ing one's] own flesh" (Eph. 5:29), that is one's church, even in its betrayals.

It is not simply problematic that betrayal exists among the commonly baptized. Such acts—capable of lengthy enumeration within the history of the Church—unveil the very reality by which Christ saves us: giving up himself for those he loves (5:25). That we are made brothers and sisters by baptism within a particular denomination, where we have been providentially placed, has, as it were, married us to each other in Christ. And the consequences of that marriage must be suffered if we are not to contradict the gospel itself, including its witness to the healing of our larger divisions. Our baptisms are deaths with Christ; we cannot escape the breadth of this reality, most especially in times of crisis and turmoil over the integrity of our church's common life and teaching. One might go so far as to call one's "spouse"—that is, baptized brother or sister—within this church "Gomer." Some would see such judgments as presumptuous, to be sure. But even such presumption can be overcome if the bond is also presumed to be unbreakable.

But we are speaking like fools here. And while I sympathize with many who lament and despair over, for example, the integrity of the Episcopal Church's current condition and of its leadership, I must judge the willingness to leave—for another denomination, for parallel dioceses, for alternative bishops—as a succumbing to temptation. "I will strike the shepherd, and the sheep of the flock will be scattered" (Matt. 26:31, quoting Zech. 13:7) is a word of judgment, not a divine hope. The shepherd may well be struck again (and by friends no less!—Zech. 13:6). But in the light of the crucified Lord, we are no longer obliged to run away. Even Jesus shared his Last Supper with Judas (Luke 22:21; John 13:21–30).

Why stay within this church, within this denomination in particular, even within this or that diocese or session or district where the burdens often seem intolerable? Because it is the most evangelical thing one might do, witnessing not to weakness, not to compromise, not to disingenuity, but witnessing to the reality of the power of the cross of Jesus Christ in history.


## The Benefits of Staying Put

And the witness is not empty. It brings with it promised and empowered benefits that must inevitably build up the kingdom of Christ from within. It is well worth detailing some of these, because the losses inherent to leaving are not merely theological; they will surely give rise to a progressive weakening of our lived faith.

*Growth in Christlikeness.* First is the matter of Christian character. If we were to ask what character aspects would be embodied by remaining with integrity within our given church, a number of elements come to mind: patience, courage, perseverance, honesty, long-suffering, mourning, peaceableness, meekness, and so on. The point here is that the form of Jesus' own life rises up into view through these embedded practices of such faithful staying put. And the range of behavioral attitudes that the New Testament variously outlines as virtues or spiritual gifts or even the beatitudes all constellate around this posture of ecclesial remaining-in-faith. Is there a comparable means of growing in Christ's image made possible by separation? It has not yet been articulated or argued by leave-takers.

*Manifesting the truth.* Second, we may trust that the truth itself is more clearly manifested and more divinely potent through its suffering contradiction within a wayward people than otherwise. After all, to be lifted up to view in the light is the act by which Jesus draws the world to himself; yet this lifting up and glorification turns out to be a dying that alone bears fruit (John 12:20–36). The truth shows itself in the peculiar form of Jesus' passion. Why then would we be anxious that staying put, in the form of Jesus, could ever obscure the clarity of the gospel? Just the opposite will be the case. And in this direction will the Great Commission move most decisively toward its fulfillment (something Jesus intimates, for example, in John 17:20–26).

*Teachability.* Third, one of the gifts of remaining will be an openness to God's own teaching. While it is hard for me to believe that there is some new truth yet to be revealed about, say, sexual behavior that will overturn the basic traditions of the Church's doctrine, nonetheless we must acknowledge the possibility of still learning something we did not know before on the matter. And where else shall we learn this than with those who challenge us about our exhausted outlooks? A pertinent analogy is the experience and understanding of something like witchcraft, the debate around which in the seventeenth century led not only to a critical reassessment of the parameters of its practice and meaning, but also, interestingly enough, contributed to a fertile burst of exploration and insight into the physical sciences. (Anglicans, in particular, had a positive role in this episode.) The basic teaching of the Church concerning the existence of the evil one and of evil in general did not change. But because of these debates, Christians now approach the question of witchcraft very differently and much more circumspectly than in the sixteenth century. That is surely a blessing. Similarly, there is every reason to hope that God might lead us into some greater light around the issue of sexuality even in our era, a hope that properly demands an embodiment in patient listening and discussion, none of which need constitute an abandonment of our basic teaching. No one should fear, from fools like us, a willing abrogation of our tradition.

*Instruments of reconciliation.* Finally, and more comprehensively, this broken world of ours cries out, if often quietly, for the witness of some power that can overcome the ravages of hostility. We believe that only one voice answers this cry. It is the voice of the one who remained in place, even in the place he had been consigned by unjust and misguided authorities. It is irresponsible to think that the habits by which we conduct our churches' life in the midst of real division has no effect on the habits of the fallen world. We have the choice and profound privilege of showing, not only other churches, but thereby the world as whole, a better way: *Solo Christo*—only by Christ. There is no other place to stand than his by which the world can be redeemed. We must not be frightened, in our church, of this place and of this remaining.

## How to Stay Put

In conclusion let me outline the practical form of the fool's vocation.

*Vow to stay.* The fool will make a renewed vow of commitment to this actual church, wherever it may be, and put aside the drawn-out and unspoken threats of further division we carry about with us. Such threats have bred nothing but prolonged suspicion, anxiety, and fear on the part of the larger body, always mistrustful of what its members might end up deciding. Can Christians not see how we have become manipulators of charity through our lack of guilelessness? Let our "yes" for this church be "yes." And then let us go on to witness to the gospel's truth in that freedom.

*Struggle for the truth.* Let the fool fearlessly maintain the integrity of our churches' venerable teaching and witness, and let him or her steadfastly refuse to participate in its open contradiction. This is a perfectly reasonable hope, and, quite frankly, the fears afoot that somehow we shall be forced to sacrifice our principles unless we separate from a fallen denomination are overblown. No one can force the fool, as a priest or pastor or layperson, to perform any rite, preach any sermon, or pray any liturgy that contradicts the gospel. From medieval Franciscans to eighteenth-century Anglican evangelicals to nineteenth-century Tractarians, successful methods of faithfully navigating a hostile church while remaining in communion with it have been developed and promoted. Our despair over such a possibility is simply contradicted by historical experience.

*Accept suffering.* Let the fool be prepared to suffer in patience the effects of the gospel's contradiction in our midst. I have already tied this imperative to the central ecclesial vocation of the Christlike disciple. What needs to be stressed is that the imperative is inescapable.

*Presume charitably.* Let the fool hold charitable presumptions toward all persons and all actions within the church. God will not condemn us for overstating the goodness of others and counting them always "better than [our]selves" (Phil. 2:3) unless we do so out of fear and servility. And this applies not only in individual relations, but in our attitude toward institutional actions. It is a matter of charity to construe decisions and documents in as orthodox a manner as possible, for it is our duty to construct a sound basis for peace even with malformed stones. We edify by hearing God's voice within the constricted tones of our brethren.

*Maintain communion.* Let the fool maintain communion with our sisters and brothers in Christ, despite our rejection of aspects of their witness and perhaps even character. Again, recall the form of Jesus in feast and supper, and let us settle ourselves into his patience in staying put, and take as our goal the form of his own communion, that is, the cross of sacrificial love, the cup he drank and shares. As persons baptized in his death, our call is to represent, as fully as possible, the perfect joining of sacrament and life together that Jesus offered at the Last Supper, shared even with his betrayer and deniers. The New Testament has no systematic theology of eucharistic excommunication or even of personal separation from communion. Where concerns with communion are addressed, as in 1 Corinthians 11, it is with an unworthy participation whose fault lies in a failure to achieve such joining of sacrament and life within the church's personal relations. Although unworthy communion in this context is therefore something to be avoided, it is only when we ourselves prove that we cannot love as Christ loved. Any subsequent historical development of the practices of excommunication and separation—practices hotly disputed and inconsistent in the Church's history—should be evaluated in this light: their purpose is fundamentally penitential, not protective of a church's order. Jesus and his Church are not injured by the unrepentant sinner who shares his body and blood. If we cannot share communion in the church, it is to our own, not another's, repentance that we are being led.

*Submit to the church's order.* Let the fool tie himself or herself to the order of our church, precisely because this order and institution provide a divine opportunity and context in which to exercise the virtues of Christ. It does this both by positive and shared encouragements and by offering structures that stubbornly insist that our decisions to love as Christ loves always be intentional and self-conscious. Submitting to bishops and canonical rules and so on, even in their patent injustices, cannot harm us if we do so with the deliberation thereby to offer humble witness. And where open dissent seems necessary, even this must take place with a willingness to suffer the ordered consequences of our disobedience, without complaint or resistance. All of this is consistent with the Scripture's outline of the Lord's own path that must be ours. And only in this path can religious institutions find their fulfillment, like the temple's, in the form of Christ.

*Be open to correction.* Let the fool always be willing to listen to his or her colleagues' admonishment and corrective counsel. This is why, in part, institutional communion is so important: we cannot hear God's prodding and correction unless we are physically bound to those who would speak hard things to us. This, after all, is how we would positively see our own role in the church. But we cannot do that, unless we are open to receiving such communication from others. "Teach and admonish one another in all wisdom" (Col. 3:16). We dare not restrict our presence in this command.

There are, of course, different kinds of fools: the fool who says in the heart "there is no God" (Ps. 14:1); the "foolish Galatians" so quick to be bewitched away from the cross of Christ (Gal. 3:1); the fool (2 Cor. 11:21) who suffers weakness (11:30) so that grace may abound (12:9–10); the fool who is tied, strongly and firmly, to the suffering of Christ, who is "the wisdom of God" because "the foolishness of God is wiser than men, and the weakness God is stronger than men" (1 Cor. 1:24–25). There is also the Church of fools, filled with waiting, filled with patience, filled with persevering, filled with prayer, filled with endurance, filled with hope. This is the Church of God. It is even here, where we stand, fools all.

# 12

## "One New Man"

### *The Calling of the Gentile Church*

## The Providential Character of the Gentile Church

In this concluding chapter, I shall not ask the question, "What is the Church?"—the question of ecclesiology since the Reformation. Instead, I shall ask the very different question, the question hovering over our reflections throughout this volume: "How is God using the Church?" I would go so far as to say that the most destructive discussions to come out of the Reformation division of the Church have centered around the questions, "What is the Church?" or "What is the 'true' Church?" These questions have fueled ongoing separations among Christians and led to preposterous conclusions regarding essences and forms and hopes of the Church, virtually none of which have ever been seen in the world as it really exists and whose promotion has only led to further division and conflict. In any case, given the way our denominations (and Anglicanism, my own especially) are unraveling as coherent institutions in our day, it seems clear to me that posing the "what is" question is no longer fruitful.

Still, we are here: so what is God doing with us? How is God using this or that church, this or that denomination? How is God using, to take the particular case, the Anglican Church? And we need special tools to answer this question, tools we have not been very adept at taking up over the centuries. When we ask questions about the Church, we are really speaking out of and to a *particular* church, among many, distinguished by name and experience; yet in general when we speak of our denominations, we speak of churches whose names and historical details do not even appear in Scripture. How, then, do we talk about the Lutheran Church or the Reformed Church or the Anglican Church without turning it into a discussion about something that no one has ever actually seen (because it is some invisible essence)? At the same time, how do we talk about, for example, the Anglican Church without losing sight that we are interested in doing so because we are interested in the one Church of Christ, whose explicit scriptural referent does not even mention Anglicanism at all?

A traditional way of dealing with the historical particularity of the church in time, a way that has avoided both essentializing the Church and relativizing its meaning and purpose, has been, as we have already discussed, to talk about the Church in terms of divine providence. If we define providence as simply as possible, we can say that it is the ordering of historical particularities by God for a single divine purpose.[1] And so, as this or that church, in this or that place, at this or that time, becomes the object of our reflection, we can look at that church in all of its specificity as something that God is using to fulfill his purpose.

Although some modern theologians worry about the mechanics of divine order and human freedom, it is not necessary to resolve this in order to speak coherently of providence. All we need to say is that God has a comprehensive purpose, which is good and true and encompasses all of creation (in its freedom) and all of time (in its contingency); and all the particulars of space and time—including churches—exist as a part of that purpose, as the pieces in the mosaic of history that, altogether, make up the great picture of that purpose.[2] Although the topic of providence proved a major and complicated category of medieval scholastic metaphysics, its early source and foundation in Christian theology, from the New Testament through Irenaeus, Cyprian, and Augustine, lay in the conviction that God's ordering of the world, in all of its variety, is reflected

---

1. See Thomas Aquinas, *Summa theologiae* 1 Q. 22.

2. Cf. Paul Helm, *The Providence of God* (Downers Grove, Ill.: InterVarsity, 1994), for a clear discussion by an evangelical scholar of what providence is, in Christian terms, from the point of view of philosophical theology.

through the particular forms and figures of Scripture, held together in Christ (esp. Eph. 1; Luke 24:27; 1 Cor. 15:4).[3]

Providence as a serious theological concept began to lose its explanatory power in the eighteenth century (although imperial governments liked to use it for political purposes!). But in the mid-twentieth century, attempts were made to revive the classical notion of providence within ecumenical circles, just because the category was helpful in trying to make sense of the diversity of Christian churches as something God could do something good with. Phrases like *the history of salvation,* drawn from biblical theology, proved helpful in this regard.

I have been arguing, then, that in talking about ecclesiology in our day is a good way to look at the question is in terms of God's providence, as it encompasses a particular church, rooted in the particularities of its history as shorn from the wholeness of the Church catholic. Let me try to do this now, as a kind of brief and final example of a way of thinking, by addressing the reality of the Anglican Church, not in terms of "what is the church (or what is *this* church)?" but in terms of "how is God using the church (or this church)?" And from a human point of view, if we can get a sense of what that might be, we can frame our response in terms of the question, "What is God's *calling* to this church?"

But where do we start with this kind of examination of the providential meaning of the Anglican Church? I doubt if there is a systematic foundation for such an endeavor. In fact, we can probably start in all kinds of places, as long as we start with things as they are, things that are particular in time about this church, things that have happened to and through it. Then, in looking at these happenings, we can try to correlate them (or collate them, to use a traditional Anglican phrase) with the breadth and direction of Scripture.

For instance, we can start with the name itself, and with the history that name points to: Anglican, that is, English. Anglicanism's peculiarity, vis-à-vis other churches, is primarily its nationality somehow, at least in its origins—and perhaps in those theological structures that support or grow out of this element. Communion with the See of Canterbury remains a visible and historical criterion for identifying an Anglican Church (enshrined, for instance, in the Episcopal Church's own constitution), and this, in the end, is a purely national standard, in that it has to

---

3. Augustine's *City of God*, esp. book 3, contains classic descriptions of God's providence ordering the course of human history, including the "two cities" of Church and world. Irenaeus's *Demonstration of the Apostolic Preaching* gives a clear illustration from the early Church of the providential reading of the Church's life in terms of scriptural historical figures.

do with a relationship to a particular people (and in a way that is quite distinct from the largely structural linkage between Rome and the wider Roman Catholic Church).

I think it is fair to say, however, that the Englishness of Anglicanism has been seen as a problem for the Anglican Church (or churches), especially in relation to its larger, global reality. There is that wonderful theological twist—if scripturally incoherent—that John Pobee made famous with his discussion of the "Anglo-Saxon captivity of the church." After all, should churches in Polynesia, the Arctic, or Francophone Africa really be identified in terms of their English origins, and what negative effects has this linkage had? Furthermore, is there not an element of irrelevance in holding on to this historically particular character, especially as the English side of the linkage seems to be decidedly weakening in numbers and vitality? Lutherans ask analogous questions, as do Presbyterians (in an age where eldership is hardly a mark of authority) and even non-denominational churches.

Thus, part of the peculiarity of Anglicanism's nationality is its very problematic status. It does not quite fit. And if we are interested in the providential meaning of this particular church, we must also be interested in the providential meaning of this lack of fittedness at the center of its particularity. These two elements are what I will underline now: the providential meaning of Anglican nationalism and how that character itself can—providentially again—embrace its own incompleteness (Michael Ramsey's characterization).

Nationalism is not something that only the English possess. But there is something peculiar to English nationalism that is noted by historians reflecting on this particular people's self-understanding in the sweep of evolving time. To take but one recent example: not long ago, well-known historian Robert Darnton wrote a widely diffused essay on European unity and lifted up England (and its Church) as an example standing in sharp contrast to the dynamics of a proper development of the European Union's euro-values. The charges are familiar: whereas the Germans and the French, for all their self-regard, are willing to push for a united Europe, England's long history of insular idiosyncrasies and autonomy stubbornly stands in the way.[4]

4. Cf. Robert Darnton, "A Euro State of Mind," *New York Review of Books* 49.3 (Feb. 28, 2002), which offers a wonderfully confused plea for a return to Enlightenment political universalism, with a few traditional swipes at English nationalism.

Ecclesially, England's extended struggle with and final break from the papacy paralleled its national self-distinction from Europe; its promotion of a uniform national religious character in the form of a church establishment, while not unique, has been uniquely steadfast (as Newman pointed out long ago); its bequest of this character to its colonial and political progeny has been consistent (starting with American Independence); and eventually the Anglicanism of independent states has become part of the cloth of a single historical continuum among Anglican churches. Few historians familiar with the phenomenon of English nationalism on a political and cultural level would be surprised at the current and conflicted tension within religious Anglicanism between autonomy and communion: Anglican churches have been simply *formed* through time to press their commonality through their national self-identity and interest, and the Englishness of these churches—which include all Anglican churches, even those who do not speak English—lies not in the language of prayer and confession primarily, but in this bequest of character.

But here we come back to the main question: does such ecclesial nationalism—and that's where I believe we must start with the historical particularity of Anglicanism—have a providential meaning? Viewed scripturally, it clearly does. For the place of the nations in their distinctions, according to Scripture (Gen. 11; Deut. 32:8), stands as a supreme mark of the providential ordering (nations are overseen by God's angels) of human sin for the outworking of universal redemption (Rev. 6:9; 22:2). The multiplicity, distinction, and maintained diversity of the nations are the result of human sin, but seen historically they are also bound up with that sin's reordering toward the creation's ultimate reconciliation with God in a common variegated praise.

Nationalism, ecclesially understood, then, is a part of the providential order of what the Scriptures point to as the purpose of the Gentiles. I will coin a word to refer to this category of providential purpose: "Gentilism." Gentilism is not a synonym of nationalism, certainly; I use it to refer to the historical movement by which God uses the nations who are joined to Christ to mold humanity into "one new man" in conjunction with Jewish Israel. And, in scriptural terms, we can outline three ways in which God does this: the Gentile provocation of the Jews, through the holiness of Christian tribulation, for the purpose of displaying the reconciliation of sinful Jew and Gentile in Christ's cross.

First, the nations, or Gentiles, exist in a relationship of grace (unnaturally) to Israel, which is naturally Jewish: and the Gentiles' providential role lies in drawing Jewish Israel back to God through their own provocation to holiness (jealousy) and thereby through their eventual usefulness in making Israel whole—that is, catholic—within the embracing redemptive purposes of God (Rom. 11). St. Paul goes so far as to raise the stakes in this relationship by noting that it is given under a terrible shadow of judgment if it fails: "You too will be cut off," he says of the Gentile Christians in 11:22.

Second, as the Book of Revelation makes clear, this movement into Israel's wholeness, a movement that the Gentiles pursue in ultimate relation with Jewish Israel, takes its form in the historical experience of tribulation, of suffering for Christ in the way of Christ: "Who are these? . . . These are they who have come out of the great tribulation . . . [and] washed their robes . . . in the blood of the Lamb" (Rev. 7:13–14's summary statement).

Finally, these two themes of Gentile purpose are brought together in Scripture's discussion of the cross of Christ (e.g., Eph. 2), which is seen both as the single instrument and as the ongoing figure in history by which the wholeness of human Israel is given in the healing of the Jewish-Gentile distinction: "For he is our peace, who has made us both one . . . creat[ing] in himself one new man in place of the two . . . reconcil[ing] us both to God in one body through the cross" (Eph. 2:14–16).

Gentilism, therefore, describes the providential purpose whereby the diversity of humankind is incorporated into Israel's form, given uniquely in Jesus Christ and the figure of his cross. Conversely, Israel (Rom. 11:26; Gal 6:16.) is the specific form given to the ungodly—Jew and Gentile together—through the redemption wrought by Jesus Christ on the cross. To speak of the Gentiles, providentially, is to speak of "all Israel" that grows from the cross of Christ, so that in and through him, creation can behold and praise God for this "light . . . to the Gentiles" and the "glory to thy people Israel" (Luke 2:32), who is the Son incarnate.

Let me stress that this way of describing scriptural Gentilism is really a way of speaking prophetically, of saying how history will unfold in God's order, how it is already unfolding. But it does not describe particular events within that process. That is what, in a sense, theologians are called to do: to discern the meaning of particular things in front of our nose in relationship to the promises of God. And if we want to talk about Gentilism within the Church as it is (and has been)—what we can call ecclesial Gentilism—we are faced with a glaring challenge to the prophecy itself: there *is no present* church of Jew and Gentile made into "one new man." What we see instead in the history of the Church to this day is the almost complete *disappearance* of Jews from the Christian Church very early on and the rise of a *purely* Gentile Christianity. The early Church fathers seemed happy enough about this development and focused almost exclusively on Gentile conversion, with Jews coming into the picture only as an example of well-deserved punishment. So that by the early medieval period the Christian Church was called, by Jews themselves, "the Gentile way," a negative characterization that, only in the twentieth century, became reinterpreted positively by Jewish theologian Franz Rosenzweig, who wished to offer an optimistic reading of Christianity as a special covenant made by God exclusively with Gentiles. But there is something very odd—and providentially wrongheaded—in making *Christian* and *Gentile* synonyms.

For better or for worse though—surely worse—the temporal reality of the Church has become one marked by the nationalism of Christian diversity. (Curiously, the more nationalistically diverse the Church became, the more anti-Semitically it behaved; modern Christian division, after the Reformation, is arguably a case in point.) So in light of the scriptural witness, we discover—we have revealed to us—the Christian Church's historical constriction, spiritually understood, even within the outworking of the historical process. As time has gone on, the Church has moved *away* from embodying its ultimate goal of the "one new man," made up of the two major elements of humanity—Jew and Gentile—and toward a more narrowly and diversely inculturated view of Christian identity that has divided the Gentiles among themselves and abandoned their calling to provoke the Jews through holiness of life.[5]

The major question arises then: is it possible to see this denial of the Gentiles' true vocation as some movement within the providential process as well? That is, can we say that the Gentile Church, in seemingly flirting with the outcome of its own sin—"you too will be cut off"—is, in this very process, struggling to grow forward into its divine mission of universal wholeness with and within Israel? This is a very hard question, rarely confronted and rarely answered. Certain English and French Christians of the seventeenth and eighteenth centuries tried to grapple with this from an apocalyptic perspective amid civil war, persecu-

5. Cf. Kwame Bediako, *Theology and Identity: The Impact of Culture upon Christian Thought in the Second Century and Modern Africa* (Oxford:Regnum, 1992), which is an interesting, if perhaps misleading, attempt to draw parallels between the early Church's Gentile separation from Jewish Israel and modern forms of African Christian "inculturation." It is nonetheless a useful stimulus to thinking about the Church's providential calling in terms of Israel and the nations.

tion, and revolution—marginalized Puritans, Anglicans, and Jansenist Catholics; nineteenth-century Darbyites; and in the last century Dutch theologian Kornelis Miskotte tried to do the same from the vantage of biblical theology after the European conflagration of World War II and the Holocaust. The question I am raising is not how to convert Jews to Christianity, or whether that is a good idea under present circumstances in our churches.[6] These are interesting questions, but tangential to the character of Gentile Christianity *as we now live it.* We have failed to convert them, it seems, because we have ignored them and our own calling to provocative holiness. Rather, the question I am raising is how nationalistically tethered churches—Gentilism gone extreme—are being used by God to fulfill his purposes for the world in Christ. And this question is not an easy one to resolve.

In part, this is because the modern era, in the wake of Christian division and the gross cruelties of ethnic and national warfare, has come to see nationalism in any guise (including ecclesial garb) as a nefarious promoter of sectarian violence. This has been one of the great ideological engines behind the press, for example, for the European Union, from among countries whose nationalistic self-understandings have undoubtedly dragged the world into untold suffering. Surely, we wonder, God cannot (or would not wish to) use such vessels of destruction for good!

Other social analysts, of course, have responded to this kind of criticism by pointing out that alternative secularism, in its promotion of universalist values supposedly free of religious particularism, has itself led to the brutal unleashing of human corruption. Witness the "failure of happiness on earth" (Darnton's phrase) as a political goal pursued, for example, by French, Soviet, and Chinese revolutions as well as by forms of capitalist utopianism. Why would God, therefore, want anything less than the maintenance of Babel's mutually competing peoples? Adam Smith would have agreed.

In short, from a purely human and political point of view, there is a truly difficult balance to be struck—and it has perhaps never been struck at all—between the sectarian dangers of nationalism and the

---

6. See Richard Popkin and Gordon M. Wiener (eds.), *Jewish Christians and Christian Jews from the Renaissance to the Enlightenment* (Dordrecht: Kluwer 1994), which contains essays that cover a range of early modern attempts at rethinking the relationship of Christianity to Jewish Israel. Kornelis Miskotte's *When the Gods Are Silent* (San Francisco: Harper & Row, 1967) is a unique and uniquely provocative essay in biblical theology that seeks to understand the meaning of the scriptural revelation and the purposes of God for human history; his willingness to see the "Gentile way" of the Christian Church held accountable to Jewish Israel was groundbreaking. More recent explorations of this theme can be found in Tikva Frymer-Kensky et al., *Christianity in Jewish Terms* (Boulder, Colo.: Westview, 2000).

self-restraining powers of nationalism to disperse power and check corruption through mutual competition and cooperation.

And lest we think this has little to do with the Christian Church in general, let us note how Philip Jenkins, a student of global Christianity, underlines the potentially world-changing influence of this tenuous balance among growing non-Western churches (and over and against Islam).[7] Furthermore, if we think it has little to do with, say, the Anglican Church in particular, we need only look at the kinds of discussions taking place today within Anglicanism's wider communion—at Lambeth, among the Primates, and within ecumenical dialogues and local synods—over practical realities concerning decision-making and authority: arguments about top-down hierarchies, bottom-up grassroots, local options, general councils, subsidiarity, confessional standards, books of common prayer, and so on. These arguments, shared with so many other denominations' internal struggles, are tied, I suggest, in an emblematic way to the unresolved and ambiguous character of Gentilism as a whole, as it has embodied itself in the Church's life and, we believe as Christians, in the outworking of God's purposes for humanity.

How, then, *is* God using this ambiguous reality, a reality fraught with conflict? In light of the scriptural witness concerning Gentilism itself—its struggle to become one with Israel, its tribulational experience, its posture in the face of assaulted hostility between Jew and non-Jew—religious Gentilism can be seen, I believe, only as a providential way station to the ecclesial revelation of the cross of Christ Jesus itself, the cross as the sole power of peace. That is, the process of internal ecclesial struggle in the world, which Gentilism historically represents, must constitute the purgation of the Church of Jesus as it moves toward its consummation with and as Israel for and in the world. To apply, as it were, our three scriptural elements of Gentilism: Romans 11 becomes a prophecy, Ephesians 2 its ultimate form, and Revelation 7 its historical experience. We shall become holy, as we grasp again our vocation to reconciliation in the form of Christ crucified, given in our acceptance of suffering from the world's hands.

Indeed, I would go so far as to assert that Anglicanism is in fact a paradigmatic, an exemplary case of ecclesial Gentilism, indicative for the whole of the fractured Church. *This* is how we should look at ourselves, whoever

---

7. Philip Jenkins, *The Next Christendom: The Coming of Global Christianity* (New York: Oxford University Press, 2002). Jenkins's popular book lays out some of the major trends underlying the shift of Christian numerical balance to the South and explores some of the implications of this evolution, especially on devotional, theological, and political (including the question of nationalist political) levels.

we are as Christians. Although virtually all Christian churches today are in fact Gentile churches, devoid of their reconciled Jewish purpose, not all are ordered in such a way as to exhibit this reality politically (that is, canonically, ecclesially, and communally) in the way that Anglicans are. We Christians are virtually all Gentiles. Oddly enough, Anglicans actually glory in this fact, given their celebration of global diversity and national multiplicity; they structure their lives so that these distinctions are embodied in Christian relationships and experiences of authority. From the West Indies to Hong Kong, from Minneapolis to Harare, from Sao Paolo to Winchester, Anglicans are both linked by this common identity and ensnared by it through their histories and present practices.

But if we are honest, we must also admit that this structural boasting has a dark shadow in terms of our ultimate destiny in God's hands. And in this sense above all, if we are indeed to speak providentially, if we are to take seriously the particularity in time of our own church, we must say that Anglicanism is a peculiar sign of God's history for Christ's body. A sign of irony as well as of paradox—I write here as an Anglican in particular—given in our attempt to spin a web of autonomous Anglican selves: for history itself, if you will, is unmasking Anglicanism's incompleteness, while also driving it forward—displaying us, calling us—as the Church Defective for the life of the world. As the newer churches of the South gradually assume a larger share of the direction of global Christianity, it is crucially important that their leadership avoid ignoring this calling that has been too long, if unsuccessfully, suppressed by the North.

### The Providential Calling of the Gentile Churches

So let me now turn to some specifics about this calling, the shape in time of this church that is ours, what we are and must become. Let me discuss certain elements of denominational Gentilism, from the viewpoint of an Anglican, as they describe our common vocation.

Gentilism, as I have indicated, appears to be a divine mission whose temporal irresolution and practical defeats are bound up, as it in fact turns out, with the historical character of incompleteness: we are a church that has somehow gone on a journey away from our goal and has, until now, missed its mark of the "one new man" of Jew and Gentile. But we are still moving, still aiming. How, in this light of continued mission, should we say that God is using the Gentile Church in its sinful penultimacy? In a sense, what we are looking for are characteristics of historical life that turn what is imperfect into an instrument of conversion—both of the Church and of the world. And we are looking for this within a particular denomination, like Anglicanism, specifically.

Anglicanism's identity in Gentilism means that we must look at the divine characteristics of our life in just these terms of providential self-conversion for the sake of the world. There are doubtless many entry points to this discussion, but, for the sake of (venerable) simplicity, let me take the "four creedal marks of the Church" and reread them in terms of this vocation: one, catholic, holy, apostolic.

### One

Clearly the most blatant historically contradicted sign of the Church's life is the mark of our oneness. We are manifestly *not* one in the sense of "one new man" in Ephesians, nor are we even one within the universal Christian body itself (the two are linked). Further, our own mutual Anglican relations are, in places, close to the breaking, if not already broken. Any affirmation of the oneness of the Church, then, can be made only insofar as a given Church stands under the judgment of its division, that is, as it is able to say, "Lord have mercy on me, for I have failed in being one as you and the Father are one." The Gentile Church, if providentially still church, must therefore see its mission as one pursued under such judgment and propelled by it. If we *are* a church, then our oneness will—in God's hand—become a kind of search whose character is humility, a "seeking for what is not" with a repentant openness to being changed in the face of Jew and Gentile alike.

Note Paul's vision in Romans 11 of the ongoing division of Gentile from Jew, permitted by God, but for the sake of spurring the humility of the Gentile Church as a sign of virtue that will "make . . . jealous" the continued condemners of the gospel. Division in incompleteness, in other words, fulfills its providential purpose of moving toward oneness, only as it drives the Gentile to a profound virtue of life in the face of that historical gift of faith that has made it part of Israel in the first place.

The Gentile is first of all driven backward to the origin of this gift tied to Israel: to the covenants, the law, the prophets, the forms of historical existence embodied in Israel (exodus, kingship, warring and its failures, exiles, restorations, and new commands). In sum, Scripture and Israel together become the bond of a unity still to be grasped through this search back amid these realities to be reappropriated with thanks and in repentance. One of the problems of Western Christianity, including evangelical Anglicanism, is that it has effectively renounced the Old Testament as sacred Scripture. This must be turned around.

This mission, in some way, fits the historical Anglican commitment to the ever reiterated appropriation of the whole Scripture: searching, studying, avoiding the too-clear dichotomies of old and new that have plagued Protestant and, to a lesser extent, Catholic exegesis and that have created terrible problems for contemporary Anglicanism in the hands of revisionists of almost neo-Manichean proclivities. Anglican common prayer is a gift under threat. Thus, the Beroean character of this search—set, it should be said, by Jews (Acts 17:11)—remains both rare and criticized among other divided churches, for, as we know, it has characterized an Anglican refusal to tie Church too closely to confession. Apostolicity (see more below) from this vocational Anglican perspective is not simply true doctrine in standard Protestant fashion, nor is it simply received structure, but it is given in a lived relationship with the Scriptures themselves. I have never been much convinced that there is such a thing as a peculiar Anglican theology; but there is in Anglicanism a kind of confluence between liturgy and scholarship that defines the form and focus of the consecrated life, wherein prayer and study meet through a common scriptural immersion. Today this is an almost romantic ideal: what we see around us, rather, is theological education's failure, in the North to approach Scripture in such an adoratively integrated way and in the South a dangerous lack of scriptural scholarship altogether in newer churches in favor of academic systematic theology, ethics, and evangelical polemics.

But if humility before the incompleteness of our being one drives us backward, it also drives the Gentile body forward as well, in an openness to realities of the churches and world that call for change and for conversion. The basic scriptural division within humanity is between Gentile and Jew; and if we have yet failed in reconciling this division, we can at least live out the oneness of the Gentile body. The ecumenical challenge remains one of Anglicanism's most clearly accepted missions, and that mission is properly founded on humility in search of its fulfillment. Up to the present, however, we must measure negatively that mission by the ease with which we can seemingly embrace some Christians, even while the embrace itself does little to change us, and we remain aloof from the vast majority of others. (Consider the continued exclusion, in the West, of Pentecostals and evangelicals from Anglican partnerships.) The assessment of world Anglicanism's ecumenical relationships—too

often and too narrowly confined to Western discussions and now openly
subverted by autonomous actions—needs to be made far more openly,
shared far more widely, and held accountable far more rigorously to the
vocation of thwarted Gentilism than it has been. This is as much true
among younger churches as it is among older ones.

If, in any case, Anglicanism has been a leader, of sorts, in a divine
project for unity, that leadership can be effective only as it is accomplished in a diaconal posture. The church's concern for its distinctive
institutional structure and ethos—in itself increasingly wobbly—has
proven a stumbling block over and over again in terms of the vocation
of repentance and conversion that marks the providential usefulness of
Gentilism. American and African, English and Asian together, Anglicans,
like all the Gentile Christians of the world, must be humbled. That is
who we are called to be, and thus, that is what the Anglican Church is,
in judgment or mercy, in God's providence.

### Catholic

Oneness and catholicity are certainly not equivalent terms, but they
are, in the Church's life, historically coordinated. The incompleteness of
the Church's oneness is what makes catholicity or wholeness necessary in
historical terms. But what can wholeness within the context of defective
oneness mean, apart from a wishful regret? It must mean dependence—the
searching for and waiting upon the other, who may not yet be in view.

And in a real sense, the Gentile Church is the universal sign of human
dependence: it depends upon Israel and, through it, upon God; it is the
temporal outcast, lifted up even in the face of nonelection, yet subjugated
to promises made to others (i.e., the Jews). In Scripture, the examples of
Ruth and the Syrophoenician woman embody this universal sign given
over to the Gentile Church. Part of the purpose of Romans 11 is to describe the historical character of this sign: Paul explains how the Gentiles
are preeminently the objects of grace, because they remain continually
unnatural to the historical forms of God's providence as figured in the
scriptural promises, and thus they hang in a perpetual dependence upon
the forms of divine mercy.

In historical terms, then, dependency means existing through the grace
of others. And if we call the Christian Church "catholic," it can only be
in light of the living structures of such dependency on others around
which the Church is built. These include the whole array of structured
forms of dependent life: political, jurisdictional, ministerial, liturgical,

and ethical. To be sure, these are all worth analyzing in this or that moment of the Church's life; Anglicans love to argue about the episcopacy and about synods and dispersed authority and prayer-book traditions and so on—all matters that do indeed embody our dependencies. But none of them are immutable forms. The point here is that viewing these forms of catholicity in terms of their embodiment of dependency cuts against many traditional notions of catholicity seen as an adherence to or participation in the given essence of the Church or in primary terms of structure and liturgy. The catholic forms of the Church's existence are given for the purpose of dependency on others and are to be measured on this basis. For the strong must always be willing to become the weak when living with the weak, and that means giving up as much as holding on. All denominations are called to this relativization of their structures, as well as to a deepening of their subjecting powers.

The Gentile Church's dependency is first on God, of course, next on Israel, and next upon the Scriptures given by Israel (including the New Testament). This has been said. Within the limited sense of Gentilism, however, we can also say that dependency (and hence catholicity) is given *particular* shape in the structures of communion that have so emerged in recent decades as important to defining the life of the Church, especially within ecumenical discussions. This cannot be overemphasized, since even in the face of current tensions and conflicts a separate denomination like Anglicanism has taken communion as something of a gentle talent and rather prided itself in this. But communion cannot be this if it truly is an expression of Gentilism's *necessary* catholicity. Communion represents, in scriptural terms, the form in which dependency or subjection can take place in mutual terms (1 Cor. 12–13; Rom. 12–13; Eph. 4; Col. 3); and this involves, clearly, patterns of authority and obedience, sacrifice and suffering—patterns that are stringently tied to the cross and admit little comfort or cultural malleability.

Anglicanism's structure of national or provincial or even diocesan autonomies is a given of its Gentilism; its reveling in such autonomies is a logical extension of Gentilism's historical defection; and its struggle against the victory of such autonomies is clearly the only providential redemption possible to Gentilism's defection. Thus, the struggle for communion that the very structures of Anglicanism have thrust upon our churches is a gift, however hard, whose purpose must be to revive dependency as the mode of catholic Christianity. Denominations should watch carefully the groaning contortions of their fellows in seeking out life together; these are the patterns, in their sweat, that are being marked out as shared gifts.

This is a harsh path, particularly in light of the long historical struggle, politically, for independence that has characterized both the nations and national churches, especially within Anglicanism. The point is not to minimize the value of this, in some cases ongoing, struggle. Instead, I need to emphasize that, beneath the motive for political self-direction, in national or ecclesial terms, there must be a more profound set of ties and limits that turn Christian churches toward sacrifice in the face of the articulated needs of others—other churches, other Christians, other historical pressures.

To this degree, many official Anglican documents rightly speak of communion as an organizing concept for ecclesiology, but they generally fail to press the point to its foundation, which is the willingness to die for the other. This is proven by the way that agreed reports with the Roman Catholics are routinely negatively received by many supporters of communion ecclesiology on the basis of their giving away too much vaunted collegiality by suggesting that there is a place where universal primacy would set redemptive limits to autonomous choices among the churches and bishops and dioceses. But the notion that churches exist in communion and that authority derives from and articulates itself within such communion can make sense only if its roots are given in a dependency posture.

Finally, as I have argued throughout this volume, this posture is a mark of the Church in other areas of our life, to the degree that they are held or exercised in common. The current debate over sexual behavior is a case in point. Dependence in this matter clearly covers a number of relationships: to Israel's Scriptures, to the past teaching of the Church, to the communion of other Anglican churches, and to the ecumenical search that marks our repentant defectiveness—even to the life of homosexual Christians in our midst. Faithfulness can lie only in finding a way to hold this array of dependencies in order. It is worth reexamining the way, indeed *any* way this can be done.

### Holy

Embracing the right answers to these kinds of questions reflects the church's sanctified life. And certainly holiness is a large reality that touches the very center of redemption in Christ and the life of the Spirit. Ecclesiologically, however, the topic can be broached only in terms of the historical figure of the Church in its actual choices and conditions. The holiness of the Gentile church in particular, then, represents the vocation of its calling to "make . . . jealous," and it takes its shape beneath the warning of its defection from this calling. Within the context of the Church's intransigent incompleteness, its Gentilism, holiness must therefore be seen as an urgent act of repentance through the ongoing forms of life that seek after oneness and are embodied in catholic communion—humility and dependence.

Most denominations, Anglicanism among them, have had long histories of "holy living." In England they move from the impulsions to reform in the face of ecclesial abuses in the sixteenth century to the disciplines of seventeenth-century devotion, and they include the Methodist revival and various evangelical movements, not to mention the Tractarian renewal. The histories are sufficiently marked that the Pelagian overtones of much of them have worried some. The category of holiness as a whole, however, has dropped from the religious screen in the West in contemporary times, except as a descriptive of the experiential contours of individual spirituality (encountering the holy), which has even appropriated to itself elements that were once regarded as intrinsically sinful (e.g., the use of "holy love" to describe autonomous fulfillment of individual sexual desire).

The result, of course, has meant the extreme impoverishment of the kind of life that properly could uphold the providential vocation of a Gentile Church, forms of holiness that, as described in Scripture, involve continence and self-sacrifice. These are the particular forms of submission to the historical promise of the root, the Old Testament figure of Israel, whose own life is a reflection, in judgment and mercy, of the holiness of God.

One way to describe any kind of renewal of the Gentile Church's mark of holiness is to inquire into the forms of discipline that could undergird scriptural searching, subjection to the promises of Israel, communal dependency, ecumenical humility, and so on. Some of these disciplines have had their ancestry already in Anglicanism—forms of scriptural and historical study, liturgical scripturalism and sacramentalism (a discipline of communal scriptural subjection taken in the face of promised grace that deserves its own treatment), deferral to the past, innovatory reticence, prayerfully multiplied councils and dialogues, and the like. It is important to see how many, even most, of these disciplines have been either threatened or outright subverted by the alternative virtues of contemporary global culture—the mitigation of study as a sanctified vocation in favor of apology, scriptural consumerism, liturgical commodification, the rejection of the past and its authority as itself judaizing and hence as incapable of being graciously authoritative (vs. the "God of the living, of Abraham, Isaac, and Jacob"), the cult of revision, the demand for immediacy, the promotion of agenda as strategically maximal. These contemporary virtues have engulfed all sides of the Church and in most parts of the world.

Once we can see this, we can also see how Gentilism, in its own sinfulness and in its providential instrumentality, presses toward a reintegration with Jewish Israel, in a way that was perhaps not immediately obvious in the dawn of the Christian Church: becoming like and becoming one with Jewish Israel cannot mean a denial of Christ, of course; it means, rather, the Church's accepted conformance to Jerusalem besieged and beset, whereby Jew and Gentile will indeed be made one through the sacrifice of the cross—the revelation of God's holiness in Christ, by which alone we can be "present[ed] . . . holy and blameless" (Col. 1:22; Eph. 1:4). That is, the Gentile Church must be joined to the fate of Israel in its historical extent so that the holiness of the cross can be made visible in it.

Holiness, in this particular context, a context that focuses upon the extremes of exemplary Gentilism like Anglicanism, will carry the particular character of patience since it is aimed at the process of historical conformance over time, in the midst of trial: "For to this you have been called, because Christ also suffered for you . . . that you should follow in his steps" (1 Pet. 2:21). And this character of demanded patience, after all, is currently that facet of the Christian conformance that is most attacked within the wider Church of contending parties. The attack itself, in my mind, is a goad to the present complaints of the left and the right: who dares to wait for the future any longer, in the face of so many changes and threats? But such daring to wait represents the patience of Israel (Ps. 130).

The reflections and decisions of churches in our day will have value to the degree that they foster or reconstruct relationships of patience among the willful and prideful self-assertions of the Gentiles (and we too are Gentiles).

### Apostolic

The character of the apostolic Church is one that has found renewed interest of late among non-Anglican and Anglican Christians alike. In general, this interest is tied to the work of the Great Commission, and the term *apostolic* has been identified primarily with evangelism among the nations, something surely appropriate to the Gentile Church. In light of Gentilism's intrinsic deformation of the Church, however, this view of what is apostolic needs some qualification.

Certainly, the contemporary Church's Gentile character must stamp it inescapably as in the lineage of the Great Commission one way or another. And to some degree, this aspect of Anglicanism, among many churches, has been borne out historically in a vigorous and impressive manner more visible today than almost at any other time, even as the spur to evangelism among all peoples remains resisted in some ecclesial quarters. This resistance is something that rightly must be overcome. The apostolic church is one, after all, that aims at overcoming its own incompleteness and in this way is defined more in terms of a mission outward, toward a transformation of relationships among real people, than in terms of maintaining some deposit of either structure or confession, let alone of simple social habit. The calling of the Gentile apostleship is ever aimed at this end, which coincides with the "ends of the earth."

But the posture of this apostolic work is one of *conversion* toward this end, in the midst of a history that has too long denied the fullness of the end itself. The apostle is the one called and used for the witness of life that demonstrates and builds up this converted character of (in creedal terms) humility, dependency, and patience as it reorients the life of the Church toward its true end of the "one new man," of Gentile and Jew together. If there is movement out in apostleship, then, this can be done only within defected Gentilism as a conscientious effort to integrate the nations into the fold of an Israel whose renewal as "one, catholic, and holy" represents a profound recharacterization of evangelism altogether; conversion outside of such a church is simply not apostolic.

Anglicanism is certainly distinctive from other Protestant denominations in its ostensive commitment to church building, to the structured formation of a people visibly linked to other churches. But even more than this, Anglicanism's apostolic vocation is tied to its own current struggles within its communion of autonomous jurisdictions. For in this very struggle—which calls on the virtues of humility, dependence, and patience—the formation of a people is being providentially focused on the work of preparing for the reconciliation of that larger division in the Church's aborted mission to draw Jew and Gentile together, a division carried yet further in the Church's own internal schisms.

The character of relation between various Anglican churches is therefore not irrelevant to the apostolic calling, nor is the ecumenical openness that the Church's oneness demands, nor finally is the jealousy of holiness vis-à-vis the non-Christian world as whole. It is not enough to preach the gospel to the ends of the earth, unless the "one new man" is both the goal and agent of this action. The challenge that all this represents to Anglicans of evangelical, Catholic, and liberal commitments is obvious.

In confronting this challenge, the providential distinctiveness of Anglicanism—and any other church that is willing to face its peculiar brand of Gentilism—surely will find its clarity: converting Gentiles to conversion itself before the great goal of all Israel, converting them to humility before the whole Scriptures, before the holiness of Israel, before the life all the nations yearning for Israel; converting them to a dependency upon Israel of the flesh, upon its gifts, upon each other, upon the calling of the past; converting them to a waiting for God's uplifting, to a patience for God to use humility and dependence as his weapons of power, to a perseverance in hope that contemporary measures of time cannot begin to span or fathom. Where once Israel stood in the face of the nations around it, today we stand in the face of a calling whose encounter will necessarily transform the very shape of who we are.

In 1936, Michael Ramsey published what was to become a small classic in Anglican ecclesiology: *The Gospel and the Catholic Church*. What made the book notable at the time—its elegant discussion, with a late Caroline flavor, of Anglicanism as a third way—now seems a little anachronistic. However, the book's stature has grown enormously over the years, due to another feature, less remarked upon seventy years ago, but now more obvious in the face of ecclesial changes of the late twentieth century: the breadth of coherent scriptural foundation that Ramsey laid, rarely seen in Anglican discussions of the Church, in describing its life providentially in terms of the fate of Christ's body in passion and self-giving—an incompleteness divinely opened to the divine gift of new life.[8]

8. Michael A. Ramsey, *The Gospel and the Catholic Church* (London: Longman, Green, 1936). A. G. Hebert's *Throne of David: A Study of the Fulfilment of the Old Testament in Jesus Christ and His Church* (London: Faber & Faber, 1941) is a rare Anglican exploration of the relationship of the Church to Israel and the Scriptures of the Old Testament, which explicates classical typological views on this matter; his conclusions, however, remain firmly traditional in their refusal to allow the Church's calling to be judged by its identity as Israel. For more recent Anglican approaches to scriptural and providentialist figuralism, see Christopher Seitz's *Figured Out: Typology and Providence in Christian Scripture* (Louisville: Westminster John Knox, 2001) and my *Spirit and Nature: The Saint-Médard Miracles in 18th-Century Jansenism* (New York: Herder & Herder/Crossroad, 2002), which offers a systematic reading of providential history in scriptural terms and its relationship to the doctrine of the Holy Spirit, based on theological discussions of the seventeenth and eighteenth centuries.

Ramsey perhaps saw then what history is only now unveiling. The Anglican Church, in its recent and astonishing expansion among diverse national groups, in the shift of its vital devotion away from its Northern and Western roots, in the midst of a withering of traditional denominational self-identities around the world, now appears less as a culture or an institution than as an instrument (among many) within God's hands for the reshaping of humanity within a chastened Israel. Given that many of the unexpected changes in world Christianity in our era have been disturbingly and ironically mixed with the expanding reach of a cruelly materialistic common global culture, it is imperative that this instrumentality not become unwitting like Balaam's and that the cross at the center of the "one new man's" abode toward which we walk be seen not solely as the mark of judgment upon our churches, but as our tree of life as well. Our providential character, of course, can be grasped in either form—as warning or example; that is up to us. But one way or the other, Israel will be made whole, through Jesus himself: "For he is our peace, who has made us both one . . . creat[ing] in himself one new man in place of the two . . . reconcil[ing] us both to God in one body through the cross" (Eph. 2:14–16).

# Index